Teaching Literature Rhetorically

Teaching Literature Rhetorically

Transferable Literacy Skills for 21st Century Students

Jennifer Fletcher
Foreword by Leila Christenbury

STENHOUSE PUBLISHERS
PORTSMOUTH, NEW HAMPSHIRE

Stenhouse Publishers
www.stenhouse.com

Credits

p. 5 Figure 1.4a Shaun Robinson/Shutterstock.com

p. 5 Figure 1.4b Cholpan/Shutterstock.com

p. 6 Figure 1.5 NancyS/Shutterstock.com

p. 26 From *Fables You Shouldn't Pay Any Attention To* by Florence Parry Heide and William C. Van Clief. Text copyright © 1978 by Florence Parry Heide and William C. Van Clief III. Reprinted with the permission of Atheneum Books for Young Readers, an imprint of Simon & Schuster Children's Publishing Division. All rights reserved.

p. 43 "You Fit Into Me" from *Power Politics* copyright © 1971, 1996, by Margaret Atwood, reproduced by permission of House of Anansi Press Inc., Toronto. www.houseofanansi.com.

pp. 44–45 "The Ways We Lie." Originally published in the November/December 1992 issue of *Utne Reader*.

pp. 74–75 Reprinted from *Prairie Schooner* Volume 88, Number 4 (Winter 2014) by permission of the University of Nebraska Press. Copyright 2014 by the University of Nebraska Press.

p. 133 Figure 5.6 From *American Born Chinese* © 2006 by Gene Luen Yang. Reprinted by permission of Roaring Brook Press, a division of Holtzbrinck Publishing Holdings Limited Partnership. All Rights Reserved.

pp. 227–229 From *Fostering Habits of Mind in Today's Students: A New Approach to Developmental Education* edited by Jennifer Fletcher, Adela Najarro, and Hetty Yelland, copyright © 2015, reproduced with permission of Stylus Publishing.

Library of Congress Cataloging-in-Publication Data

Names: Fletcher, Jennifer, 1972- author.
Title: Teaching literature rhetorically : transferable literacy skills for
   21st century students / Jennifer Fletcher.
Description: Portland, Maine : Stenhouse Publishers, [2018] | Includes
   bibliographical references.
Identifiers: LCCN 2018020328 (print) | LCCN 2018021369 (ebook) | ISBN
   9781625310712 (ebook) | ISBN 9781625310705 (pbk. : alk. paper)
Subjects: LCSH: Language arts (Secondary) | Literature--Study and teaching
   (Secondary) | English language--Rhetoric--Study and teaching (Secondary) |
   English language--Composition and exercises--Study and teaching (Secondary)
Classification: LCC LB1631 (ebook) | LCC LB1631 .F628 2018 (print) | DDC
   428.0071/2--dc23
LC record available at https://lccn.loc.gov/2018020328

Book design by Tom Morgan Blue Design (www.bluedes.com)

Manufactured in the United States of America

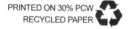

PRINTED ON 30% PCW
RECYCLED PAPER

23 22 21 20 19 18   9 8 7 6 5 4 3 2 1

To my students past, present, and future: Thank you for being my teachers.
And in memory of Robbye G. Kimble: Librarians make the best storytellers.

CONTENTS

Foreword
Leila Christenbury

The opening scene of the classic Victorian novel *Hard Times* takes place in a classroom, and a rather intimidating man, a guest speaker, is lecturing the assembled students and their schoolmaster. The author paints the scene:

> [A] plain, bare, monotonous vault of a schoolroom and the speaker's square forefinger emphasized his observations by underscoring every sentence with a line on the schoolmaster's sleeve. The emphasis was helped by the speaker's square wall of a forehead . . . the emphasis was helped by the speaker's mouth, which was wide, thin, and hard set. The emphasis was helped by the speaker's voice, which was inflexible, dry, and dictatorial. (Dickens [1854] 1965)

And what is the guest speaker's message, delivered for the benefit of the schoolmaster and his students? The memorably named Thomas Gradgrind declaims:

> Now, what I want is Facts. Teach these boys and girls nothing but Facts. Facts alone are wanted in life. Plant nothing else, and root out everything else. You can only form the minds of reasoning animals upon Facts: nothing else will ever be of any service to them. . . . Stick to Facts, sir! (Dickens [1854] 1965)

And how is the schoolmaster to do this? The author tells us explicitly, for the students who sit in desks before the guest speaker and the schoolmaster are described as no more than "little vessels then and there arranged in order, ready to have imperial gallons of facts poured into them until they were full to the brim" (Dickens [1854] 1965). Mr. Gradgrind, indeed, seems to be "a kind of cannon loaded to the muzzle with facts, and prepared to blow [the students] clean out of the regions of childhood at one discharge" (Dickens [1854] 1965).

This is the gripping opening scene of the 1854 *Hard Times*, in which Charles Dickens articulates only too precisely the grim outline of an education circumscribed by "facts" and a teaching modeled on direct transmission of those facts to students as if they were totally empty-headed and only too eager to be filled up. Today, Dickens would clearly recognize those who proclaim that education should convey only facts, that it should be oriented only toward obtaining a job, and that education's ultimate goal is financial success, measured solely by salary. Dickens would not be surprised by today's public comments that the study of the humanities, art, music, and literature are now non-revenue-producing frivolities that are wholly optional in a money-driven, Darwinian, winner-take-all, zero-sum society. These arguments, and those who make them, the Gradgrinds of the world and the secular proponents of a prosperity gospel, would be familiar to Dickens, and we can safely assume that he would once again scorn the kind of impoverished instruction and exclusive devotion to the direct utility of financial gain that they posit.

Jennifer Fletcher's admirable book, *Teaching Literature Rhetorically*, is the opposite of Mr. Gradgrind's message in *Hard Times*. Born of practical experience working with students and based on a palpable devotion to the power of the humanities to provide intellectual ground for exploration, *Teaching Literature Rhetorically* provides specific and well-tested paths to both celebrating the power of literature and giving students real-world skills. Written with an eye to the soul and heart, as well as to the realities of the world in which we and our students live, this book moves beyond its pedagogical focus. Fletcher invites us and our students to have a "flourishing life," which, she maintains, encompasses both the real and the ideal: "A good job is important. A life well-lived is even more important." Arguing that we can indeed move from academic proficiency to true intellectual passion, Fletcher conclusively answers the Gradgrinds of the twenty-first century, noting that

> When we analyze literary texts, we engage in conversations that . . . may last [as Shakespeare writes] "so long as men can breathe, or eyes can see."

It is rare to encounter a book on teaching literature that also highlights the intensive need for a study of the humanities. This vision of literature, indeed what a study of the humanities can do for all of us, is similarly articulated by the writer Marilynne Robinson, who describes the humanities "as a powerful testimony to human capacities, human grandeur, the divine in the human. . . . [Alexis de Tocqueville's] arsenal open to all, where the weak and the poor could always find arms" (Robinson 2017). Like Dickens and others before her, Robinson sees in the "contemporary assault on the humanities" a belief that "workers . . . should learn what they need to learn to be competitive in the new economy. All the rest is waste and distraction." The message of Mr. Gradgrind lives.

But he has his opponents.

Socrates' examined life is a full life, and while critics would prefer that workers at any level simply hew to competition and the getting and spending, the humanities, literature in specific in this argument, consistently ask us to calculate the cost of that getting and spending. Thus, the critical skills of consideration, the look at argument, and, yes, the sheer beauty of the craft, make literature enduring as a study and make our devotion to its teaching worthwhile and, even in a society that questions the economic utility of the humanities, wholly defensible.

If today as a culture we have lost our faith in organized religion, we find ethics and morality in literature. If in our public discourse we have descended into coarseness and impoverished our vocabulary, we can experience precision of expression and richness of language in literature. If in our comfortable society we no longer live near the other and are safely insulated from poverty and war and the perils of immigration, we can experience them—and perhaps what empathy they engender—in literature. If we live in a world circumscribed by terrorism and tribalism and suspicion, in literature we can dream and dare and articulate a brave new world.

And how do we bring this into our classrooms? In *Teaching Literature Rhetorically*, Fletcher gives us paths in and direct advice on instruction. She does not stick to the facts. And we as her readers and students are all the richer for it.

WORKS CITED

Dickens, Charles. (1965) 1854. *Hard Times*. New York: Harper & Row.

Robinson, Marilynne. 2017. "What Are We Doing Here?" *New York Review of Books*, November 9. http://www.nybooks.com/articles/2017/11/09/what-are-we-doing-here/.

Leila Christenbury is Commonwealth Professor at Virginia Commonwealth University in Richmond. She is a past president of the National Council of Teachers of English, a past editor of English Journal, *and recipient of the David H. Russell Award for Distinguished Research in the Teaching of English.*

Acknowledgments

A book's acknowledgments are a chance to write a thank-you note for some of the greatest gifts a writer can receive. This note goes out to a long list of people who gave me gifts of time, expertise, insight, and support while I was writing this book. Their generosity and brilliance are the reasons this book exists.

I wish especially to thank my students for being my vision keepers. Day after day, they kept me honest, letting me know which of my crazy ideas supported their learning and which ones weren't worth the time and effort. They were wonderfully gracious about trying new things. Their willingness to share their work and their experiences is a gift not only to me but also to the teaching profession.

My colleagues, too, have been remarkably generous. I want to thank the following people for their excellent feedback on draft chapters: Meline Akashian, Patrick Belanger, Nelson Graff, Debian Marty, Mridula Mascarenhas, Marcy Merrill, and DeShea Rushing. Extra thanks are also due to Nelson for the use of his "Comparing and Learning from Communication Autobiographies" and for allowing me to participate in a Teaching for Transfer pilot course. I learned so much. Robby Ching, Glen McClish, Kathleen Rowlands, and Maria Villaseñor deserve special thanks for their ongoing support and encouragement. Diana Garcia was exceptionally kind in responding to my interview questions. I owe a special debt of gratitude to my colleagues in the School of Humanities and Communication at California State University, Monterey Bay; their work significantly informs my understanding of effective and ethical communication and cooperative argumentation. It is a privilege working with such superb educators.

The community of teachers involved with the California State University's Expository Reading and Writing Curriculum (ERWC) continues to be one of my greatest sources of inspiration and new learning. I'm especially indebted to John Edlund for alerting me to the rhetorical dimensions of academic citations through his "Negotiating Voices" section of the ERWC Assignment Template. Nancy Brynelson is my role model and hero. If I were ever to become an administrator (which is not likely), I'd want to be just like her. Robby Ching has helped me develop a more nuanced understanding of rhetorical grammar and genre analysis. Adele Arellano, Lisa Benham, Loretta Bernasconi, Debra Boggs, Virginia Crisco, Kim Flachmann, Shirley Hargis, Carol Jago, Cheryl Joseph, Marcy Merrill, Chris Street, David Swartz, and Norm Unrau have all enriched my thinking in important and lasting ways.

Much thanks to Stylus Publishers for granting permission to reprint sections from Chapters 4 and 6 of *Fostering Habits of Mind in Today's Students: A New Approach to Developmental Education* (2015) and to *California English* for permission to reprint a portion of the article "Reconcilable Differences" written with Kathleen Dudden Rowlands (and shout-out to Carol Jago, *CE's* editor, for her exceptional kindness and service to our profession). The California Reading and Literature Project (CRLP) has generously allowed me to include materials developed for its Secondary Academic Language Tools (SALT) program.

I am also deeply grateful to the members of my writers' group: Tiina Kurvi, Undine Lauer, and Camilla Mann. You are amazing writers and dear friends.

To my editor, Bill Varner: It has been a great pleasure working with you and getting to know you through this project. Poets make the best editors—a wonderful example of how literary knowledge helps writers communicate effectively in any genre and context. To Jay Kilburn, Stephanie Levy, Chandra Lowe, Chuck Lurch, Grace Makley, Zsofia McMullin, Dan Tobin, and Drew Yemm: Thank you for bringing this book to life. The whole Stenhouse team is first rate in every way.

Jenn Benge: Your artwork is brilliant. I so appreciate your ability to translate my wacky thought experiments into practical classroom activities.

I also wish to thank a particularly astute reviewer, Heather Rocco, who provided much-needed redirection at a critical moment.

To my parents, Dan and Dorothy Kimble, who fostered my love of literature and teaching: I am forever grateful for all you've done for us. To my sister, Coreen Cardenas, one of the best teachers I know: Thank you for always being there when I need you.

And, finally, I want to thank my family: Ken, Dryden, and Ellerie. You all are the best thing to ever happen to me.

Concepts for Transfer

A high school principal once said to me, "Literature is great, but how many of us use literature in our jobs?" I'm guessing that you've heard comments like this, too. As English language arts teachers, we're often in the uncomfortable position of defending a core element of our discipline—the study of literature—from skeptics who question its practical value. I can say this for sure: if more of us used what we learned from literature on the job, the world would be a better place.

First, a little backstory. I started writing this book with the idea that rhetorical knowledge could help students get more out of literary texts—that doing things like analyzing arguments in poetry, for example, would make students better readers and writers. From literature, we learn about the transformative power of stories, the gifts of imagination, the pleasures of reading, and the importance of craft. From rhetoric, we learn about critical reasoning, the structure of arguments, the tools of persuasion, and the significance of context. Combining the two gives students the best of both worlds.

But then I began thinking about what exactly I wanted students to get out of their literary learning and *where* I hoped that learning would go. And I wrestled with the question we literature teachers are sometimes asked, *When are students going to use this?* The more I thought about it, the more I realized there was a higher goal to pursue.

I came to see a rhetorical approach to literature as a way to promote the kind of deep and transferable learning that prepares students to be adaptive thinkers and communicators who thrive across the diverse contexts of their lives. It wasn't just that literature and rhetoric could productively be combined but that doing so accomplished something special.

Not only does rhetorical knowledge help students communicate effectively in a variety of situations, it also helps students repurpose their learning for new tasks and settings. In other words, rhetorical thinking promotes transfer of learning—the single most important goal we can have as teachers if we hope to have a positive impact on our students' future lives. If students can't transfer what they learn from one setting to the next, then we have to question the value of the education we've provided.

Literary learning is too important not to be applied outside of the English language arts classroom. Those of us who love to read and teach novels, poetry, short stories, and drama know that literary study offers students tremendous benefits, today and tomorrow. Literary study develops all the academic literacy skills and dispositions that form the basis of this book—from reading closely, to negotiating different perspectives, to communicating with self and others in mind. When we teach these high-utility competencies with an eye to their future applications, we increase the likelihood that what our students learn in our classes will be put to good use.

Like where, for instance? Let me give you an example. How about the field of medicine? Can a literature education make for better health care professionals? Rita Charon thinks so. In *Narrative Medicine: Honoring the Stories of Illness* (2006), Charon, a physician and professor of clinical medicine at Columbia University, argues for the importance of "narrative competence" in the medical field. For Charon, narrative competence means the capacity to listen empathetically to patients' stories, understand the significance of their narrative choices, and synthesize various accounts into a cohesive whole. The ability to facilitate and interpret storytelling as a means of better understanding a patient's illness can literally be a matter of life or death. This is not something doctors, nurses, and therapists just naturally do, says Charon, who notes that "although everyone grows up listening to and telling stories, sophisticated knowledge of how stories work is not attained without considerable effort and commitment" (2006, ix). Charon provides narrative training for medical students at Columbia by introducing them to literary texts and theories and giving "them the tools to make authentic contact with works of fiction, poetry, and drama" (2006, x).

If prestigious medical schools are trying to reap the rewards of a literature education, is it any wonder that other fields and sectors also have a new appreciation of literature's relevance? Many employers and universities now see literary study as a powerful means of developing the creative problem-solving and communication skills essential to success. Note how the following headlines all herald a humanities education—of which literature is a central part—as a hot commodity in the twenty-first century:

- From *Scientific American*: "Science Is Not Enough: Politicians Trying to Dump Humanities Will Hobble Our Economy" (October 2016)

- From *American Express Open Forum*: "Why English Majors Are the Hot New Hires" (July 2013)

- From *Education Drive*: "Why Tech Industries Are Demanding More Liberal Arts Graduates" (July 2016)

Teaching literature is one of the best things we can do for all our students, regardless of where they're headed in their careers and lives. Literature is still the heart of our discipline. Former National Council of Teachers of English president Leila Christenbury rightly calls literature "the backbone of English language arts" (2000, 124). We just need to help students figure out how, when, where, and why they can put their valuable literature education to good use. That's where a rhetorical approach comes in.

Teaching literature rhetorically makes the works we love to read and teach, the books with the power to change our students' lives, more exciting, accessible, and relatable. As students move from a passionate engagement with art to a rigorous study of argument, they develop rhetorical reading and writing skills they will be able to apply flexibly, independently, and compellingly to future tasks and contexts.

Transfer of Learning Is a Matter of Educational Equity

What students do with their learning once they leave our classrooms has become an increasingly important concern to educators. The National Research Council shaped much of the recent discussion on this topic through the 2012 publication of the report *Education for Life and Work: Developing Transferable Knowledge and Skills in the 21st Century*. Then, in 2013, Elon University published the *Elon Statement on Writing Transfer*, the framework that emerged from the work of forty-five writing researchers who participated in a three-year seminar on key transitions in students' educational journeys.

For those of us working hard to improve college access and completion, the recent scholarship on transfer of learning offers important insights about how we can help students negotiate the critical transitions that increasingly determine postsecondary success—such as the transition from high school to college, from school to work, and from first-year college courses into the major and beyond. Teaching for transfer promotes students' agency and resilience by empowering them to adapt and apply their learning to new settings.

These capacities are key to retaining and graduating more students. For first-generation and nontraditional college students, unfamiliar experiences are a daily reality. A convergence of equity agendas has helped us to rethink how we prepare today's students for their future lives by paying closer attention to those moments in the educational pipeline when students are most likely to leave school.

What's more, college access is no longer seen as an issue that affects a minority of graduating high school students. According to a report by the Institute for Higher Education Policy (Miller, Valle, and Engle 2014, 6), 65 percent of all job openings will require some form of postsecondary education and training by the year 2020. "Higher education," the report states, "is now a minimum requirement for most jobs in the knowledge economy" (Miller, Valle, and Engle 2014, 10). Access to higher education—which includes adequate preparation—is now regarded as "a basic right for all" (Miller, Valle, and Engle 2014, 10).

The same report also notes that twenty-first-century learners do not fit the traditional profile of the college-bound student:

52 percent will be the first in their family to complete college

51 percent are low to moderate income

42 percent are from communities of color

18 percent are nonnative English speakers

10 percent are immigrants

Their prospects don't fit the traditional mold either. In an age of start-ups, innovators, and entrepreneurs—and the boom-and-bust cycles that accompany them—it's far more likely that today's graduates will experience a working life characterized by multiple career changes and disruptions rather than a thirty-year stint with the same company capped off by a steady pension.

Teaching for transfer prepares twenty-first-century learners for a changing world. To be clear, transfer of learning doesn't mean a wholesale carryover of knowledge and skills from one place to another, like transferring funds between bank accounts. Rather, the theoretical model of transfer is much closer to the idea of transformation. Think about the transformations effected by successful film adaptations. As *San Francisco Chronicle* film critic Mick LaSalle writes on the adaption of stage plays into movies, "You can't just take one thing from one place and slap it into something else" (2017, 15). Whatever is being carried from one context to the next undergoes significant redesign and repurposing before it can be put to effective use.

The founders of my university know all about strategic redesign and repurposing. Our campus was created from a converted army base—the famous Fort Ord, site of basic training for Jimi Hendrix, Jerry Garcia, Leonard Nimoy, and Clint Eastwood. At its peak capacity, the base employed roughly 35,000 people, a regional powerhouse that drove the economies and identities of the surrounding communities. When the base closed in 1994, it must have seemed as if life as they knew it was ending for local residents. Yet in the face of radical change, educators, civic leaders, military personnel, business owners, and local community members came together to find innovative new purposes for the shuttered base. California State University, Monterey Bay, opened as a new educational hub (see Figure I.1). Other portions of the old army base are now dedicated to recreational use and cultural preservation, including the Fort Ord National Monument and Fort Ord Dunes State Park. The region has learned to adapt and thrive.

When our students encounter radical change and novelty, they won't be able to do what they've always done. But they will have valuable skills, knowledge, and cultural and personal resources they can draw on. Rhetorical thinking and a spirit of transfer can help them leverage those assets appropriately.

Teaching for Transfer Requires Expansive Framing

It's not enough that our students have advanced literacy skills by the time they graduate from high school; we also need to carefully consider the uses to which they put those skills. How we teach affects not only what our students learn but also how they apply what they learn.

FIGURE I.1
A repurposed army tank garage is now a university art studio.

In a 2012 issue of *Educational Psychologist* dedicated to research on transfer of learning, David N. Perkins and Gavriel Salomon describe some of the challenges of teaching for transfer. As they note in "Knowledge to Go: A Motivational and Dispositional View of Transfer" the generally agreed upon purpose of schools is to offer "knowledge-to-go, not just [to] use on site" (2012, 248). However, substantial research suggests that the intended take-away learning often gets left behind. "Besides just plain forgetting, people commonly fail to marshal what they know effectively in situations outside the classroom or in other classes in different disciplines," Perkins and Salomon write (2012, 248).

If we want students' literary learning to have a positive impact beyond their English classes, we need to help them figure out how to take their learning with them. Students need knowledge and the ability to repurpose it. Beyond developing the ability to interpret, analyze, and respond to literary texts, students also need to ask questions about the applications of their literary learning:

- When am I going to use this again?
- How else can I use this?
- Where else can I use this?

We help students develop this mind-set for applied learning through what Perkins and Salomon call "expansive framing," or instructional framing that promotes transfer of learning. Perkins and Salomon distinguish between expansive framing and bounded framing: "Expansive framing emphasizes the meaningfulness and usefulness of what's being learned and its potential to relate to a range of other circumstances. Bounded framing treats what's being learned as for the unit, for the class, for the quiz" (2012, 254).

Expansive framing gets at the idea of transfer as almost a sort of time machine; through the portal of transfer, we see beyond our immediate present into our future lives and past experiences. Transfer bridges different sites and phases of learning, knitting together prior knowledge with new skills and understandings, as we adapt to the changing circumstances and demands of our lives.

We're not framing instruction for transfer when we tell students we just have to cover the content or get through the required material. An example of bounded framing would be telling students they have to be able to identify genres for the SAT without explaining *why* the SAT measures this ability in the first place or what it has to do with their future success.

A rhetorical approach, on the other hand, is a type of expansive framing because it focuses on use, relevance, and circumstances. We can set students up to apply their learning by explicitly modeling "transfer-focused thinking" (Moore and Bass 2017, 7–8), including metacognition and rhetorical analysis.

Literary learning needs to be knowledge-to-go.

A Rhetorical Approach Prepares Students for a Complex World

Considering the challenges our students will face in their future lives, they're going to need to leverage all the learning they have. We live in a time that sociologist Zygmunt Blauman has described as "liquid modernity" (2007, 1), a period of profound dynamism and flux. Perhaps never before has the ability to adapt to changing conditions been requisitioned with such frequency and need as in our current age.

Yet literature is often taught as the study of "timeless voices and timeless themes," as the title of one popular textbook series puts it. Many students still learn to read literature by searching for fixed, universal meanings, and they learn to write about literature by following rules and formulas, as though literary study is in its own time warp, disconnected from the social, political, technological, and economic changes that our students will have to navigate in order to thrive in the twenty-first-century world. Something is out of joint.

In contrast, a rhetorical approach to literature heightens students' situational awareness and responsiveness by engaging the various voices of literary texts and conversations, not as timeless voices but as unique components in particular rhetorical situations. Rhetoric's fundamental concern is how to communicate effectively in diverse contexts. We learn from studying rhetoric how elements of the rhetorical situation—including audience, purpose, occasion, and genre—impact the effectiveness of communication choices. Literary scholar James Phelan says the rhetorical approach "seeks to be a portable approach by developing concepts and tools . . . that are powerful enough to give us insights into the dynamics of specific texts and flexible enough to apply across a range of texts" (2010, 217–228).

What is *not* a rhetorical approach to reading literature? One that attempts to keep literature in its own box and that ignores the communicative functions (or "uses") of literature in real-life contexts. Kenneth Burke describes this nonrhetorical approach in *A Rhetoric of Motives*, using the example of John Milton's 1671 poem "Samson Agonistes":

> One can read it simply *in itself*, without even considering the fact that it
> was written by Milton. It can be studied and appreciated as a structure of
> internally related parts, without concern for the correspondence that almost
> inevitably suggests itself: the correspondence between Milton's blindness
> and Samson's, or between the poet's difficulties with his first wife and
> Delilah's betrayal of a divine "secret." (1969, 4; italics in original)

As Burke notes, reading the poem this way ignores some of its most important work and meaning: that it "is not sheer poetic exercise" but rather the rhetorical action of "a cantankerous old fighter-priest … whose very translation of political controversy to high theologic terms helps, by such magnification, to sanction the ill-tempered obstinacy of his resistance" (1969, 5). Milton the fighter-priest speaks to a particular audience (seventh-century Royalists and Puritans) for a particular purpose (self-justification). This is poetry "for use" (4).

What is *not* a rhetorical approach to writing about literature? One that sets out a list of rules or prescriptions for students to follow instead of offering them situational contingencies to consider.

The world we live in certainly doesn't operate by fixed rules. The kinds of problems we now face are anything but fixed. Researchers talk about the 21st century as being the era of "wicked problems"[1]—problems that are fluid, constantly changing, and unpredictable, including terrorism, poverty, and climate change. An example of a wicked problem in which a solution might work one time only to fail the next is the Zika virus: incomplete and contradictory data, rapid developments, lots of components in play. Students need flexible competencies to deal with these kinds of dynamic, unpredictable problems. In essence, we want students to face a problem they've never seen before without freaking out and to understand that we don't solve complex problems by oversimplifying them.

Rhetoric Is the Art of Adaptation

Rhetoric is interested not so much in the timeless and universal as in the unique and particular: in other words, to paraphrase Aristotle, in the available resources in a given situation. This kind of adaptive thinking helps people succeed in school, work, and life. Fixed thinking and one-size-fits-all approaches typically do not.

----

1. *See, for instance, "'Wicked Problems' and the Work of School" by Stephen Murgatroyd in a 2010 issue of the* European Journal of Education.

Linda Adler-Kassner, a University of California professor who writes about transfer and educational reform, argues that success in a particular context depends on a person's ability to identify what is valued and necessary in that context: "Even in a globalizing economy, the on-the-ground specifics of schools, workplaces, and individual experiences have distinct elements and qualities. . . . No class, no school experience, can teach students to be successful in *all* of these contexts for practice" ("Transfer and Educational Reform" 2017, 18; italics in the original). Instead, students need to learn the art of adaptation.

When Am I Going to Use This Again?

How do students know what and how to adapt? The research on transfer suggests students need deep learning, including an understanding of underlying principles, to effectively repurpose their knowledge and skills in new contexts. In other words, they need expert learning. According to the National Research Council, "Experts have not only acquired knowledge, but are also good at retrieving the knowledge that is relevant to a particular task" (2000, 43). That is, they have developed conditional knowledge—knowledge of when, where, and why to apply their learning. Many of our students can demonstrate proficiency on individual worksheets or tests but don't know the conditions under which they can appropriately use their knowledge again. They can't answer the question "When am I going to use this?"

Consider this. How we drive depends on the conditions: wet or dry weather, light or heavy traffic, rough or smooth roads, good or poor visibility. How we communicate also depends on the conditions: the setting, the people involved, the unique moment in time. In real-world communication, a text's context (i.e., the set of conditions) is ultimately a more important determiner of meaning than the text itself, a point made by Russian philosopher and literary critic Mikhail Mikhailovich Bakhtin. Michael Holquist, editor and translator of *The Dialogic Imagination: Four Essays by M. M. Bakhtin*, explains Bakhtin's idea of *heteroglossia* this way: "At any given time, in any given place, there will be a set of conditions—social, historical, meteorological, physiological—that will ensure that a word uttered in that place and at that time will have a different meaning than it would have had under any other conditions" (1981, 428). Change the conditions, and you change what the text means.

Yet we often teach in a way that limits our students' ability to respond to changing conditions. If we instruct students to follow one-size-fits-all rules and formulas, we ill equip them to deal with the metaphorical icy roads in their future. In fact, formulaic approaches can actually impede students' academic preparation. Citing multiple studies, Adler-Kassner describes this problem in "Transfer and Educational Reform":

> Research on writing indicates that the more strongly writers believe that writing always takes place within or always extends from specific forms (e.g., argumentative, informative/explanatory, and narrative) and the more rigid

the ideas they have about what those forms look like, the less able they are to understand that successful writing requires flexibility. (2017, 21)

In other words, rule-based instruction of the "always" and "never" kind can make students less prepared for the literacy demands of the postsecondary world.

A rhetorical education, however, gets students ready for real-world job opportunities. Take a look at this Facebook job posting from January 29, 2017:

> ### Brand Optimization Analyst
> Execute, optimize, and measure the impact of the brand across channels. (*San Francisco Chronicle*)

Analyzing the effects of communication choices across contexts is precisely what a rhetorical education prepares students to do. I take seriously first-generation college students' desire to get a good job after graduation. They and their families have made real sacrifices to enable them to pursue their college dreams, and they want to know that those sacrifices will pay off. "When am I going to use this again?" is not a trivial question for them. But when I ask students what they want for their future, they say more than just a high-paying career. They want to make a difference. They want to grow and travel. They want to be happy. They want their families to be happy.

Literature is often the means by which we learn who we are and what makes us happy; it helps us grow beyond the limits of our own experience, encouraging us to embrace complex problems and diverse perspectives, while empowering us to make the contributions that only we can make. A good job is important. A life well-lived is even more important.

By engaging literature rhetorically, students develop abundant intellectual and personal resources they'll be able to use to make a living and a life.

This Book Is a Guide to Making the Most of Our Opportunities

You can think of this book as a resource for making the most of our opportunities to promote transferable learning through literary study. Transfer and rhetoric are all about taking advantage of available opportunities, not following a rigid system. That's why you'll find lots of nonliterary examples and activities in this book, too. Keeping literary skills, concepts, and texts separate from informational texts is a missed opportunity. What I hope you'll find throughout are friendly ways to help students develop versatility as readers, writers, and thinkers.

The chapters are accordingly organized around eight portable literacy skills and practices that help students thrive long after they leave our classrooms:

- Integrating skills and knowledge
- Reading closely and critically

- Assessing the rhetorical situation
- Analyzing genres
- Negotiating voices and meaning
- Developing and supporting a line of reasoning
- Communicating with self and others in mind
- Reading and writing with passion

These are broadly applicable skills, valuable in all content areas. They're also the skills that help students adapt their literary learning to new tasks and contexts. A literature program that develops these skills prepares students to be successful in the lives they are likely to live.

Transformative learning of this kind doesn't happen overnight. A rhetorical approach sparks a big shift in students' thinking; it takes time, lots of practice and reflection, and support for students to internalize their new understandings. Modeling and mentoring are essential.

There are a couple ways to read this book, depending on what you want to get out of it. I've tried to load the chapters and appendixes with practical strategies you can use right away if you're flipping through this book while lesson planning on a Sunday night. Other sections are probably better suited to slow reading done with a cup of tea or a glass of wine by the fireside.

The works of literature in this book are a mix of what literacy scholar Katie Egan Cunningham calls "mirrors" and "windows" (2015, 6): texts that reflect students' own backgrounds and identities and texts that offer insights into alternative perspectives. As Egan notes, changing times call for changing texts (2015, 22-24). I include examples from award-winning young adult novels, such as Sherman Alexie's *The Absolutely True Diary of a Part-Time Indian*, Jacqueline Woodson's *Brown Girl Dreaming*, and Gene Luen Yang's *American Born Chinese*, as well as from enduring classics, such as *Hamlet*, *The Canterbury Tales*, and *Beowulf*. The texts also present a range of difficulty levels, from highly accessible works such as the Harry Potter series or Rodman Philbrick's *Freak the Mighty* to Kazuo Ishiguro's *The Remains of the Day* and Joy Kogawa's *Obasan*, which offer older readers an intellectual stretch.

You'll notice that I take an integrated approach to written communication in this book. Chapters typically address reading and writing, and high-utility concepts such as audience, purpose, context, ethos, pathos, and logos appear throughout the book. There's a good reason for this: The reading strategies *are* writing strategies, and the writing strategies are reading strategies. Transfer of learning from reading to writing and vice versa is one of the most important applications of students' knowledge and skills we can promote in our classrooms.

You'll notice, too, that I use the phrase "ethical and effective communication" throughout this book. This is one of the values I bring to this discussion. *Ethical* communication, for me, means informed and respectful communication that promotes understanding. *Effective* communication means communication that reaches its target audience and achieves its intended purpose.

What doesn't this book do? It's not a tech resource. It might seem odd that a book about preparing students for the future has so little to say about technology, but there are a couple reasons for this. First, I'm not a tech expert. I'd recommend Diana Neebe and Jen Roberts's *Power Up* (2015) for a fabulous guide to bringing your classroom into the digital age. Second, the tech skills students need today are not the tech skills students will need tomorrow. Teaching for transfer means preparing students to adapt to situations they haven't encountered before and that, in many cases, do not even exist yet. What critical thinking and communication skills, problem-solving abilities, and habits of mind will students need to continue to adapt in order to thrive in a constantly changing world? That's the question I'm inviting you to explore with me.

Finally, I can't write about preparing students for the future without tipping my hand to the kind of future I'd like to see. You'll notice that I have a commitment to collaborative problem solving, that I think we need to understand before we argue, and that I believe diversity benefits us all. I invite you to contribute your own values, beliefs, and priorities to this conversation and let me know how I can deepen my thinking. You can contact me at jfletcher@csumb.edu.

What ultimately matters is what our students know and can do when we're not there to give them directions. Can they adapt to unfamiliar situations? Figure out how to communicate in new settings and forms? Find innovative solutions to problems? Collaborate? Contribute to their own and others' well-being? This is the real test of life readiness.

I'm excited by the learning I've seen happen in my own classes and the thought of where it might go. I want you to be excited by the possibilities, too.

CHAPTER ONE

Integrating Skills and Knowledge

Writing transfer is inherently complex. It involves approaching new and unfamiliar writing tasks through applying, remixing, or integrating previous knowledge, skills, strategies, and dispositions.

—JESSIE L. MOORE

Our fondest wish as teachers is that our students will use what we've taught them. This is what it means to make a difference—that our work continues to have an impact long after our students have left our classrooms. Much of the time, this impact is obscured from our view; we see our students' future lives through a glass darkly and can only hope their intellectual journeys proceed along the course we helped to set.

But sometimes we get a clear view of where and how our students apply their learning beyond our classes. A few years ago, I received an e-mail from a former student who went on to become a technical writer for the US Department of Defense:

> *Dr. Fletcher,*
> *You would not believe what I just did at work today. . . . My team is putting out a "thought paper" to persuade different departments and services (Army, Navy) to use this new technology. I was sent an article about converging technologies.*
>
> *To the point. I was able to critically analyze the structure of the article, the ebb and flow of ethos/pathos and logos, and even some of the grammatical elements enhancing*

the rhetoric. . . . My teammate was very impressed, and now I get to take the lead on the paper.

I just wanted to share this with you because this is exactly what I wanted to get out of the class.

Thank you for the tools.
Cody

Of course, Cody's e-mail made my day. It also helped me think more intentionally about what students get out of my English classes, that is, what learning they carry with them and where it goes. I wondered: *What helped Cody use what I'd taught him?* Looking back, I'd say it was the following qualities:

- A mind-set toward connection-making
- An ability to hold onto thinking[1]
- Rhetorical knowledge and skills
- A habit of creative problem solving
- A habit of leveraging prior knowledge

Instead of shaking the dust off his heels when he left my class, Cody lived with his learning for an extended period, saving his skills and knowledge for a fresh opportunity to repurpose them.

Adaptive thinkers like Cody are the "makers" of the educational world, reveling in creative redesigns of existing models. Like the steampunk artist who integrates the old with the new in a fantastic reimagining of Victorian culture, the student who can successfully integrate skills and knowledge acquired in different settings is a master of remix. Prior knowledge becomes a storehouse of novel possibilities—the maker's inventory of spare parts waiting to be recombined. A student who has developed this mind-set for connection-making leaves a class thinking, *What am I going to make out of all this interesting stuff in my brain?*

Fostering Integrative Learning

Cody's account of how he transferred rhetorical knowledge and skills acquired through an undergraduate humanities course to his new job working for the military beautifully illustrates the idea of *integrative learning.*

In its Integrative and Applied Learning VALUE Rubric, the Association of American Colleges and Universities (AACSU) defines *integrative learning* as "an understanding and a disposition that a student builds across the curriculum and co-curriculum, from making simple connections

----

1.   *Kelly Gallagher describes the importance of teaching students to "track their thinking" over time in* In the Best Interest of Students. *(2015, 148)*

among ideas and experiences to synthesizing and transferring learning to new, complex situations within and beyond the campus" (2009; see Appendix 2). Integrative learning is at the heart of the twenty-first-century competencies most educators agree are needed to thrive in a changing world. David N. Perkins, for example, repeatedly stresses the importance of boundary-crossing and connection-making in his discussion of broad educational trends that are "expanding the universe of what's worth learning," trends he calls "the six beyonds" (2014, 2). Among these trends, Perkins identifies the following movements toward integrative thinking:

- A movement beyond traditional disciplines toward hybrid disciplines (e.g., bioethics)

- A movement beyond discrete disciplines toward interdisciplinary topics and problems (e.g., reducing poverty or increasing access to clean water)

- A movement beyond regional perspectives toward global systems and studies (2014, 3)

In describing an additional "beyond"—beyond content mastery toward applied learning—Perkins notes that educators are now "encouraging learners not just to master content academically but to also notice where content connects to life situations, yields insights, and prompts productive action" (2014, 3).

Integrating Literature and Rhetoric

A rhetorical approach to literature helps students make meaningful connections. Rhetoric is a powerful tool for seeing the big picture, for moving beyond a silo mentality toward a more interconnected understanding of our world. As Aristotle says, "Rhetoric is not bound up with a single definite class of subjects, but is as universal as dialectic [i.e., reasoned discourse]" (1984, Book 1, Chap. i). Rhetoric is a metadiscipline.

Like a universal decoder ring, rhetoric can thus speak the language of all other approaches to literary analysis, including critical theories such as New Criticism and reader response. In *The Mirror and the Lamp* ([1953] 1971), literary critic M. H. Abrams identifies the following coordinates of art criticism: the universe, the work, the audience, and the artist (see Figure 1.1).

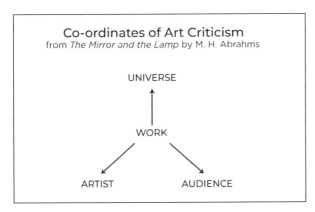

FIGURE 1.1

Coordinates of art criticism from *The Mirror and the Lamp* by M. H. Abrams

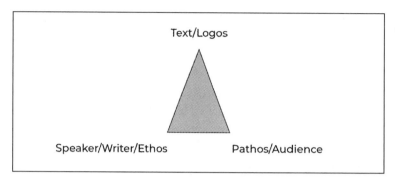

FIGURE 1.2

The rhetorical triangle

Abrams uses these coordinates to identify different critical theories, or lenses, with each lens emphasizing different coordinates. For example, mimetic approaches (such as neoclassicism) foreground the relationship between the work and the universe, while objective theories (such as New Criticism) focus on a close reading of the work itself.

However, a rhetorical approach simultaneously engages the dynamics of all four coordinates. Rhetoric is interested in how all meaning-making agents—text, writer, reader, and context—contribute to the effect of a work. (See Figure 1.2.)

Consider Aristotle's description of a rhetor's tasks:

> But since rhetoric exists to affect the giving of decisions . . . the orator must not only try to make the argument of his [sic] speech demonstrative and worthy of belief; he must also make his own character look right and put his hearers, who are to decide, into the right frame of mind. (1984, Book II, Chap. i)

In this description of effective speech, we find an even emphasis on three of Abram's coordinates: the work, the audience, and the artist. Elsewhere in *Rhetoric*, Aristotle gives equal weight to *kairos* (the immediate social context) or what Abrams might call "the universe." Rhetoric, in other words, is a sort of superlens. Because skilled rhetors must understand multiple views and fields simultaneously, rhetoric can serve as a foundational practice on which advanced and portable competencies in other content areas, including literary studies, are built.

Combining literature with rhetoric thus amplifies student learning while enhancing its transferability. Think about the added benefits your students could get from integrating literary and rhetorical approaches to textual analysis, for instance (see Figure 1.3):

LITERARY ANALYSIS	RHETORICAL ANALYSIS
characterization setting point of view plot theme conflict imagery	rhetorical situation audience context purpose ethos pathos logos

FIGURE 1.3
Combining literary analysis with rhetorical analysis

If students can analyze a novel's plot, point of view, and theme, as well as its audience, context, and purpose, they'll have twice the interpretive power. Bringing together these two ways of knowing gives students the best of both worlds.

Why Integrative Thinking Matters

If you want to give your students a quick idea of what we mean by integrative thinking, show them a few screen grabs from films like *Mad Max: Fury Road* (2015) or *The League of Extraordinary Gentlemen* (2003) and ask them what artifacts and ideas have been creatively combined and repurposed (e.g., cars, trucks, transportation, defense).

The two images in Figure 1.4 also offer intriguing examples of integrative thinking. You can share images like these with your students and ask the following questions: *What do you notice about these images? What strikes you as interesting or important? What other examples of repurposed objects, buildings, or things can you think of?*

FIGURE 1.4A
A repurposed shipping container now serves as a restaurant.

FIGURE 1.4B
Old car parts make a fine fish.

While we hopefully don't need to prepare our students to survive in a postapocalyptic wasteland, we do need to educate them for a changing world. Whenever we invite students to consider multiple perspectives, engage diverse contexts, explore various modes of inquiry, leverage their prior knowledge, practice real-world problem solving, and communicate rhetorically, we are fostering the integrative thinking central to a flourishing global society. As the AAC&U observes, "Students face a rapidly changing and increasingly connected world where integrative learning becomes not just a benefit . . . but a necessity" (https://www.aacu.org/value/rubrics/integrative-learning, 2009).

To see why, we need only look at a couple of real-world examples from our own century. First, a case of failure to practice integrative thinking, with tragic consequences: the Flint, Michigan, water crisis. The interconnections between the environment, the human population, and the economy profoundly affect access to clean water. The crisis that began in Flint in 2014 resulted from ignoring these interconnections. Economic interests eclipsed human and environmental concerns when an emergency city manager, looking to save money, switched the water source from the Detroit Water and Sewerage Department to the Flint River without considering the risks to public health. The corrosive river water stripped lead from the one-hundred-year-old pipes, contaminating the tap water and poisoning the population.

When integrative thinking is effectively practiced, however, the result can be inspiring. For example, Dr. Frank Fish, a researcher at West Chester University in Pennsylvania, looked to the natural world to help solve a problem faced by twenty-first-century humans: the challenge of designing efficient wind turbines that can produce cleaner energy. Fish noticed that the leading edge of a humpback whale's flipper was bumpy, a fact that seemed to run counter to accepted wisdom on aerodynamic design. The edges of windmill blades and airplane wings had always been straight. Straight edges reduce resistance, right? Yet when Fish applied the humpback whale's leading bumpy edge design to the blade of a wind

FIGURE 1.5
Whale flipper

turbine, he found it actually increased the turbine's efficiency by 20 percent. You can find out why by viewing the video "Whales to Windmills" (2011) at www.youtube.com/watch?v=OpLzI27febM. (See Figure 1.5.)

Dr. Fish's creative combination of marine biology and aerodynamic technology exemplifies the disposition for making "connections among ideas and experiences and . . . synthesizing and transferring learning to new, complex situations within and beyond the campus" (AAC&U 2009), —a disposition central to integrative thinking. Integrative thinking helps us see the familiar in new ways. This ability is key to finding innovative solutions to problems.

Take the example I share in the introduction: narrative medicine. Medical schools have found that combining study in literature and science leads to more effective patient care. In a blog for the *New York Times*, Dr. Richard Panush, a department chair at a major teaching hospital, notes that "studies have repeatedly shown that such literary training can strengthen and support the compassionate instincts of doctors" (2008). Integrative learning helps health care professionals think differently about their work, ultimately resulting in improved quality of care.

> While "transfer of learning" may be a newer term for many teachers, the idea of integrative learning dates back to John Dewey and beyond. In *The School and Society*, Dewey calls for schools to be connected with real life "so that the experience gained by the child in a familiar, commonplace way is carried over and made use of there and what the child learns in the school is carried back and applied in everyday life, making the school an organic whole, instead of a composite of isolated parts" (1889, 91).

Throughout this book, I share strategies for supporting specific acts of transfer made possible by a mind-set for connection-making (Figure 1.6):

TRANSFER OF LEARNING FROM . . .	
reading to writing	English language arts classes to other content areas
literary texts to informational texts	high school to college
rhetorical analysis to literary analysis	school to career
home to school	literature to life

FIGURE 1.6
Acts of transfer[2]

To use David Perkins's words, these are "lifeworthy" acts of transfer that are "likely to matter in the lives learners are likely to live" (2014, 8).

- - - - - - - - - - - - - - - - - -

2. *Nearly all of these also work in reverse.*

Where Do We Start?

All this might sound pretty aspirational. So where do we start? I think we start by fostering a disposition toward connection-making. This is the "spirit of transfer" Haskell writes about that helps students apply their learning to new tasks and contexts (2001). Valuing prior knowledge and seeking creative ways to redeploy it can be a big shift in thinking for adolescent learners. According to Perkins, a problem with some conventional teaching is that it "neglects the dispositional side of learning by not fostering sensitivity and inclination to engage the content and connect it widely" (2014, 112). Many students come to our English language arts classes doubting the relevance of what they already know and can do. They may wait for us to tell them the new "rules" and believe they're not "allowed" to adapt their prior skills and knowledge to the work they're doing for our class, especially if they're used to more formulaic approaches to instruction. Some students may even see bringing together learning from different classes or assignments as a form of cheating, or "double dipping."

This puts a special obligation on teachers to invite students to integrate their skills and knowledge in meaningful ways. We need to tell students that it's not only OK but actually a fantastic idea to take their learning beyond traditional academic boundaries. This, in fact, is the pathway to deeper understandings and more transferable competencies. We also need to help students develop the situational awareness and rhetorical sensitivity necessary to adapt and apply their learning appropriately, so that they don't think we're simply asking them to rehash their tenth-grade oral report on animal rights for their twelfth-grade research paper on the industrial food complex. Students need encouragement and support to make meaningful connections.

So. We start by making the connections visible. Picture one of those maps of flight paths in the back of an airline magazine. Think of all those graceful arcs connecting the airline's different destinations, the hubs bright with converging lines. Now picture your own intellectual journey—the places you've been, the books you've read, the subjects you've studied, and the degrees and credentials you hold. How have the connections among these learning experiences shaped the person you've become? In what sites and paths have you spent the most time? What routes were the most transformative?

To help students develop a mind-set toward connection-making, ask them to draw their own map, linking the different sites of their learning, including classes, projects and assignments, home, work, sports, music, electronic environments, and so forth. Encourage them to include in-school and out-of-school learning experiences. Tell students to draw a line between "destinations" if they have transferred learning from one task or context to the other. The purpose of this activity is for students to find their "connecting cities," those sites of learning that interact with the others. Students may even find they have a learning "hub" (think of all those American Airlines flights that connect in Dallas, Texas). See the model and student sample in Figures 1.7 and 1.8.

TRANSFER MAPS

Directions to Students: First, look at a picture of an airline's flight paths. You can find this image online if your teacher doesn't provide one for you. Notice all the different destinations the airline flies to and how many of those cities are connected by the airline's itineraries. With this image in mind, now draw a map of your own sites of learning, including classes, projects and assignments, home, work, sports, music, electronic environments, and so forth. Include in-school and out-of-school learning experiences. Draw a line between destinations if you have transferred learning from one task or context to the other.

Try following up with these questions:

- What are you learning now that will be useful in college and in the workplace?

- How is what you learned in one area of your map related to another? For instance, what have you learned from playing sports that you've used in school?

- What opportunities do you see to connect your learning that you haven't taken advantage of yet?

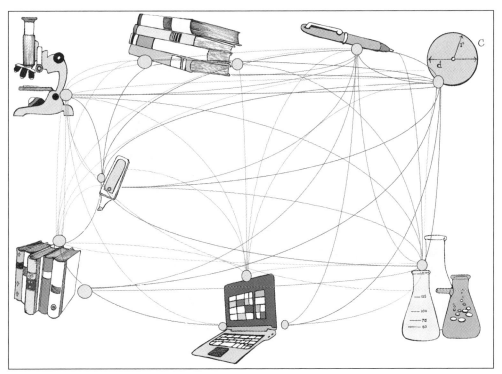

FIGURE 1.7
Transfer of learning map

Students can write their responses to these questions before discussing their answers with a partner or a small group.

To extend students' thinking further, you can ask them to write an "integrative narrative" that tells the story of how their different sites of learning are connected.

> **Directions to Students:** Choose three or four learning contexts that are especially important to you: for instance, work, school, home, and sports. Other options could include music, dance, social media, and faith-based activities or specific content areas, such as math or English. Reflect on your experiences in each of the areas you selected. What are the major lessons you've learned? What are your most important achievements? Now think about how these areas are related. What are the overall big ideas you're learning across these different contexts? How does one context support your learning in another? Write an integrative narrative that tells the story of how your different sites of learning are connected. Your task is to synthesize and interconnect what you are learning in the areas you identified.

By the way, when I have my students do this, I'm surprised by how many of them identify YouTube as a major site of their learning. Electronic environments are a huge part of their transfer maps.

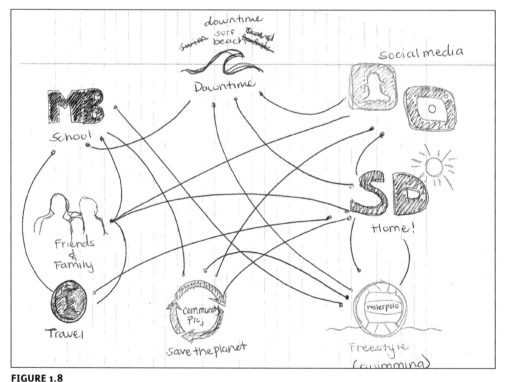

FIGURE 1.8
Student example of a transfer of learning map

Tech Twist: Instead of drawing their maps, students can use Google My Maps to drop pins on important sites of learning and describe the experiences in those locations that have shaped their identity as a learner. My Maps is great because it allows students to add images of themselves and to choose colors and icons that are symbolic to them. My Maps will also allow students to draw lines connecting sites of learning. (Thank you, Mark Vermillion, for teaching me about this tool!)

CAREER CHANGER QUICK-WRITE

Another opening gambit I've used to foster a disposition toward integrative learning is the career changer quick-write. Like the transfer map, this activity helps students to see that intentional cross-context connections can lead to higher levels of understanding and performance.

> *Directions to Students*: Choose one of the statements that follow to respond to in a quick-write. In your response, explain why that statement might be true. Support your position using reasons and examples. (If you're skeptical that any statement is true, then try at least to play the "believing game" with one statement.) What transferable skills and knowledge might that person bring from their prior experience that would help them be successful in their new profession? What are the similarities and differences between the two jobs? Feel free to be creative and come up with your own career change if you prefer.
>
> Someone trained as a poet might make a particularly good lawyer.
>
> Someone trained as a DJ might make a particularly good computer programmer.
>
> Someone trained as an architect might make a particularly good fashion designer.
>
> Someone trained as an athlete might make a particularly good business manager.
>
> Someone trained as a rapper might make a particularly good journalist.
>
> Someone trained as a farmer might make a particularly good teacher.
>
> Someone trained as a teacher might make a particularly good police officer.
>
> Someone trained as a _____ might make a particularly good _____.

Notice the way students compared contexts and extracted generalizations in the following examples:

> A DJ would make a good computer programmer because both work with technology. To be a good programmer, you need to be able to identify patterns in order to create more complex coding. DJs also look for patterns when they are working with their technology.

> Someone trained as a teacher might make a particularly good police officer. A teacher always has to be aware of what is going on. Whether it's regular teaching or reacting to emergency situations. So does a police officer. They are both the people you first turn to in need of help.

Someone trained as a rapper might make a particularly good journalist. A lot of good rappers like to tell stories within their songs in a very poetic way.

The skill you can transfer from being an athlete to being a businessman is being organized with a schedule. A schedule is important when trying to be consistent with activities such as weight training. It's similar to a businessman's perspective because if you miss a day of anything you have a negative result. Another skill that can transfer is patience. As an athlete it takes time for your body to become how you want it to be. It's similar to being patient about a growing business. It takes long periods of time for it to be successful.

Examples from Literature

Let's also start making the connective thinking that goes on during literary reading and writing more visible. Figurative language is often cited as a distinguishing feature of literary texts, a specialist concern germane only to the English language arts classroom. However, a figure of speech, by its very nature, is an act of integration. Take metaphor. Both the word *transfer* and the word *metaphor* have morphemes that mean "to bear or carry"; each term represents a bridging of differences. The *Oxford English Dictionary*, in fact, defines *metaphor* as "a figure of speech in which a name or descriptive word or phrase is *transferred* to an object or action different from, but analogous to, that to which it is literally applicable" [emphasis added]. Not for nothing does Aristotle say in *Poetics* that mastery of metaphor is a sign of genius "since a good metaphor implies an intuitive perception of the similarity in dissimilars (1984, chap. 22)."

Consider the deft use William Shakespeare makes of metaphor in *King Lear*. In the following example, Shakespeare transfers the image of a weapon to his title character's emotional state. When the loyal Kent attempts to intercede on the wrongfully disinherited Cordelia's behalf, an outraged Lear warns him that the "bow is bent and drawn; make from the shaft" (act 1, scene 2, line 141), meaning that Kent had better get clear of Lear's rage. This martial metaphor both expresses the intense aggression Lear feels toward those who oppose his will as well as foreshadows the imminent destruction of his kingdom by civil war. The mental discipline required to create a metaphor that can do this much heavy lifting for a text is indeed a mark of genius.

METAPHOR WRITING

You might try this next activity as part of your poetry or short-story unit: Give your students a set of items to observe and compare, noting the "similarity in dissimilars" (Aristotle 1984, chap. 22). For instance, you might pair a red lava lamp with a painting of poppies by Georgia O'Keeffe or a seashell with a photograph of a human ear. First, instruct your students to describe the items, noting qualities such as shape, color, and texture. They can do this by creating a cluster, drawing, or Venn diagram. Then, ask your students to write an implied comparison of these two dissimilar things using colorful, imaginative language. See where this is going? That's right. You just asked your students to create a metaphor.

Here are some of the creative comparisons my tenth graders produced in response to the lava lamp/O'Keeffe pairing:

The lava bloomed in a field of red poppies.

The petals of the poppies were magma-red.

The petals flowed in molten rivers.

The field of flowers burned bright in the sun.

Now take the learning one step further, toward integrative thinking and transfer. As I noted in the introduction, successful transfer of learning depends on a *metacognitive awareness* of the similarities and differences between tasks and contexts. Students need both a mind-set for connection-making and the analytical skills that tell them if and how different forms of knowledge can be meaningfully combined. That's why a rhetorical approach, with its keen attention to audience and context, is so important. To develop this spirit of transfer, try asking your students the following kinds of questions after any activity:

- How is this activity similar to work you've done in other classes? How is it different?
- To what extent did your prior knowledge contribute to your success on this activity?
- Where do you see yourself using this knowledge and these skills again?
- How might you need to adapt what you've learned for another genre or discipline?
- What did you most enjoy about this work? What would you like to do again?

Our students need explicit help seeing the transfer opportunities inherent in literary study. Literature is rich with integrative thinking, an excellent reason for keeping literary texts front and center in the twenty-first-century English language arts classroom.

Another figurative device that is a creative act of integration is the pun. Like metaphors, puns are jam-packed with meaning potential; they're redolent with interconnected nuances, semantic bridges joining disparate moods and messages. Look at the flurry of meanings Shakespeare invokes when Claudius says to Hamlet, "But now, my cousin Hamlet, and my son," and Hamlet sulkily responds, "A little more than kin, and less than kind!" (act 1, scene 2, lines 64–65):

- Hamlet doesn't have kind (i.e., loving) feelings toward his uncle.
- Hamlet sees himself as a different kind of person from Claudius.
- Hamlet is not Claudius's son by birth,[3] making their relationship unnatural.

----

3.   See the Oxford English Dictionary *for older definitions of* kind *meaning "derived from birth."*

As Sylvan Barnet notes in an introductory essay to another of Shakespeare's plays, *As You Like It*, "The puns evidently were not put in as sops to the groundlings; they are an important way of communicating a complex meaning" (1998, xx).

When we teach puns as part of a literature unit, we can point out to students that they are developing a transferable competency—that the ability to integrate different meanings this way has applications outside of an English language arts classroom. The study of literary devices is not an outdated hobby of English teachers with no connection to the real world. We need only look to books such as *Who Moved My Cheese?* (1998) and *What Color Is Your Parachute?* (1970) to see the business world's fondness for figurative thinking. Figures of speech, like metaphors and puns, are a vibrant part of our living language and are powerful tools for comparison, synthesis, and integration.

MOTIF JOURNALS

The study of motifs is yet another way students can practice integrative thinking during a literature unit. I like using motifs both to focus on the internal connections within a single text and to help students make thematic connections across texts. When my juniors read *The Great Gatsby* (1925), for example, they tracked and analyzed F. Scott Fitzgerald's repeated references to vision and misperception over the course of the novel (e.g., the billboard for Dr. T. J. Eckleburg, "Owl-Eyes," characters' blurry vision at parties, moments of mistaken identity). If your students read a series of thematically related readings, you can have them track a motif across multiple texts. This enables them to "analyze how two or more texts address similar themes or topics in order to build knowledge or to compare the approaches the authors take" (NGA/CCSSO 2010, CCSS.ELA-Literacy.CCRA.R.9.) I use the following motif journal to help students connect and analyze recurring images and actions in Shakespeare's plays, but this activity can be adapted for any thematically related set of readings.

> **Directions to Students:** Choose one of the following motifs to track across the major texts we read for this course:
>
> - Land, territory, and/or borders
> - Possessions (people and things)
> - Abuse of authority
> - Self and other
> - Wonders and marvels
> - Storms
> - Travel and/or exile

Then for each text, choose one quotation on your selected motif to respond to in an analytical journal entry. Your journal response should explain how your chosen quotation relates to the meaning of the work as a whole. Each journal entry should be roughly a half page or more in length.

Remember, you will only be tracking one motif throughout the course of the semester for this assignment. That means you'll be looking for quotations on the same motif in each of the following texts we read:

> *The Tempest*
>
> *The Merchant of Venice*
>
> *Othello*
>
> *King Lear*
>
> *A Thousand Acres* (a novel by Jane Smiley)

Note: Consider how your selected motif changes its meaning and function across the texts. For example, how is the storm motif in *The Tempest* similar to and different from the storm motif in *King Lear*? What is the purpose of this motif in each text?

The journal entries and quotations can then be integrated into a literary analysis essay examining the significance of these connected examples.

When students can not only recognize literary devices such as metaphors, puns, and motifs but also explain *how* and *why* the writer is using them—and can make skillful use of such devices in their own writing—then they've developed some highly portable and valuable literacy skills they can carry over into other areas of their lives. Let's start telling students, "When you create and analyze figures of speech, you are doing things with your brain that will help you solve complex problems in a changing world."

INTEGRATED QUESTIONS

Integrative thinking helps students understand the complexities of a text. Questions that ask, for instance, how two elements of a text work together to create meaning are terrific for rhetorical analyses. Integrated questions help students understand the relationships between part and whole:

1. How do the diction and imagery contribute to the text's meaning?

2. How do the syntax and structure contribute to the text's meaning?

3. How do the audience and occasion relate to the text's purpose?

4. How do the diction and evidence affect the logic of the text?

5. How do the diction and syntax affect the tone?

6. How do the claims and evidence affect the writer's ethos?

7. How do the tone and diction affect the writer's ethos?

8. How do the emotional and logical appeals affect the writer's ethos?

Invite your students to do a quick-write on one or more of these questions in response to a work of literature they're reading. The answers to these questions can then become integrated thesis statements that make arguments about a text's meaning (the thesis statements are integrated because they combine two or more functional elements of the text), to be developed and supported through a process essay.

Teachers can even make a game out of this kind of mix-and-match questioning by putting several rhetorical and literary elements together in a grab bag and then having students randomly draw two to work into a question about a text they're reading. The point is that all of a writer's choices interact to create meaning. Complex, connection-making questions like these additionally help prepare students to meet the Common Core's standards on integrative thinking, such as the ability to "determine two or more central ideas of a text and analyze their development over the course of the text, including how they interact and build on one another to provide a complex analysis" (NGA/CCSSO 2010, CCSS.ELA-Literacy. RI.11-12.2).

> Students' transfer of learning may not look the way we want it to at first. And that's OK. If we approach rhetorical reading and writing as acts of creative problem solving, then we should expect students to have their share of productive "fails."

Making Connections Through Stories

In a literature classroom, this mind set toward connection-making additionally gets a big boost from the boundary-crossing power of stories. Stories are everywhere; they're important to all academic disciplines and discourses. As education scholar Katie Egan Cunningham notes, stories are "the heart of literacy learning" (2015). Storytelling is a best practice in business, politics, law, the STEM (science, technology, engineering, and math) fields, and, of course, in the arts and humanities.

After many years as a high school English teacher, I now work with future teachers and first-year students in a humanities and communication program at a university. My interdisciplinary department includes the fields of literature, philosophy, journalism, history, ethnic studies, prelaw, communication, and creative writing and social action. One colleague described what our fields have in common: "What we do in communication is tell stories. What we do in oral history is tell stories. What we do in creative writing is tell stories." The same may be said of other fields in the humanities. But storytelling is also important to the sciences, technology, mathematics, and engineering. Take, for example, the following story from National Public Radio.

In an article on the hypercompetitive world of biomedical science, Story Landis (real name), the director of the National Institute of Neurological Disorders and Strokes, described the fight for funding that has tempted some researchers to take shortcuts:

> Getting a grant requires that you have an exciting story to tell, that you have preliminary data and you have published. . . . In the rush, to be perfectly honest, to get a wonderful story out on the street in a journal, and preferably with some publicity to match, scientists can cut corners. (Harris 2014)

In the race to be the first to publish a compelling narrative that will secure additional resources, some scientists have advanced research studies based only on flimsy evidence. Of course, this example highlights the importance of ethical and effective storytelling. The narratives we construct about our work and its impact need to be informed and responsible. We want students to apply high standards of integrity to any act of communication. But it also makes clear that empirical evidence and reasoning aren't enough to convince decision makers, even in the world of the hard sciences. Human beings need to feel a human connection.

I've recently experienced a more positive integration between storytelling and the STEM fields through my son's participation in the Tech Challenge, an event sponsored by the Tech Museum of Innovation in San Jose, California. Located in the heart of Silicon Valley ("the most inventive place on earth," according to the museum's website), the Tech Museum has become a hub of learning for the next generation of coders, engineers, builders, and scientists. But it also offers a creative space for future artists, writers, designers, dreamers, and problem solvers of all stripes.

The Tech Challenge is the museum's annual team design challenge for students in grades 4–12. The 2016 challenge was to design and build a glider that could take off at a zero-degree angle, demonstrate lift by flying over a mountain, fly around a storm cell (represented by a six-foot pylon), and deliver its payload of ping-pong balls on target twenty-six feet away (see Figure 1.9). Not so easy. But here's my favorite part: two-thirds of the students' score was based on their critical thinking and oral and written communication skills. In addition to an engineering journal the students kept (hooray for writing to learn!), the students also demonstrated their learning through a postflight interview and (the best bit) an original story they'd written explaining a real-world application of the glider they'd designed. The first few lines of my son's team's story show the power of narrative for bringing science to life:

> March 5th 10:47 AM 2016
> Five scientists have been chosen to build a glider that can transport medicine to rural villages in Africa: Dr. Galiguis, Dr. Fletcher, Dr. Geronimo, Dr. Pattawi, and Dr. Steinbruner. Each scientist specializes in a certain area. Dr.

Galiguis is in charge of getting the glider in the air. Dr. Fletcher is in charge of launching the glider. Dr. Pattawi is in charge of the body of the glider. Dr. Geronimo is in charge of the cargo and flight path. Finally, Dr. Steinbruner is in charge of the wings.

"Ready to launch," Dr. Galiguis says through the intercom.

The glider slowly moves back as the launcher is pulling it back.

"Ready . . . Go!" Dr. Galiguis says releasing the glider from the launcher. The glider gets off the launching pad and then explodes. Parts of medicine go flying everywhere, and one giant wing comes crashing back onto the launcher, but it's all in flames. Two months of hard work goes down the drain.

The English teacher in me couldn't help feeling deeply gratified that in this event, held at the center of the tech universe, the English language arts are even more important to a team's overall success than science and technology.

Before I get carried away by the triumph of the humanities, I want to make the point that integrative learning is the real hero in this case. As the Tech Challenge makes clear, solving real-world problems requires the ability to bring together diverse forms of knowledge and

FIGURE 1.9
The Tech Challenge at the Tech Museum of Innovation in San Jose, California

experience, along with a range of twenty-first-century skills, including curiosity, flexibility, and persistence.

Storytelling and Career Readiness

Although the Common Core places great emphasis on the value of integrative thinking—reading anchor standards 7–9 are titled "Integration of Knowledge and Ideas"—some of this emphasis may be getting lost in translation. First, as Kelly Gallagher notes in *In the Best Interest of Students* (2015, 49), there's a real problem with telling students they need to "stay within the four corners of the text," as some of the authors of the Common Core have recommended (Wilson and Newark 2011). While this recommendation doesn't appear in the standards themselves, the fact that CCSS framers David Coleman and Susan Pimentel are saying it elsewhere has a significant impact on how teachers view the pedagogical intentions of the Common Core. If integrative thinking and transferable literacy skills are the goal, it makes no sense to raise artificial barriers between sites of student learning.

Second, as Gallagher also notes, the CCSS undervalues the reading and writing of narrative texts (2015, 10)[4]. I'd add that the CCSS similarly undervalues the importance of pathos, or the audience's frame of mind, in academic argumentation. This approach frankly strikes me as being out-of-touch with the literacy demands of the twenty-first-century workplace.

By steering the curriculum away from the study of narrative and pathos, narrow implementations of the Common Core may actually end up making students *less* career-ready. Andy Goodman, a nationally known consultant in the field of strategic communications, sees storytelling as a "best practice" of successful organizations, calling stories "the single most powerful communication tool" available to corporations, nonprofits, foundations, educational institutions, and government agencies (2010; see also www.thegoodmancenter.com/about). Goodman's corporate clients include Bank of America, General Electric, and Intel. Writing to an audience of public interest professionals, Goodman makes clear the problem with privileging "objective" reasoning over the power of personal stories:

> We remain a sector devoted to data and enamored of empirical evidence. And while we will always need hard facts to make our cases, we often fail to realize that the battle for hearts and minds *starts with the hearts*. The audience you seek will only give its attention to things it cares about, and caring is not an entirely rational activity. (2010, i; italics in original)

If your organization's goal is to educate or persuade, Goodman recommends you tell your audience a story. "In a two-hour speech," Goodman says, "people will remember a two-minute story" (2010, 2).

----

4. *See the description of "Key Shifts in ELA": www.corestandards.org/other-resources/key-shifts-in-english-language-arts/.*

In language that offers a striking counterpoint to Coleman's infamous claim that "people don't really give a shit about what you think or feel" (Wilson and Newark 2011, 10), Goodman tells private industry and public-sector leaders that a compelling personal account is precisely what's needed to jolt audiences out of their evidence overload:

> Even if you have reams of evidence on your side, remember: numbers numb, jargon jars, and nobody ever marched on Washington because of a pie chart. If you want to connect with your audience, tell them a story. (2010, 2; italics in original)

Lest we take umbrage at Goodman's admittedly anti-intellectual tone here, allow me to note that Goodman's clients include some of the most prestigious institutions and foundations in the world of higher learning: Harvard University, Stanford University, UCLA, MIT, Princeton University, the MacArthur Foundation, and the Bill & Melinda Gates Foundation. His audience includes people who excel at making arguments in their own fields; what they're often not so good at (as the shrinking budgets of colleges and universities show) is convincing donors and legislators to fund their programs.

Again, it's the ability to integrate skills and knowledge, to combine ways of knowing and communicating, that leads to the most successful responses to twenty-first-century challenges. Effective communicators, Goodman shows, know how to give their audiences the nitty-gritty data *and* the compelling story that shows why the data matter. Thomas Newkirk echoes this important idea in *Minds Made for Stories*: "We will need narrative to accomplish the fuller rhetorical aim of persuasion" (2014, 7).

> **Gerald Graff, one of my favorite thinkers on academic culture, makes a similar point about the integration of narrative and argument: "There is no necessary quarrel between arguments and narratives. Good stories make an argumentative point, and arguments gain punch from embedded stories" (2003, 4).**

Integrating Literature and Argument

In an educational context dominated by the Great Common Core Curriculum Shift, we sometimes see literary analysis as taking a back seat to argument—or at least presented as significantly different academic work. For instance, for the anchor standard calling for students to "delineate and evaluate the argument and specific claims in a text, including the validity of the reasoning as well as the relevance and sufficiency of the evidence" (NGA/CCSSO 2010, CCSS. ELA-Literacy. CCRA.R.8) the CCSS notes that this standard is "not applicable to literature." Missy James and Alan P. Merickel, authors of *Reading Literature and Writing Argument* (2005), would disagree. James and Merickel's made-for-each-other description of literature and argument remind me of those old you-got-your-peanut-butter-on-my-chocolate commercials: "*Literature liberates thinking, and argument disciplines it. The combined and com-*

plementary forces are inspiring and empowering" (2005, xv; italics in original). Delineating and evaluating the argument in a text is absolutely applicable to literary reading.

In fact, literary interpretation isn't just compatible with argumentation; it requires it. Gerald Graff and Cathy Birkenstein explain why in their popular book *They Say, I Say: The Moves That Matter in Academic Writing*: "Since the same piece of evidence in a literary work will often support differing, even opposing interpretations, you need to argue for what you think the evidence shows—and to acknowledge that others may read that evidence differently" (2014, 195). Furthermore, because literary works don't explicitly state their themes, their meaning is always arguable (Graff and Birkenstein 2014). Literature makes arguments by developing and supporting explicit and implied claims about the meaning of human experience. And people have arguments about literature; they disagree about what those textual arguments mean.

In some literary works, arguments appear as debates between characters: for instance, John Savage and Mustafa Mond arguing the value of social stability versus personal freedom in Aldous Huxley's *Brave New World* ([1932] 2006). Other times, the debates manifest as internal struggles: e.g., Huck Finn reasoning out the moral, legal, and theological implications of helping a runaway slave escape from his owner (Twain [1884] 1995).

Reading with an eye to these kinds of conflicts is an excellent pathway to a text's theme, Graff and Birkenstein suggest, because "these debates can provide you with points of entry into the issues raised by the work, its historical context, and its author's vision of the world" (2014, 193).

Graff and Birkenstein recommend the following questions to help students discover their own stance on a literary text's meaning:

> The Common Core clearly values integrative thinking, calling in its literacy standards for students "to know how to combine elements of different kinds of writing—for example, to use narrative strategies within argument and explanation within narrative—to produce complex and nuanced writing" (NGA-CCSSO 2010, 49).

1. What is the central conflict?

2. Which side—if any—does the text seem to favor?

3. What's your evidence? How might others interpret the evidence differently?

4. What's your opinion of the text? (2014, 192)

Literature and Life Readiness

Despite fantasies I may have to the contrary, I understand that not all high school students aspire to be college English majors. Heck, I understand that some students can barely tolerate their required four years of high school English. In my current work teaching first-year composition and summer bridge courses to college freshmen, I often encounter newly minted math, science, and business majors who say they have never been good writers. Some of these students are hoping their nonhumanities majors mean that their days of struggling with literacy tasks are behind them, and I gently try to disabuse them of this notion. Reading and writing, of course, are at the heart of any academic discipline. And, in some places, the study of literature is playing an increasingly important role in preparing all students to be life ready.

Consider what Yale University has been up to in Singapore. In 2011, Yale University became the first Ivy League school to open a new version of itself in Asia. With the goal of creating "a new generation of leaders for Asia's companies and governments," the 300-plus-year-old university has partnered with the National University of Singapore (NUS) in a unique experiment to see whether Yale's venerable educational model can be replicated in a different setting (Norton 2015, 23). The hope is that Yale alumni from Singapore will be as distinguished as their American counterparts, whose graduates include US presidents, Supreme Court justices, and top CEOs. The new Yale-NUS campus has decided to take the long view of learning, to measure the success of its students in terms of how they apply their learning in future contexts. Yale president Peter Salovey identified key questions the university will ask about its graduates: "Do they go on to the best graduate and professional programs? Do employers say they find these students articulate, creative, capable of teamwork?" (Norton 2015, 23–24). Outcomes, in other words, will be assessed in terms of transfer of learning.

To make sure Yale-NUS receives glowing reports of its alumni, the university has chosen a heavy emphasis on the liberal arts—including required courses in literature and philosophy—to prepare the next generation of leaders. The belief is that by doing such things as studying the characteristics of a hero in epic poetry, students develop the habits of mind that enable them to make critical leadership decisions. According to Singapore education minister Ng Eng Hen, Yale-NUS's turn toward the humanities will have a profound impact on Singapore's schools:

> It signals to students and parents that critical thinking, analysis, and deliberation—hallmarks of liberal-arts education—will be needed and valued. . . . It will hopefully move us from a system that is now world-renowned for students who answer set questions well to one that produces students who want to start asking the right questions to produce solutions to complex problems. (Norton 2015, 24)

As Yale-NUS's liberal arts curriculum suggests, a focus on transfer of learning as an instructional target isn't simply about producing the best workers for the labor market. It's a far loftier goal. The ability to effectively apply learning to new situations—whether in college, career, or life—depends on a high degree of intellectual agility. At the heart of transfer of learning are habits of mind we deeply value as liberal humanists: creativity, openness, and adaptability.

In addition to its transfer potential in college and career, a literature-based curriculum also prepares students for informed and conscientious civic participation. Nearly eighty years ago, Louise Rosenblatt argued that literary study "might be made the very core of the kind of educational process needed in a democracy" ([1938] 1995, 261).

Literature, she wrote, has the power to increase students' capacity to make positive social contributions:

> As the student shares through literary experience the emotions and
> aspirations of other human beings, he can gain heightened sensitivity to the
> needs and problems of those remote from him in temperament, in space,
> or in social environment; he can develop a greater imaginative capacity to
> grasp the meaning of abstract laws or political and social theories for actual
> human lives. Such sensitivity and imagination are part of the indispensable
> equipment of the citizen of a democracy. ([1938] 1995, 261)

Rosenblatt's inspiring words describe a transformative learning experience that goes beyond academic boundaries. Taking a rhetorical approach to literature acknowledges that our students are going to carry their literary learning into contexts far beyond the world of English studies. And that's a good thing.

Conclusion

In many ways, this chapter is itself an act of integration; it maps the many different learning sites I engaged during the time I was writing it: books I read, conversations I had, classes I taught, conferences I attended, schools I visited, and even my own children's school projects. Writing creates a hub of intersectionality; it knits together the various identity components, sites of learning, and personal experiences that compose our lives. We're happy when we feel everything is coming together.

As teachers, we practice the integration of skills and knowledge when we embed a new approach—like the rhetorical approach or teaching for transfer—in what we're already do-ing. We match up what we already know and do with the new strategies and concepts we're trying to learn.

Students who practice integrative thinking and develop a spirit of transfer have acquired academic superpowers. These abilities allow them to simultaneously view the past and future, to see around corners and through barriers, to travel across space and time. They've become big-picture thinkers, adaptive and responsive problem solvers who can operate outside of narrow formulas and categories. In a job interview, they can describe how they might apply their learning to a real-world scenario. In academic settings, they can bring skills and knowl-edge together from various disciplines to address a complex problem, such as the need to rid the ocean of trash without harming marine life.

The ability to integrate skills and knowledge is a gateway competency that leads to other transferable literacy skills. In Chapter 2, I show how reading literature rhetorically helps students to develop an essential transferable literacy skill: the ability to read closely and critically. This, too, is a competency that ultimately helps twenty-first-century learners "to solve difficult problems or explore complex issues in original ways" (AAC&U 2009).

When we teach for transfer of learning and teach rhetorically, it's clear that what we do with literature as English language arts teachers is fresh and exciting and deeply relevant to the lives our students are likely to live.

CHAPTER TWO

Reading Closely and Critically

Many of the standard concepts of rhetorical analysis we employ when we teach expository texts—claim, evidence, appeal, ethos, pathos, logos, strategy, premise, context, and so forth—meaningfully explicate the elements and workings of literary texts.

—GLEN MCCLISH

I've been making the case that one of the best ways to prepare students for success in education, work, and life is to teach for transfer of learning. I've further argued that, if we want students to transfer their learning, we need to help them integrate their skills and knowledge across a variety of contexts.

I now want to explore how the power of integrated learning—of combining rhetoric and literature—can help students become better readers who ultimately get more out of their English classes. Rhetorical knowledge not only helps students adapt and apply their learning but also amps up students' power as critical readers. Adding rhetorical knowledge to literary knowledge is like adding a protein boost to your favorite fruit smoothie—you get more bang for your buck. Let me show you what I mean.

For years, I used a fabulous collection of stories called *Fables You Shouldn't Pay Any Attention To* by Florence Parry Heide and Sylvia Worth Van Clief (1978) to introduce short-story elements to my ninth graders. The stories include the account of a discontented cow who learns the grass really is greener on the other side and a greedy fish who is rewarded for her gluttony. Students always enjoyed a subversive thrill when the protagonist in each tale does well by doing bad (except in the final tale, when the protagonist learns it *doesn't* pay to be honest), and I enjoyed the brief period of resistance-free reading in my classroom.

My lesson plan was simple. I'd arrange students in small groups and give each group a different fable to analyze. Their task was to identify the story's setting, protagonist, antagonist, conflict, inciting incident, rising action, climax, falling action, resolution, and theme and then present their work to the class through a plot diagram and setting illustration. You can see from the following fable about Cyril the selfish squirrel from Heide and Van Clief's book why this unit was popular:

> Cyril and Jennifer were squirrels. They lived in the forest. Cyril was very, very, very selfish.
>
> That wasn't very nice. You're supposed to share. Jennifer shared. But not Cyril.
>
> "Hey, can I have some of your nuts?" one of the other squirrels would ask Jennifer.
>
> "Help yourself," Jennifer would say.
>
> "Hey, can I have some of your nuts?" one of the other squirrels would ask Cyril.
>
> "Drop Dead," Cyril would say.
>
> "You're selfish, Cyril," the other squirrels would say.
>
> "You're supposed to share, the way Jennifer does."
>
> Jennifer kept giving her nuts to the other squirrels.
>
> Cyril was too selfish. He kept his nuts to himself.
>
> "Hey, can I have some of your nuts, Jennifer?" asked Cyril.
>
> "Help yourself," said Jennifer.
>
> Winter came. Jennifer had given all of her nuts away.
>
> "Hey, can I have some of your nuts, Cyril?" asked Jennifer.
>
> "Drop Dead," said Cyril.
>
> And she did.
>
> "I'm glad I was selfish," said Cyril. "It pays." (1978, 15–19)

(I confess to changing the word "nuts" to "acorns" when I used this text with freshmen for reasons that will be obvious to anyone who has taught this age group.) To me, the fables were just a quick and entertaining way to teach the literary terms and concepts I was going to ask students to apply to more complex works of literature down the road.

But then I made a fascinating discovery. The most interesting aspects of the fables weren't on my list of short-story elements. We were leaving a lot of good stuff untouched on our plates.

After using a rhetorical approach to texts as part of the California State University's Expository Reading and Writing Course (ERWC), I decided to try adding a rhetorical twist to our reading to see whether there was more to these brief stories than met the eye. Instead of just looking for traditional literary elements, I now asked students to think about how considerations of audience, purpose, genre, occasion, ethos, pathos, and logos contributed to their understanding of the text. Here are my updated questions:

1. How does the title impact the writers' ethos? How would you describe the tone or attitude of this title? What kind of people would write a book called *Fables You Shouldn't Pay Attention To*? Can we trust these writers?

2. What is the function of the title? Is it supposed to be a warning? Or something else?

3. What do we expect of this genre? What do the writers give us instead?

4. Who is the audience? What kind of readers would appreciate and enjoy these stories? The full title includes the phrase "For Every Good Kid in the World." Who is the "You" in the title? Do the writers really mean that good kids shouldn't pay attention to their book? What assumptions are the writers making?

5. What, if anything, is being satirized here? What do readers need to know about the purpose of traditional fables or didactic literature to understand these stories in context?

6. How did you feel when reading these stories? Were you offended? Amused? Which characters, if any, did you identify with? The good characters or the selfish/greedy/discontent/careless characters? Could you relate to the writers' sense of humor?

The conversations suddenly became much more lively and nuanced. Instead of dealing only with the surface of the text, students were digging into the dynamics of the rhetorical situation. When we discovered the following cautionary note to the reader on the dust jacket, we grew even more intrigued:

> The only part of this book you are supposed to take seriously is the title.
> Do not read these fables unless you are prepared to ignore them. Don't be
> moved by the fate of Genevieve, who was careless; or Chester, who was lazy;
> or Gretchen, who was greedy. After all, *you* don't want to be careless or lazy or
> greedy . . . or do you?

Wait, what? Really?

"What's up with that last line?" I asked my students. "What are the writers implying about human desires, motives, and morality? What are they suggesting they know about *us*?"

We now found ourselves in deep psychological waters indeed.

I then asked students to revisit their plot outline, this time examining how the writing *works*:

- What are the writers *doing* at each point in the story?

- What are the purposes behind the choices they've made?

- How do you think they expect readers to react to their choices?

Last, I posed a challenge question to the class: *Do the writers take morality seriously?* Their responses reflect the many different directions students can take their thinking:

- "Yes, they do because if they didn't take morality seriously, people wouldn't read the book. But I think the writers did not take morality seriously when they were kids. When they were told to do something, they probably didn't want to listen."

- "Yes, because they warn people at the beginning of the book. They are concerned about people learning from these stories, and the sole purpose of the stories is for fun."

- "No, because they forget that young kids are not good at following instructions."

- "They're not trying to be serious. They're being ironic. These aren't real fables."

- "My answer depends on whether the book was written for children or adults."

- "Maybe. Adults can understand the ironic message, but kids would be confused by the ending."

- "Yes, they're making a serious point about how people are hypocrites."

- "No, they're just trying to be funny."

Notice how the students' responses now include considerations of audience, purpose, genre, message, and ethos, instead of just my original list of short-story elements.

Taking a rhetorical approach to the fables showed me and my students the value of being adept in multiple ways of reading. If one angle of approach doesn't deliver the deeper, richer understandings we're after, there are others we can try. Having both literary and rhetorical knowledge in our interpretive tool kits gives us greater insight into how writers' and readers' choices create meaning. What's more, showing students the choices we have as readers helps them develop more transferable and adaptable literacy skills.

> **Students need multiple angles of approach to meaning. Teaching students to read rhetorically gives them more opportunities to make exciting textual discoveries.**

Annotating and Analyzing the Text

Of course, to be able to answer the more sophisticated questions that come with a rhetorical approach, students need robust analytical reading skills. Close reading and annotation are among the most challenging and important literacy skills we teach. The Common Core College and Career Readiness Anchor Standards for Reading privileges these abilities, calling for students to "read closely to determine what the text says explicitly and to make logical inferences from it" (NGA/CCSSO 2010, CCSS.ELA-Literacy.CCRA.R.1), to "interpret words and phrases as they are used in a text" (NGA/CCSSO 2010, CCSS.ELA-Literacy. CCRA.R.4), and to "analyze the structure of texts" (NGA/CCSSO 2010, CCSS.ELA-Literacy.CCRA.R.5). In a rhetorical approach, annotation isn't a dissection of an inert specimen; it is a dialogic interaction with a text.

The authors of the college textbook *Reading Critically, Writing Well* give a helpful description of annotation:

> *Annotating* means underlining key words, phrases or sentences; writing
> comments or questions in the margins; bracketing important sections of
> the text; connecting ideas with lines or arrows; numbering related points
> in sequence; and making note of anything that strikes you as interesting,
> important, or questionable. (Axelrod, Cooper, and Warriner 2008, 597; italics
> in original)

Annotation is particularly important to a rhetorical approach to texts because of rhetoric's interest in the purpose, effects, and functions of writers' choices.

Over the years, I've found that it's hard to get students to interact with texts, to highlight evidence and mark writers' choices, to note what writers are saying and how and why they are saying it. It's much easier for students just to bubble in an answer on a test or wait for a teacher to tell them what the text means. I've often watched in dismay as some of my students stared passively at a reading passage I'd asked them to analyze and annotate. When I push individual students to do more than look at the page, some reluctantly underline a single phrase and then look at me as if to say, "There, are you satisfied?" Nope, I want more. I've learned that students need explicit instructional support to see the range of choices they have as meaning-makers.

Ultimately, annotation should be driven by intellectual curiosity and authentic engagement, not compliance with a teacher directive.

Show Students What Goes On in Readers' and Writers' Brains

Students need to see the behind-the-scenes processes—and benefits—of multiple ways of reading. One of the best ways to help students learn how to read closely and annotate texts is to model our own thinking as expert readers. Too often, students don't get to see what goes on in fluent readers' brains when they interact with a text. I love Thomas C. Foster's description of the differences between students' and teachers' ways of reading—and the distrust those differences breed—in *How to Read Literature Like a Professor*:

> A moment occurs in this exchange [about literature] between professor and
> student when each of us adopts a look. My look says, "What, you don't get it?"
> Theirs says, "We don't get it. And we think you're making it up." We're having
> a communication problem. Basically, we've all read the same story, but we
> haven't used the same analytical apparatus. (2003, xiii)

Our challenge is to show students what we're doing when we make sense of challenging texts, so that they have a greater appreciation of the analytical apparatuses available to them.

We can help students take note of what is "interesting, important, or questionable" (Axelrod, Cooper, and Warriner 2008, 597) in a text by demonstrating how we look for weird writerly DNA, those markers of a writer's unique style and thinking. Look at how Pulitzer Prize–winning novelist Jhumpa Lahiri describes her approach to annotation in the essay "My Life's Sentences":

> In college, I used to underline sentences that struck me, that made me look up from the page. They were not necessarily the same sentences the professors pointed out, which would turn up for further explication on an exam. I noted them for their clarity, their rhythm, their beauty and their enchantment. For surely it is a magical thing for a handful of words, artfully arranged, to stop time. To conjure a place, a person, a situation, in all its specificity and dimensions. To affect us and alter us, as profoundly as real people and things do. (2012)

Opening sentences, in particular, Lahiri says, "need to contain a charge," "a live current, which shocks and illuminates (2012)." It's that chemical reaction Lahiri describes that we want to help students be alert to. Lahiri's description of her reading process beautifully makes the point that readers have roles and responsibilities when it comes to constructing meaning. Annotation is about having a relationship with a text, about responding to the vitality of a writer's words. David Bartholomae and Anthony Petrosky describe the give-and-take dynamic of reading this way:

> Reading involves a fair measure of push and shove. You make your mark on a book and it makes its mark on you. Reading is not simply a matter of hanging back and waiting for a piece, or its author, to tell you what the writing has to say. (2002, 1)

As students practice making their mark on a text, they develop a nose for noteworthy writer behavior. They develop, in other words, their rhetorical sensitivity. I tell students that when we read rhetorically interesting texts, our annotation scorecard should light up like a Christmas tree. We know we're on the right track with our readings when we get excited about potential connections and meanings. Fluent readers have a goofy enthusiasm for the thrill of discovery that transcends academic assignments. We read because the texts are interesting; they do intriguing things to words and ideas.

The following are several strategies for teaching annotation that can help strengthen students' close-reading skills while developing their rhetorical sensitivity.

INTERRUPTED READING

This strategy works to help defamiliarize the reading process so students can view a text with greater critical attention. In an interrupted reading, students see only a few lines from a text at a time. I like to use a few sentences or less from a text on individual PowerPoint slides to focus students' attention on the effects of a writer's choices at the word, phrase, and sentence level. As I show each slide, I ask students, "What do you notice?" If students need prompting, I then ask what they think about individual words, phrases, images, punctuation marks—anything that catches our eye. For each item we notice, we talk about what it suggests or means and why it could be important.

When I introduce this activity, I remind students that they've engaged in similar practices in other classes and that they can adapt this approach to other subjects of study. Examining discrete pieces of evidence in isolation is a common activity in the sciences, for instance. A biologist studies the function of individual cells in relation to the organism. In all academic areas, analysis involves working from part to whole. Framing our interrupted reading of a text in this way keeps the focus on transfer of learning.

The following example of an interrupted reading comes from the final chapter of Gary Soto's lyrical novel *Buried Onions* (2006). I like to use this activity with unfamiliar text, so that students examine the writer's words with fresh eyes. In the case of Soto's *Buried Onions*, my students have already read the preceding chapters, so they are bringing their prior knowledge of the novel to bear on their interpretation of the slides. For each slide, I ask a different student to read the sentence or sentences aloud, and we all just take in the words for a moment. Then we have a whole-class discussion about what catches our attention. Notice how the student and teacher comments interrupt the regular flow of reading to create more room for closer analysis.

Slide 1: "I walked toward the car and hopped a barbed-wire fence into the field, where huge, land-locked seagulls were picking at the earth."

> **Me:** What words stand out to you? What's interesting or important here?
>
> **Celeste:** "Barbed-wire fence." Sounds like a prison.
>
> **Joey:** The seagulls are land-locked. That makes it seem like they're trapped away from their natural home.
>
> **Erin:** "Picking" is what scavengers do.

Slide 2: "I didn't know the crop, but whatever it was had already been harvested."

> **Me:** Now what do you notice?
>
> **Enrique:** The harvest is already gone.

Stephanie: The field's been picked over.

Jonathan: It's like he arrived too late. He's missed out.

Slide 3: "My attention was on two men, both black, both in tattered clothes, who were gathering what was left after the harvest."

Me: What do you notice? What's going on with the grammar and imagery?

Cory: There are other people now, two men.

Jasmine: He repeats himself—"both black, both in tattered clothes."

Me: What else?

Bryan: Their clothes are tattered. The men seem like survivors or scavengers, like the seagulls.

Slide 4: "I hesitated in the field, hesitated because what were these men but miracles?"

Me: What's happening with Soto's language here? What's significant about his punctuation or syntax?

Joey: More repetition—"hesitated" is mentioned twice. This slows the scene down.

Courtney: There's a question.

Me: Anything else? What words seem significant?

Gladys: "Miracles."

Me: OK, what does the word *miracles* suggest? How does that word strike you at this moment?

Jasmine: It's kind of a surprise. It doesn't really go with the other sentences.

Bryan: Calling the men "miracles" makes this sound like a religious experience.

Slide 5: "'No, it can't be!' I cried to myself as I hurried toward them."

Me: What do you think now?

Nicole: The pace is faster and more exciting.

Will: There's an exclamation point.

Me: Good observation! What's important or interesting about Soto's verbs?

Juan: "Cried" and "hurried" are more intense. He seems upset. Does he know these men?

The point is not to teach students to read all texts this way but rather to show students what they might be missing if they just try to take in a whole text at a glance. This activity also serves as a slow-motion demonstration of annotation. The isolated frames give students the opportunity to learn the process of marking text without the pressure of real-time reading.

ANNOTATION CUE CARDS

This activity provides extra support for a whole-class demonstration of annotation. Start with a rhetorically interesting text. The weirder and more wonderful choices the writer has made, the easier it will be for students to find things to talk about. Then distribute Annotation Cue Cards to the class on which are written sample marginal comments and questions. Using a document camera or projector, model how to mark a text and write marginal comments, calling for students with Annotation Cue Cards to contribute their responses. The cards serve as prompts for a group discussion of the writer's choices and can help students see the kinds of comments and questions fluent readers write during a close textual analysis.

You'll find a sample set of Annotation Cue Cards and directions to students as part of the extended rhetorical reading of Saki's "The Storyteller" later in this chapter. See Appendix 3 for a list of Annotation Cue Cards to use with a collaborative analysis of William Shakespeare's Sonnet 15.

MEGA-MARGINS

Giving students extra room to write their marginal notes can help extend their thinking. Much thanks to Raquel Topete in the Eastside Union High School District for the terrific idea of using "mega-margins" to help students develop the skill of annotation. This activity

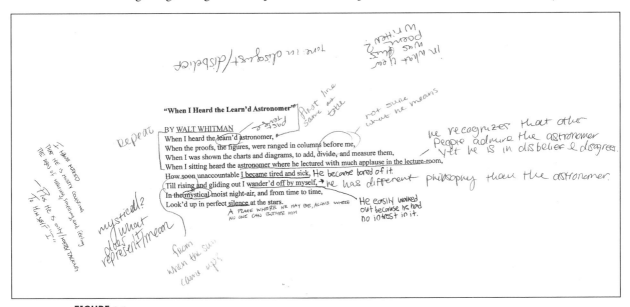

FIGURE 2.1

Student annotations of Walt Whitman's poem "When I Heard the Learn'd Astronomer" using mega-margins

works best with a text that can be printed on an 8-by-11-inch sheet of paper, like a short poem or prose passage. Glue or tape the letter size text to a sheet of legal paper, thereby giving students extra blank paper to explore their thinking (see Figure 2.1). Students can now work in groups or individually to annotate the text in the mega-margins. If you want to give students even more space for marginalia, you could glue the text to a piece of chart paper.

The group option works well for getting students up out of their seats and interacting with one another.

SAY, MEAN, MATTER, DO

Say, Mean, Matter (Blau 2003) is a popular strategy that helps students read between and beyond the lines. As the CCSS notes, close reading involves understanding what a "text says explicitly" and the ability "to make logical inferences from it" (NGA/CCSSO 2010, CCSS. ELA-Literacy.CCRA.R.1). My rhetorical enhancement to Say, Mean, Matter was to add a fourth column labeled "Do." For Say, Mean, Matter, Do, students not only have to paraphrase a writer's words and explain why those words matter in relation to the meaning of the work as a whole, but they also have to discuss the rhetorical function or effect of those words (i.e., what they are "doing" to the text or audience). Adding a Do column to Say, Mean, Matter turns the focus of the analysis toward real-world communication by asking students to think about the intent and impact of a writer's choices. This extra step requires students to read like writers, a practice rich with transfer applications. The Do column also pairs well with Descriptive Plot Outlining (see next activity).

I created the following example for South African writer Olive Schreiner's 1883 novel *The Story of an African Farm*, which describes the experiences of a man who disguises himself as a female nurse in order to be closer to the woman he loves. (See Figure 2.2.) See the student example of Say, Mean, Matter, Do for Sherman Alexie's *The Absolutely True Diary of a Part-Time Indian* in Appendix 5.

SAY, MEAN, MATTER, DO (ADAPTED FROM BLAU 2003)			
Directions: Choose several quotations from the text to record in the following chart. Then practice paraphrasing each quotation and analyzing its significance to the work as a whole. Consider what the quotation *says* and *does*.			
SAY (Quotation and page number)	MEAN (Paraphrase and/or close reading of quotation)	MATTER (Connection to the theme; significance to the work as a whole)	Do (Effect on the reader and/or text; rhetorical function or move)
When Lyndall first sees Gregory, the new man on the farm, she says, "There...goes a true woman—one born for the sphere that some women fill without being born for it" (Schreiner 164).	In this quotation, Lyndall suggests that Gregory better fits the Victorian model of the angel in the home than many women, herself included. The words "true" and "born" are ironic in this context and work against the idea of "natural" gender roles. "Sphere" suggests the notion of a proper place— again, used ironically.	This example illustrates the artificial and restrictive nature of both masculine and feminine gender stereotypes in the nineteenth century—a key theme of the novel. As a misplaced man, Gregory is peevish, self-centered, and oblivious of his effeminacy. When he later lives as a woman, he becomes deeply caring, generous, and empathetic.	Lyndall's blunt comment surprises the reader and foreshadows Gregory's later cross-dressing. This direct statement moves the novel toward a more candid and experimental exploration of gender roles.

FIGURE 2.2
Say, Mean, Matter, Do

DESCRIPTIVE PLOT OUTLINING

My favorite new strategy for analyzing literature rhetorically is something I've been calling Descriptive Plot Outlining. Descriptive outlining is about seeing the rhetorical moves other writers make. When students create a descriptive outline of an op-ed article, for instance, they note both what the writer is saying and what the writer is doing, that is, the moves the writer makes to achieve specific rhetorical purposes and effects. The "doing" part of the outline is about how the writer's choices function to create meaning.

In Descriptive Plot Outlining, students apply their understanding of a writer's moves to an analysis of a narrative text. Instead of just listing different plot events on a traditional plot chart or "story mountain" (see Gustav Freytag [1896] for the theoretical origin of this activity), students also describe the function and effect of each of those events. The activity thus encourages students to think of plot events as strategic moves a writer makes to achieve a desired end. A descriptive plot outline also shows the problem with reading just an excerpt from a longer work. We can't read for the arc if we only have one little slice of the trajectory. (See Figure 2.3.)

See the teacher-generated example of a Descriptive Plot Outline for "The Most Dangerous Game" in Appendix 7.

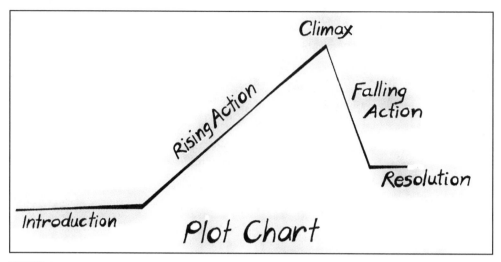

FIGURE 2.3
Plot Diagram

Directions to Students: Draw a plot diagram representing the events in your selected narrative. You may choose to diagram the narrative as a whole or to diagram the dramatic arc for a particular moment or scene. On the outside of your diagram, list what happens at each point. Then, inside the diagram, describe what each event does rhetorically. Your descriptive statements should reveal how the events function in the text. In other words, what impact does the event have on the reader, character(s), or theme? What is the effect or purpose of that event? See the following list of verbs for ideas on how to write your "does" statements.

Verbs for "Does" Statements for Literary Analysis

closes	invites	qualifies
amplifies	introduces	reverses
introduces a complication	questions	undermines
builds to a crescendo	softens	suggests
expands	counters	challenges
contracts	balances	surprises
intensifies	heightens	frustrates
pauses	increases	confuses

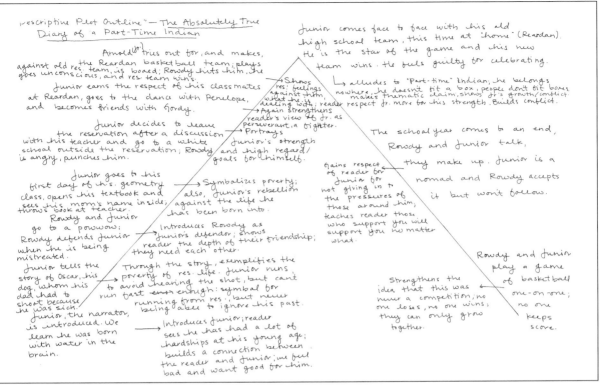

FIGURE 2.4

Student example of a Descriptive Plot Outline of *The Absolutely True Diary of a Part-Time Indian*

If your students have ever given you a plot summary when you asked for a literary analysis, try having them create a Descriptive Plot Outline of the narrative first. (See Figure 2.4.) Analytical thinking is baked into this activity.

Descriptive plot outlining is moreover an authentic practice in literary criticism; it just doesn't necessarily go by this name. See, for instance, what Seamus Heaney writes in his introduction to his critically acclaimed translation of the epic poem *Beowulf*:

> Just when the narrative seems ready to take another step ahead into the main
> Beowulf story, it sidesteps. For a moment it is as if we have been channel-surfed
> into another poem, and at two points in this translation I indicate that we are
> in fact participating in a poem-within-our-poem not only by the use of italics
> but by a slight quickening of pace and shortening of metrical rein. (2000, xiii)

Here, Heaney is describing the narrative moves the text makes ("it sidesteps") and the impact some of those textual shifts and departures has on the reader ("as if we have been channel-surfed"). This practice also goes by the name of "charting the text." By charting the progression of a writer's ideas and moves over the course of a text, we better understand the connection between structure and meaning. This is an understanding rich with transfer potential; it is "knowledge-to-go," to use Perkins and Salomon's phrase (2012, 248).

By connecting the plot structures of fictional stories to the moves writers make in nonfiction, we provide the expansive framing (Perkins and Salomon 2012) that enables students to apply their learning to future tasks, including their own compositions, as well as their reading of informational texts. When taught for transfer, plot is not merely the sequence of events in a story but is instead both a "generative concept" (Smith, Appleman, and Wilhelm 2014, 116) for discovering and organizing ideas and a tool for analyzing and evaluating thinking.

Give Students a Reason to Go Back into the Text

In addition to showing students what goes on in readers' and writers' brains, we also need to give kids reasons to go back into texts for a closer look. For many students, "I read it—I'm done" is the default response (Gallagher 2004, 80). Moreover, showing students what they can gain from deeper and alternative ways of reading helps dispel the myth that good readers understand everything they read the first time.

PRE- AND POST-ANNOTATION CARDS

Pre- and Post-Annotation Cards allow students to compare their understandings at different stages of the reading process. While I like to start a close reading with some open-ended questions that allow students to explore their first impression of a text, I know that most students will need focused help digging below the surface. After whatever prereading activities might be needed, we read a text for the first time, and I ask my students the following questions:

> Students who have learned to create descriptive outlines of expository texts can transfer this rhetorical reading skill to an act of literary analysis (see my book *Teaching Arguments* [Fletcher 2015] or *Reading Rhetorically* by Bean, Chappell, and Gillam [2014] for directions and examples of descriptive outlining using informational texts).

    What do you notice?

    What do you think is interesting?

    What do you want to talk about?

We share responses for a bit, and I have students record their initial thoughts on one side of an index card under the heading "Pre-Annotation Understanding" (see Figure 2.5). We'll respond to these same questions later on the "Post-Annotation Understanding" side of the index card after we've critically analyzed the text (see Figure 2.6). The post-annotation responses serve as a formative assessment of what students have learned through close reading, as well as a reminder to students of why "one and done" doesn't produce the most sophisticated readings. The student samples in Figures 2.5 and 2.6 are in response to Saki's short story "The Storyteller."

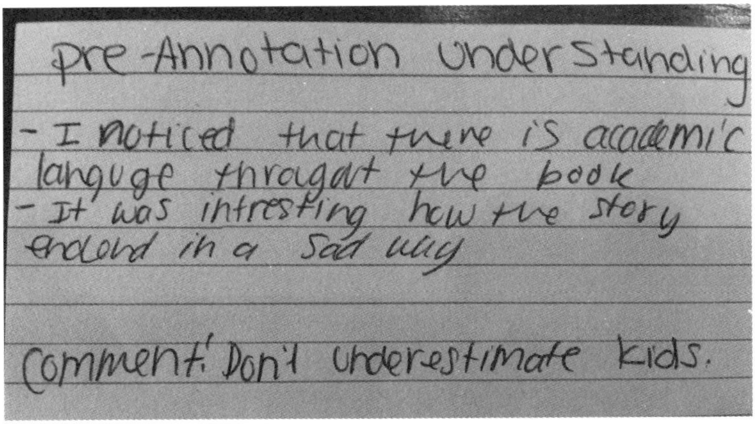

FIGURE 2.5
Pre-Annotation
Understanding

Pre-Annotation Understanding

- I noticed that there is academic languge througout the book
- It was intresting how the story endend in a sad way

Comment: Don't underestimate kids.

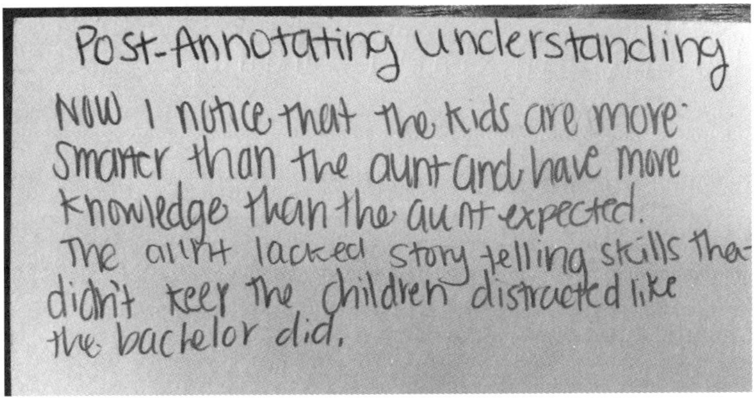

FIGURE 2.6
Post-Annotation
Understanding

Post-Annotating understanding

Now I notice that the kids are more smarter than the aunt and have more knowledge than the aunt expected.
The aunt lacked story telling skills that didn't keep the children distracted like the bachelor did.

LOOP READING

Another activity for helping students see how their insights become clearer and stronger across extended interactions with a text is one I've been calling Loop Reading. This strategy borrows from Peter Elbow's Loop Writing activity to get students to circle back to a text for a second and third look. The new insights at each stage of response provide a rationale for why a single reading of a text is often insufficient.

I introduce this activity to students by sharing the following excerpt from Sherman Alexie's powerful young adult novel *The Absolutely True Diary of a Part-Time Indian*. In the following scene, Arnold Spirit, the main character, gets a lesson on the value of recursive reading from his new friend, Gordy:

> "Listen," [Gordy] said one afternoon in the library, "The first time you read [a book,] you read it for the story. The plot. The movement from scene to scene that gives the book its momentum, its rhythm. It's like riding a raft down a river. You're just paying attention to the currents. Do you understand that?

The second time you read a book you read it for its history. For its knowledge of history. You think about the meaning of each word, and where that word came from. I mean, you read a novel that has the word 'spam' in it, and you know where that word comes from, right?"

"Spam is junk e-mail," I said.

"Yes, that's what it is, but who invented the word, who first used it, and how was the meaning of the word changed since it was first used?"

"I don't know," I said.

"Well, you have to look all that up. If you don't treat each word that seriously then you're not treating the novel seriously."

"Okay, so it's like each of these books is a mystery. Every book is a mystery. And if you read all the books ever written, it's like you've read one giant mystery. And no matter how much you learn, you just keep on learning there is so much more you need to learn."

"Yes, yes, yes, yes," Gordy said. (2009, 94–97)

Directions to Teachers: Instruct students to respond to each of the prompts below in a four-minute quick-write by copying the sentence starter and then completing the idea in their own words. Before each of the first three quick-writes, students read the text (this is why this activity works best with shorter texts, like poems). The last prompt can be completed without an additional reading. Reveal the prompts to the students one at a time, keeping the others hidden until their turn. You may need to build students' background knowledge prior to the first reading.

(First Reading)

Prompt 1: When I first read this poem, I thought...

(Second Reading)

Prompt 2: Then I read it again and thought...

(Third Reading)

Prompt 3: When I read it a third time, it occurred to me...

Prompt 4: Now I wonder...

The following student example is based on Mary Oliver's poem "The Journey":

When I first read this poem, I could relate to the first part when it is talking about people wanting help. I also thought it was a very matter-of-fact poem, because it simply said at the end that only your life matters to you. (In a way, but it was also saying that you should stop trying to help other people all of the time and focus on yourself.)

When I read it the second time, I thought that the poem was more about how people could distract you from what you really wanted. I thought the language was poetic, but it still told real truths of life.

The third time I read it, it occurred to me that the section about wind prying at foundations may be symbolic for people trying to stop you from your calling.

Now I wonder what happened to the "you" in the poem before they finally realized what they had to do.

It can also be helpful for students to stop and discuss their ideas in small groups or explore the context of the text between each reading, so that they are working toward an enriched understanding over the course of the subsequent readings.

I love when this strategy works. For the "Now I wonder . . ." prompt, one of my students landed on an insight at the heart of literary criticism. After describing the mental image she saw as she read the poem a third time, she wrote for the fourth prompt, "Now I wonder if my image is similar to what others see or try to picture." Once students start wondering about what goes on in *other* readers' heads, they're on their way to a sophisticated understanding of meaning as something we actively, collaboratively, and individually construct, not as a single right answer we find in a text.

Note: Just like loop writing, loop reading doesn't work for all students, but it does help many students get beneath the surface of a text.

READING FOR THE SHIFT

Sometimes we need to read texts closely and recursively so that we're not caught off guard when a writer pulls the rug out from under us. I like to make this point by sharing examples of texts that open with misleading statements. The texts seem to be headed in one direction but all of sudden take a radical turn, confounding the reader's expectations. If students settle for a superficial reading that accepts the opening remarks at face value and assumes that the thesis is in the introduction, they could end up with a serious misreading of a text.

I start by showing the class a set of images familiar to most of the students I've taught from Southern California: the famous "stretching portraits" in Disneyland's Haunted Mansion attraction. The portraits are the first of many unsettling illusions on this ride. At first glance, the pictures appear to be ordinary paintings on the walls of an ordinary gallery (see Figure 2.7).

© Disney

FIGURE 2.7
Stretching Portraits 1

However, guests to the Haunted Mansion quickly find themselves trapped in a stretching room with "no doors and no windows." As the room becomes disturbingly elongated, the portraits are revealed in their full horror (see Figure 2.8):

© Disney

FIGURE 2.8
Stretching Portraits 2

Disney's stretching portraits dramatically make the point that texts, whether visual or verbal, can take radical departures from what they initially appear to be. After seeing the full images, students then write or talk about how their first impressions put them on the path of a serious misinterpretation, taking note of the implications for reading comprehension.

With our reader radar alerted to these kinds of abrupt rhetorical shifts, we now take a look at a literary text, Margaret Atwood's poem "You Fit into Me" (1996).

Directions to Students: Read the following poem by Margaret Atwood and respond to the questions that follow. Then write a Stretching Portrait Poem of your own.

"You Fit into Me" by Margaret Atwood

You fit into me
Like a hook into an eye
A fish hook, an open eye

- What is this poem saying?
- What does the first line of the poem suggest?
- How does the last line change the poem's meaning?
- How does this poem play with reader expectations?
- How does the radical shift in imagery, from a hook-and-eye enclosure on a garment to a barbed fishing hook (see Figure 2.9), impact the reader emotionally?
- What can happen if we read only part of a text or read a text too quickly?

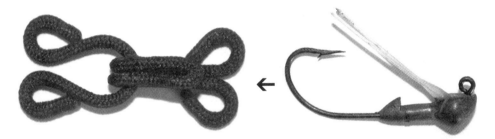

FIGURE 2.9
Hook and Eye

Directions for Writing: Write a Stretching Portrait Poem in which you give your reader a false first impression of your subject. You may want to include abrupt shifts in tone, diction, and structure, as well as content and meaning. End your poem with a surprise twist.

Zeno, one of my students, created a Stretching Portrait Poem that gave me chills:

Bright lights shining
Tall buildings in the clouds
A burning mushroom

Lina's was equally stunning:

Taken to the church,
Long black limo;
Today is a big day.
Walked down the aisle,
Father of the bride.
He awaits me,
To say my final goodbye.

Once students have written their poems, I remind them to be on their guard for these kinds of moves in the work of other writers. Here's where we can facilitate transfer of learning from writing to reading and from literary texts back to informational texts. Notice, for instance, what Stephanie Ericsson does in the opening section of her magazine article "The Ways We Lie":

> The bank called today, and I told them my deposit was in the mail, even though I hadn't written a check yet. It'd been a rough day. The baby I'm pregnant with decided to do aerobics on my lungs for two hours, our three-year-old daughter painted the living-room couch with lipstick, the IRS put me on hold for an hour, and I was late to a business meeting because I was tired.
>
> I told my client that traffic had been bad. When my partner came home, his haggard face told me his day hadn't gone any better than mine, so when he asked, "How was your day?" I said, "Oh, fine," knowing that one more straw might break his back. A friend called and wanted to take me to lunch. I said I was busy. Four lies in the course of a day, none of which I felt the least bit guilty about.
>
> We lie. We all do. We exaggerate, we minimize, we avoid confrontation, we spare people's feelings, we conveniently forget, we keep secrets, we justify lying to the big-guy institutions. Like most people, I indulge in small falsehoods and still think of myself as an honest person. Sure I lie, but it doesn't hurt anything. Or does it?
>
> I once tried going a whole week without telling a lie, and it was paralyzing. I discovered that telling the truth all the time is nearly impossible. It means living with some serious consequences: The bank charges me $60 in overdraft fees, my partner keels over when I tell him about my travails, my client fires me for telling her I didn't feel like being on time, and my friend takes it personally when I say I'm not hungry. There must be some merit to lying.

> But if I justify lying, what makes me any different from slick politicians
> or the corporate robbers who raided the S&L industry? Saying it's okay to lie
> one way and not another is hedging. I cannot seem to escape the voice deep
> inside me that tells me: When someone lies, someone loses. (1991)

"What's Ericsson saying here?" I ask my students. "What's her main point?" Here's what
I often hear in response:

> "Everyone lies."

> "It's impossible to tell the truth all the time."

> "She doesn't feel guilty about lying."

> "There are some good reasons to lie."

And so I show the image of the Haunted Mansion stretching portraits again. "Remember this?" I say. "Where does the picture Ericsson's painted start to change into something different? What are your first clues that her argument isn't what it appears to be?"

Now things get interesting. Many students identify the word "but" in the final paragraph as the key transition, so we all circle it. But some students see the shift happening earlier, at the end of the third paragraph. Ericsson's question "Or does it?" following her statement that her lies don't hurt anything puts savvy readers on their guard. By the time Ericsson says "There must be some merit to lying" at the end of the fourth paragraph, these readers already suspect that she's setting us up.

> When we teach for transfer, we encourage students to turn their reading strategies into writing strategies and their writing strategies into reading strategies.

Ericsson's rhetorical turn is fully as dramatic as Atwood's when it comes, requiring the same total reader reorientation to her meaning. Her central claim that "When someone lies, someone loses" in the last sentence in this excerpt completely undermines an interpretation of her main point as being about the inevitability and harmlessness of lying.

This activity moreover enforces the idea that we need to understand before we argue. Reading a text closely and critically shows respect for the writer's ideas.

Training Students to Monitor Their Confusion

Problems and confusion are a normal part of academic work, which is why I don't take students' struggle with reading comprehension as cause for dismay. The way I see it, it's not teaching if everyone in the room can already read complex texts independently; it's book club.

Students need to hear the message that feeling overwhelmed sometimes just means you are appropriately challenged. Think of Olympic diving. What's the difficulty level of the attempted task? The greater the challenge, the greater the rewards. If you're not starting with at least a little buzz of confusion and curiosity, I tell students, the text you've tackled may not offer much payout.

In *I Read It, but I Don't Get It*, Cris Tovani (2000) offers a list of key indicators of confusion that students can learn to watch for when they're reading. These include two I find especially important in a rhetorical approach:

- The inner voice inside the reader's head stops its conversation with the text, and the reader only hears his voice pronouncing the words.

- The camera inside the reader's head shuts off, and the reader can no longer visualize what is happening as she reads. (2000, 48)

The trick is for students to do something when they notice that either of these things has happened. Reading rhetorically entails the ability to listen for other voices in a conversation and to imagine the larger social context (i.e., the scene or setting) in which the conversation takes place. Reading rhetorically also involves paying closer attention to our own responses to a text so that our confusion is productive rather than disabling. This kind of self-awareness has important implications for transfer of learning. The National Research Council notes in *How People Learn* that "transfer can be improved by helping students become more aware of themselves as learners who actively monitor their learning strategies and resources and assess their readiness for particular tests and performances" (2000, 67).

FUZZY/CLEAR CARDS
This is a terrific formative assessment strategy I learned from my colleague Natasha Oehlman. Using index cards or half sheets of paper, students record something from the day's lesson that is still fuzzy or confusing to them on one side of the paper and something else that is now clear to them on the other side. Teachers can then address fuzzy content in a subsequent lesson.

METACOGNITIVE REFLECTION
Asking students to write about the challenges they encounter as readers and what they do to address those challenges is another way to promote self-efficacy and transfer of learning. Invite your students to respond to the following questions in a quick-write after completing a reading assignment: *What did you find difficult about the reading assignment? When did you have to work hard to make sense of the text? How did you deal with difficulties?*

Formative assessment like fuzzy/clear or metacognitive reflection help us to teach rhetorically by paying attention and responding to the immediate social situation in our classroom.

Tolerating Ambiguity

Some texts just won't give up their secrets. James Phelan describes the difference between texts that are difficult to understand and those that stubbornly resist interpretation: "The *difficult* is recalcitrance that yields to our explanatory efforts, while the *stubborn* is recalcitrance that will not yield" (1996, 178; italics in original). Phelan gives Toni Morrison's Pulitzer Prize–winning novel *Beloved* as an example of a stubborn text. No matter how many angles of approach a reader takes, the title character escapes fixed meaning. Girl-ghost Beloved is what literary critics call "over-determined." Like the white whale in Herman Melville's *Moby-Dick*, she is so full of complex and contradictory meanings that a single interpretation cannot account for all the ways she functions in the text.

We need to help students understand that sometimes the confusion they're experiencing is a rhetorical effect of the text. Ambiguity may be an aspect of the text's theme and purpose.

Reading Across Contexts

Developing students' skill in close reading doesn't mean we teach them not to look beyond the world of an individual text. In the case of *Fables You Shouldn't Pay Any Attention To*, staying within the "four corners of the text" (Wilson and Newark 2011, 1), as the authors of the Common Core recommend, kept us from seeing some of our richest opportunities for meaning-making. By focusing strictly on the literary elements within the fables, we weren't making connections between the texts and a larger conversation. A more contextualized reading of the fables—one that included a consideration of audience, genre, and function—eventually helped us relate this satire of didactic literature to the history of censorship and book banning. Ultimately, the most provocative questions arose from our rhetorical reading: *Are there some stories we shouldn't pay attention to? Are there some books we shouldn't read?*

In *Narrative as Rhetoric: Technique, Audiences, Ethics, and Ideology*, Phelan defines rhetorical reading "as the recursive relationship between authorial agency, textual phenomena, and reader response" (1996, 176–177). In this model, the text "is a sharable medium of a multi-leveled communication between author and reader, even as it takes the reader's experience of the text as the starting point for interpretation" (177). Reading is an experience at once shared and personal, one that calls on our emotions, intellect, and sense of self to construct an understanding of a text.

Taking the Rhetorical Approach to the Next Level: Extended Lesson

Sometimes it's a rhetorical approach that opens the door to a more sophisticated analysis of a literary text. And sometimes it's literary criticism that deepens our understanding of an expository text. The ability to integrate and apply the two ways of reading moves students toward much more advanced and adaptive literacy practices.

Besides being wicked fun, the stories from *Fables You Shouldn't Pay Any Attention To* give younger students an easy access point for learning the basics of literary and rhetorical analysis. When they're ready, they can try those skills with a more complex text, such as Saki's "The Storyteller" (1913), a story that offers rich material for exploring questions on moral education, children's literature, and gender stereotypes.

I teach Saki's story in the form of readers' theater to give students a richer understanding of the dynamics between the different voices in the text (see Appendix 8 for my script). Before they read Saki's story, I remind students that they have been exploring how audience and purpose affect writers' choices. They've also been exploring the topic of morality in literature. Because "The Storyteller" is a more complex text than the fables, you may want to preteach some of the following vocabulary words (note the British spellings):

adverse	assail	behaviour
transcendent	correspondingly	recommenced
sensibility	arising	commended
conveying	defence	unsympathetic
distill	rarity	
apprehending	favour	

(If you're curious, the text complexity score for "The Storyteller" is 11.3, according to the Pearson Reading Maturity Metric. See www.readingmaturity.com/rmm-web/#/.)

The original version of Saki's story can be found on the following pages.

The Storyteller

It was a hot afternoon, and the railway carriage was correspondingly sultry, and the next stop was at Templecombe, nearly an hour ahead. The occupants of the carriage were a small girl, and a smaller girl, and a small boy. An aunt belonging to the children occupied one corner seat, and the further corner seat on the opposite side was occupied by a bachelor who was a stranger to their party, but the small girls and the small boy emphatically occupied the compartment. Both the aunt and the children were conversational in a limited, persistent way, reminding one of the attentions of a housefly that refuses to be discouraged. Most of the aunt's remarks seemed to begin with "Don't," and nearly all of the children's remarks began with "Why?" The bachelor said nothing out loud. "Don't, Cyril, don't," exclaimed the aunt, as the small boy began smacking the cushions of the seat, producing a cloud of dust at each blow.

"Come and look out of the window," she added.

The child moved reluctantly to the window. "Why are those sheep being driven out of that field?" he asked.

"I expect they are being driven to another field where there is more grass," said the aunt weakly.

"But there is lots of grass in that field," protested the boy; "there's nothing else but grass there. Aunt, there's lots of grass in that field."

"Perhaps the grass in the other field is better," suggested the aunt fatuously.

"Why is it better?" came the swift, inevitable question.

"Oh, look at those cows!" exclaimed the aunt. Nearly every field along the line had contained cows or bullocks, but she spoke as though she were drawing attention to a rarity.

"Why is the grass in the other field better?" persisted Cyril.

The frown on the bachelor's face was deepening to a scowl. He was a hard, unsympathetic man, the aunt decided in her mind. She was utterly unable to come to any satisfactory decision about the grass in the other field.

The smaller girl created a diversion by beginning to recite "On the Road to Mandalay." She only knew the first line, but she put her limited knowledge to the fullest possible use. She repeated the line over and over again in a dreamy but resolute and very audible voice; it seemed to the bachelor as though some one had had a bet with her that she could not repeat the line aloud two thousand times without stopping. Whoever it was who had made the wager was likely to lose his bet.

"Come over here and listen to a story," said the aunt, when the bachelor had looked twice at her and once at the communication cord. The children moved listlessly towards the aunt's end of the carriage. Evidently her reputation as a story-teller did not rank high in their estimation.

In a low, confidential voice, interrupted at frequent intervals by loud, petulant questionings from her listeners, she began an unenterprising and deplorably uninteresting story about a little girl who was good, and made friends with every one on account of her goodness, and was finally saved from a mad bull by a number of rescuers who admired her moral character.

"Wouldn't they have saved her if she hadn't been good?" demanded the bigger of the small girls. It was exactly the question that the bachelor had wanted to ask.

"Well, yes," admitted the aunt lamely, "but I don't think they would have run quite so fast to her help if they had not liked her so much."

"It's the stupidest story I've ever heard," said the bigger of the small girls, with immense conviction.

"I didn't listen after the first bit, it was so stupid," said Cyril.

The smaller girl made no actual comment on the story, but she had long ago recommenced a murmured repetition of her favourite line.

"You don't seem to be a success as a story-teller," said the bachelor suddenly from his corner.

The aunt bristled in instant defence at this unexpected attack.

"It's a very difficult thing to tell stories that children can both understand and appreciate," she said stiffly.

"I don't agree with you," said the bachelor.

"Perhaps you would like to tell them a story," was the aunt's retort.

"Tell us a story," demanded the bigger of the small girls.

"Once upon a time," began the bachelor, "there was a little girl called Bertha, who was extra-ordinarily good."

The children's momentarily-aroused interest began at once to flicker; all stories seemed dreadfully alike, no matter who told them.

"She did all that she was told, she was always truthful, she kept her clothes clean, ate milk puddings as though they were jam tarts, learned her lessons perfectly, and was polite in her manners."

"Was she pretty?" asked the bigger of the small girls.

"Not as pretty as any of you," said the bachelor, "but she was horribly good."

There was a wave of reaction in favour of the story; the word *horrible* in connection with goodness was a novelty that commended itself. It seemed to introduce a ring of truth that was absent from the aunt's tales of infant life.

"She was so good," continued the bachelor, "that she won several medals for goodness, which she always wore, pinned on to her dress. There was a medal for obedience, another medal for punctuality, and a third for good behaviour. They were large metal medals and they clicked against one another as she walked. No other child in the town where she lived had as many as three medals, so everybody knew that she must be an extra good child."

"Horribly good," quoted Cyril.

"Everybody talked about her goodness, and the Prince of the country got to hear about it, and he said that as she was so very good she might be allowed once a week to walk in his park, which was just outside the town. It was a beautiful park, and no children were ever allowed in it, so it was a great honour for Bertha to be allowed to go there."

"Were there any sheep in the park?" demanded Cyril.

"No"; said the bachelor, "there were no sheep."

"Why weren't there any sheep?" came the inevitable question arising out of that answer.

The aunt permitted herself a smile, which might almost have been described as a grin.

"There were no sheep in the park," said the bachelor, "because the Prince's mother had once had a dream that her son would either be killed by a sheep or else by a clock falling on him. For that reason, the Prince never kept a sheep in his park or a clock in his palace."

The aunt suppressed a gasp of admiration.

"Was the Prince killed by a sheep or by a clock?" asked Cyril.

"He is still alive, so we can't tell whether the dream will come true," said the bachelor unconcernedly; "anyway, there were no sheep in the park, but there were lots of little pigs running all over the place."

"What colour were they?"

"Black with white faces, white with black spots, black all over, grey with white patches, and some were white all over."

The storyteller paused to let a full idea of the park's treasures sink into the children's imaginations; then he resumed:

"Bertha was rather sorry to find that there were no flowers in the park. She had promised her aunts, with tears in her eyes, that she would not pick any of the kind Prince's flowers, and she had meant to keep her promise, so of course it made her feel silly to find that there were no flowers to pick."

"Why weren't there any flowers?"

"Because the pigs had eaten them all," said the bachelor promptly. "The gardeners had told the Prince that you couldn't have pigs and flowers, so he decided to have pigs and no flowers."

There was a murmur of approval at the excellence of the Prince's decision; so many people would have decided the other way.

"There were lots of other delightful things in the park. There were ponds with gold and blue and green fish in them, and trees with beautiful parrots that said clever things at a moment's notice, and humming birds that hummed all the popular tunes of the day. Bertha walked up and down and enjoyed herself immensely, and thought to herself: 'If I were not so extraordinarily good I should not have been allowed to come into this beautiful park and enjoy all that there is to be seen in it,' and her three medals clinked against one another as she walked and helped to remind her how very good she really was. Just then an enormous wolf came prowling into the park to see if it could catch a fat little pig for its supper."

"What colour was it?" asked the children, amid an immediate quickening of interest.

"Mud-colour all over, with a black tongue and pale grey eyes that gleamed with unspeakable ferocity. The first thing that it saw in the park was Bertha; her pinafore was so spotlessly white and clean that it could be seen from a great distance. Bertha saw the wolf and saw that it was stealing towards her, and she began to wish that she had never been allowed to come into the park. She ran as hard as she could, and the wolf came after her with huge leaps and bounds. She managed to reach a shrubbery of myrtle bushes and she hid herself in one of the thickest of the bushes. The wolf came sniffing among the branches, its black tongue lolling out of its mouth and its pale grey eyes glaring with rage. Bertha was terribly frightened, and thought to herself: 'If I had not been so extraordinarily good I should have been safe in the town at this moment.' However, the scent of the myrtle was so strong that the wolf could not sniff out where Bertha was hiding, and the bushes were so thick that he might have hunted about in them for a long time without catching sight of her, so he thought he might as well go off and catch a little pig instead. Bertha was trembling very much at having the wolf prowling and sniffing so near her, and as she trembled the medal for obedience clinked against the medals for good conduct and punctuality. The wolf was just moving away when he heard the sound of the medals clinking and stopped to listen; they clinked again in a bush quite near him. He dashed into the bush, his pale grey eyes gleaming with ferocity and triumph, and dragged Bertha out and devoured her to the last morsel. All that was left of her were her shoes, bits of clothing, and the three medals for goodness."

"Were any of the little pigs killed?"

"No, they all escaped."

"The story began badly," said the smaller of the small girls, "but it had a beautiful ending."

"It is the most beautiful story that I ever heard," said the bigger of the small girls, with immense decision.

"It is the only beautiful story I have ever heard," said Cyril.

A dissentient opinion came from the aunt.

"A most improper story to tell to young children! You have undermined the effect of years of careful teaching."

"At any rate," said the bachelor, collecting his belongings preparatory to leaving the carriage, "I kept them quiet for ten minutes, which was more than you were able to do."

"Unhappy woman!" he observed to himself as he walked down the platform of Templecombe station; "for the next six months or so those children will assail her in public with demands for an improper story!"

Reading "The Storyteller" Rhetorically

Saki's tale is suffused with a sense of audience expectations. Both the children and the reader are repeatedly invited to anticipate the storyteller's moves—and then are delightfully surprised when the story deviates from their expectations. Phelan uses the example of Katherine Anne Porter's "Magic" to demonstrate how narrative functions as rhetoric, but the description works just as well with Saki's "The Storyteller." The character "is **telling** a particular **story** to a particular **audience** in a particular **situation** for, presumably, a particular **purpose**" (Phelan 1996, 4; emphasis added). We can use Phelan's model to conduct a rhetorical reading of Saki's "The Storyteller," noting how the following elements work together to create meaning:

1. teller

2. story

3.   situation

4.   audience

5.   purpose (Phelan 1996, 8)

Like Porter's "Magic," Saki's "The Storyteller" involves "the narrator's telling the story to his or her audience and then the author's telling of the narrator's telling to the author's audience" (Phelan 1996, 8). There are multiple tellers, stories, situations, audiences, and purposes we need to engage to understand this text. Saki's story is also a description of a rhetorical exchange involving the interaction between two competing narratives (sort of like an Edwardian rap battle). Added to this mix is a third storyteller—Saki's narrator. The three narrative threads together form a complex intersection of voices and perspectives.

Comparing Rhetorical Purposes, Choices, and Effects

The competing narratives offer a rich opportunity for comparing and analyzing rhetorical purposes, choices, and effects. For instance, we can ask students to think about the different aims of each of the storytellers:

- What is the rhetorical purpose of the aunt's story? What does she do to achieve this purpose? Is she successful? Do you think she has other reasons for telling the children stories?

- Does the aunt take morality seriously? What character traits do you think she admires? How do you know?

- What is the rhetorical purpose of the bachelor's story? What does he do to achieve this purpose? Is he successful? Do you think he cares about the moral and/or intellectual influence he has on the children? What can you infer about his values or beliefs? What, if anything, does the bachelor ridicule in his story?

- What can readers infer about Saki's purpose? What does he do to achieve this purpose? Is he successful?

We can also ask students to think about the effects of the storytellers' choices:

- Which story is the most interesting and compelling? Which story, if any, do you imagine in the greatest detail? Which story seems the most "real" to you?

We can ask questions about character and credibility:

- To what extent are we likely to share the aunt's view of the bachelor? What does the narrator do to win our trust and goodwill?

Or about genre and structure:

- Why are opening, superficial similarities between the two stories necessary and important? What do these similarities do/accomplish? What is their rhetorical function? How do the children react to them?

And we can ask about the different message, claim, or theme that each tale conveys:

- What are the different ways we can interpret each of the three stories? Do any of the stories seem to have a fixed meaning? Are any of the stories open ended? Why is this significant?
- What theme or message does the contrast between the two stories convey? What do readers learn about effective storytelling? About children? About adults?
- What title would you give the aunt's story? What title would you give the bachelor's story?

One teacher I talked to after sharing a rhetorical reading of "The Storyteller" at a workshop suggested that the bachelor might actually be flirting with the aunt by telling his story—a fascinating hypothesis that opens a whole other world of critical questions:

- How would the bachelor's story be different if the aunt weren't sitting there? What narrative choices, if any, seem made for the aunt's benefit? Are there moments when he seems to be performing for the aunt? Does he seem to talk over the heads of the children directly to the aunt (e.g., the way Mark Twain talks over Huck Finn's head)? Or does the bachelor speak exclusively to the children? What does the bachelor seem to understand or assume about the children? About the aunt? Of whom (if either) does he have a higher opinion? How do you know?

Questions that model rhetorical thinking can help students dig more deeply into texts and contexts. Try using a structured discussion strategy such as Spencer Kagan's Numbered Heads Together to engage your students with these questions. In this strategy, students are arranged in groups of four, with each student given a number from 1 to 4. A question is posed to the whole class. Students then have a set time, say, three minutes, to discuss the question. When the time is up, the teacher spins a spinner, choosing just one of the four students from each group to share that group's key insights. If the spinner lands on the number 2, for instance, only the number 2 student in each group will share a response with the whole class. This approach encourages all students to listen carefully to their peers and to develop their own ideas because anyone could be called on.

ANNOTATION CUE CARDS FOR "THE STORYTELLER"

If your students are new to annotation or reluctant to speak in class, you can use Annotation Cue Cards to support a group think-aloud. In this activity, the whole class works together to analyze and question a text, with the cue cards serving as models of the kind of thinking that goes on during close reading. The cue cards are there to help students who aren't sure how to jump into the discussion, and students aren't obligated to reveal whether they're reading a cue card or offering an original insight.

Directions to Teachers: Distribute the following comments and questions on individual slips of paper or index cards (see Appendix 9 for a full list of cue cards for "The Storyteller"). It's best if the cards aren't in order. You may not have enough cue cards for each student, but you should have enough "plants" around the room so that you have lots of responses when you ask your students to help you annotate Saki's story. A few students will receive wild cards on which they can write their own comments or questions—you can add more wild cards as students become proficient in annotation.

As part of a second reading of the text, read sections of the story aloud, calling for those students with cue cards to add their comments or questions at the relevant moments. Encourage students to put their cue cards in their own words. Add your own critical think-aloud comments as appropriate. Be sure to pause frequently to ask whether anyone has anything to contribute, and remind students to annotate their own copies of the story during this process. Let students know it's OK if they don't see a spot to share their cue card; they can make up their own comments or questions instead.

Comment: The opening description suggests a dreary atmosphere.

Comment: Sounds like a dull and boring situation.

Question: Why don't we get the bachelor's name?

Question: What is the narrator's tone when he says the children remind one of a housefly?

Comment: The children want storytellers to know the reason for everything.

Comment: The word "emphatically" suggests the children took over the space.

Question: Does the narrator see the bachelor the same way the aunt does?

Comment: Write your own annotation on this card and say it aloud whenever it naturally fits into the group analysis of the text.

(See Appendix 9 for the full activity.)

Admittedly, this activity feels a little artificial, so I try to keep the tone light. We're practicing group analysis, trying on the academic discourse for size, so it's all right if we get a little goofy. But I do find that the cue cards offer more reticent students a helpful way into the discussion. I also find that students' own observations often blend seamlessly with the cue card comments.

After completing a whole-class analysis of the text, I ask students to create their own Annotation Cue Cards as a formative assessment. I pass out index cards, and each student writes a new question and a new comment based on something he or she noticed in the story. The students often see something in the text I missed, as the following examples show:

> **Carina's Question: Why does "horribly good" hook the children's attention?**

> **David's Question: How come this aunt doesn't make an effort to keep the children more busy and distracted?**

> **Diego's Comment: The aunt is being untruthful, like saying it's rare to see something when it's common.**

> **Nathalie's Comment: The bachelor seems to have more experience with the kids than the aunt.**

> **Manny's Comment: The bachelor was on the breaking point of leaving the carriage or saying something to them.**

I can then redistribute the student-generated cue cards to the class to deepen our understanding of the text through an additional critical reading. If you want to make explicit the rhetorical reading strategies students are practicing during this activity, you can pair the group think-aloud with the following checklist.

CHECKLIST FOR LISTENING TO A LITERARY ANALYSIS

Directions to Students: As you listen to and participate in the group think-aloud, keep track of what readers do while analyzing the text rhetorically. Place a check mark by everything you hear readers do during the demonstration.

___ Identify the subject of the text

___ Postpone judgment

___ Identify figurative language and/or symbolism

___ Notice sentence patterns and choices

___ Identify the context

___ Notice text structure and organization

___ Evaluate the effectiveness of the writer's rhetorical choices

___ Analyze connotations of words

___ Paraphrase key sentences or phrases

___ Summarize the writer's theme or message

___ Identify meaningful repetition

___ Notice inconsistencies or ambiguities

___ Notice what sections of the text say and do

___ Identify the writer's purpose

___ Notice key transitions and shifts

___ Offer a personal response

___ Connect language choices to theme or meaning

___ Look for irony

___ Consider the rhetorical effect of punctuation

Increasing Task and Text Complexity: Negotiating Voices

If your students are ready for an additional rhetorical challenge, they can deepen their understanding of Saki's "The Storyteller" by examining how intertextuality—or the presence of texts within texts—contributes to its meaning.

In a rhetorical approach, a text doesn't stand alone. The traces of other voices in the conversation or literary tradition that the text participates in are important clues to its meaning and context. The appearance of Rudyard Kipling's poem "The Road to Mandalay" (1890) in Saki's "The Storyteller," for instance, points to the story's opposition to conventional morality and gender codes. The youngest girl repeatedly recites the first line to "The Road to Mandalay" as a means of escaping her aunt's stultifying attempts at moral improvement.

These are the words the little girl recites:

> By the old Moulmein Pagoda, lookin' lazy at the sea

Of course, these words don't appear in the actual text. Saki is engaging a world outside his own story and assuming his early-twentieth-century readers are familiar with this popular poem from the late nineteenth century. We can help students analyze the possible rhetorical effects of this allusion by asking the following kinds of questions:

1. Find the full text of "The Road to Mandalay." What's the rest of this poem about?

2. Why has Saki chosen to reference this poem in his story? What is the relationship between Kipling's "The Road to Mandalay" and Saki's "The Storyteller"?

3. What assumptions does this allusion suggest Saki has made about his readers? What additional information are we supposed to supply from our knowledge of Kipling's poem that can help us understand Saki's theme? Does this assumption still work for twenty-first-century readers?

4. Why is it significant that both of the tales within the story are about what happens to good little girls? Why does Saki have the youngest girl, instead of the boy, Cyril, repeat this line?

Now ask your students to consider the next three lines of the poem:

> *There's a Burma girl a-settin', and I know she thinks o' me;*
> *For the wind is in the palm-trees, and the temple-bells they say:*
> *"Come you back, you British soldier; come you back to Mandalay!"*

Here we discern a longing for romance and adventure far away from conventional British society—a feeling intensified when the poem's speaker describes his life back in England:

> *But that's all shove be'ind me - long ago an' fur away*
> *An' there ain't no 'busses runnin' from the Bank to Mandalay;*
> *An' I'm learnin' 'ere in London what the ten-year soldier tells:*
> *If you've 'eard the East a-callin', you won't never 'eed naught else."*
> *No! you won't 'eed nothin' else*
> *But them spicy garlic smells,*
> *An' the sunshine an' the palm-trees an' the tinkly temple-bells;*
> *On the road to Mandalay...*
> *I am sick o' wastin' leather on these gritty pavin'-stones,*
> *An' the blasted English drizzle wakes the fever in my bones;*

Toward the end, the poem takes an explicitly antididactic turn when the speaker expresses his desire to return to Mandalay and escape the constraints of conventional morality:

> *Ship me somewheres east of Suez, where the best is like the worst,*
> *Where there aren't no Ten Commandments an' a man can raise a thirst;*

The words "where the best is like the worst" and "there aren't no Ten Commandments" offer an especially interesting clue to the meaning of Saki's story. If you have your students read "The Road to Mandalay" in connection with "The Storyteller," you can expect them to experience a significantly greater reading challenge. This is not an easy text for most of today's high school students. Furthermore, the poem's 1890's treatment of race and gender will prompt many students to read it against the grain—with excellent reason. Reading "The Storyteller" rhetorically, however, could involve taking on the challenge of situating the text in its post-Victorian social world, a world characterized by imperialism, orientalist fantasies, and strict gender norms. Appreciating this textual and historical context can help students see the youngest girl's compulsive recitation as not just a response to boredom but also an act of subversion. In choosing *this* particular poem and *this* particular character to recite it, Saki makes the poem another voice against the sanctimonious idealization of "good" little girls.

From Literature to Argument

In reading a short story like "The Storyteller" or a poem like "The Road to Mandalay," we are already reading rhetoric and arguments. As Glen McClish (n.d.) notes in "Teaching Poetry Rhetorically," creative writers "write to direct the attention of their readers, suggesting what is important, significant, admirable, pitiable, or evil. They set forth subjective claims, positions, and stances about the world, human relations, and experiences—they present cases and argue" (4). McClish's point concerns poets in particular, but the remark applies equally to novelists, playwrights, and other writers of literature.

Students can further develop their rhetorical literacy skills and understanding by writing arguments about literature. Kelly Gallagher talks about the importance of getting kids to "track their thinking" (2015, 147–149). We do this when we ask students to participate in an ongoing conversation. We want them to explore a line of inquiry over the course of their reading, discussion, and writing, to discover their thinking on a text or topic through a thoughtful exchange with the other people involved in the conversation. When we understand reading and writing as acts of communication, there's no place for decontextualized, one-and-done approaches to texts.

The following argument prompts offer opportunities to extend students' thinking about moral education and children's literature.

PROMPT 1: MORAL EDUCATION AND CHILDREN'S LITERATURE

The passage that follows is adapted from the introduction to *The Book of Virtues: A Treasury of Great Moral Stories* by William J. Bennett (1993). Read the passage carefully. Then write an essay in which you explain Bennett's argument and discuss the ways in which you agree or disagree with him. Support your position with reasons and evidence from your reading, as well as from your observations and personal experience as relevant.

> Moral education—the training of heart and mind toward the good— involves many things. It involves rules and precepts—the *dos* and *don'ts* of life with others—as well as explicit instruction, exhortation, and training. Moral education must provide training in good habits. Aristotle wrote that good habits formed at youth make all the difference. And moral education must affirm the central importance of moral example. It has been said that there is nothing more influential, more determinate, in a child's life than the moral power of a quiet example. For children to take morality seriously they must be in the presence of adults who take morality seriously. And with their own eyes they must see adults take morality seriously.
>
> . . . The vast majority of Americans share a respect for certain fundamental traits of character: honesty, compassion, courage, and perseverance. These are

virtues. But because children are not born with this knowledge, they need to learn what these virtues are. We can help them gain a grasp and appreciation of these traits by giving children material to read about them. We can invite our students to discern the moral dimensions of stories, of historical events, of famous lives. There are many wonderful stories of virtue and vice with which our children should be familiar.

... If we want our children to possess the traits of character we most admire, we need to teach them what those traits are and why they deserve both admiration and allegiance. Children must learn to identify the forms and content of those traits. They must achieve at least a minimum level of moral literacy that will enable them to make sense of what they see in life and, we may hope, help them live it well.

> **Effective writing prompts repeatedly take students back to the text—not to "hunt and peck," as a colleague says, but to really understand what the writer is saying and how the text works.**

PROMPT 2: WARNING LABELS FOR IMPROPER STORIES

Read the passage that follows carefully. Then write an essay in which you explain the writer's argument and discuss the ways in which you agree or disagree with her. Support your position with reasons and evidence from your reading, as well as from your observations and personal experience as relevant.

It's time to think more carefully about the effect inappropriate reading material can have on young minds. Maybe we don't need to ban books with harmful or immoral messages, but readers should at least be aware of potentially offensive or inappropriate content in books. Parents, in particular, have the right to know if a book might be sending a message they don't want their children to hear. We have a rating system for movies and video games, and we have warning labels for music albums with explicit song lyrics; shouldn't we have warning labels for books, too? That way, people can choose reading materials that will help them lead better lives and develop stronger moral characters instead of choosing books that waste their time with trashy entertainment.

Expanding the Conversation

Making text-to-text connections across a larger conversation in literary studies can help kids hold onto their thinking. What other texts could be a part of this same discussion? How about Chaucer's Wife of Bath's prologue and tale or Polonious's "few precepts" speech to his son Laertes in *Hamlet*? Think how your students might respond to the following kinds of questions:

- How does the Wife of Bath feel about her husband's book about wicked women?

- How would you describe Polonius's ethos or image?

- What is the tone of his speech?

- What motivates him to give this advice to his son? What does Polonius say? What does he do? What assumptions does Polonius make about Laertes?

- How does the audience view this moment in the play?

- How does Polonius's speech compare to other examples of didactic (teaching) literature?

- How do we feel about advice books? What are the characteristics of this genre?

- Who is the market for advice books?

- How do adult children typically respond when their parents give them advice?

> Reading across contexts and engaging increasingly complex tasks and texts help to develop intellectual capacities essential for transfer of learning. These include the following:
>
> 1. **A mind-set toward connection-making**
>
> 2. **Ability to hold onto thinking**
>
> 3. **Rhetorical knowledge and skills**
>
> 4. **A habit of creative problem solving**
>
> 5. **A habit of leveraging prior knowledge**

This kind of rhetorical analysis prepares students for the moral ambiguity of texts like F. Scott Fitzgerald's *The Great Gatsby* (1925), Albert Camus's *The Stranger* (1942), or Mark Twain's *The Adventures of Huckleberry Finn* ([1895] 1995).

Conclusion

A rhetorical approach balances close textual analysis with other strategies for meaning-making. In a rhetorical framework, the text is one of several agents of meaning. In addition to spoken or written words, the audience, writer, or speaker, and context also affect how and what messages are expressed and how those messages are received and understood. The text doesn't stand alone but functions as part of a whole act of communication in a complex social world. Teaching students to combine their literary knowledge with their rhetorical knowledge prepares them to respond flexibly to a variety of changing literacy tasks and genres—and to value their own experiences and choices as meaning-makers.

CHAPTER THREE

Assessing the Rhetorical Situation

With milieu comes attendant expectations.

—TIM GUNN

I f we're not teaching for transfer of learning—that is, if we're only teaching for success on school-based performance tasks, and what happens beyond those tasks isn't our concern—then we don't need to teach students how to assess different rhetorical situations. We can just tell students what to do, and they can follow our directions (or not). However, if transfer is the goal, then the ability to analyze the demands of unique rhetorical situations and respond appropriately is an essential literacy skill.

Experienced readers and writers take the time to assess a rhetorical situation—including the audience, occasion, purpose, and genre—whenever they encounter a new context of communication. This is the lurker, or reconnaissance, stage of communication. Before I felt confident enough to host my first Twitter chat, for instance, I lurked in several other chats to get a sense of how it was done. When I mentioned to my daughter that I'd be listening in on other conversations, she raised an eyebrow and said, "Stalker much?"

"I'm not a stalker," I said, "I'm a lurker," and then added in a burst of inspired self-defense, "Lurkers are learners!" We do this kind of detective work, I explained, when we have to learn how to act in a new situation.

I don't think any of us expect that our students will only encounter literacy tasks and contexts exactly like the ones they experience in our classrooms. Yet many of our students feel painfully unprepared to deal with the unfamiliar.

I think of Tony, for instance. Tony was one of those spark plugs who brought a wonderful energy to our classroom discussions from the very first day of class. A thoughtful reader and passionate speaker, Tony showed every sign of genuine intellectual engagement. It wasn't until our first essay assignment that I discovered he was struggling in my course. He waited after class one day until all the other students had left and then approached me with my writing prompt in hand.

"I don't know how to do this," he said, gesturing to my instructions to write a three- to four-page reading-based argument essay. "I've only written short essays," he explained and then added with a look of dejection, "I don't know why I never learned this before." After reassuring Tony that this wasn't a problem, I showed him some models of this type of writing, and then we explored ways for him to gather and sort evidence in preparation for building an extended argument.

> Preparing students to be college and career ready doesn't mean we give them advance exposure to every possible literacy task they can encounter in the postsecondary world (many of which, of course, don't exist yet). It means we give them the rhetorical tools and sense of self-efficacy needed to adapt to any situation.

What struck me wasn't the fact that Tony hadn't written a longer essay before (it turned out, he'd only written five-paragraph essays). This was no big deal. In fact, many students who take advanced placement courses arrive on college campuses with little to no experience writing multidraft process essays since their focus has largely been on mastering a forty-five-minute on-demand essay. What concerned me was that Tony felt like he was already supposed to know how to write the kind of essay I was asking him to write and that something was wrong with him because he didn't. He wasn't seeing my assignment as a new rhetorical situation that would take some figuring out. Faced with an unfamiliar task, he didn't know where to start.

We can better prepare students to face the unfamiliar by helping them to develop the rhetorical knowledge needed to adapt to new situations. Students need flexible and diversified literacy skills, not preloaded sets of instructions.

Teaching the Rhetorical Situation

In its most immediate, cut-to-the-quick sense, assessing a rhetorical situation means finding the things people care about and are talking about. This can include problems, needs, relationships, events, and expectations for how people should communicate (i.e., discourse conventions). It can also include available information or data. Of these components, a critical need or problem—what rhetoricians call the *exigence*—may be the most important. Lloyd F. Bitzer famously defines *exigence* as "an imperfection marked by urgency," a "something waiting to be done" (1999, 221). A rhetorical exigence is a problem or obstacle that can be changed by rhetoric. Something lights a fire in our belly, and, oh my goodness, we feel a powerful impulse to respond. Speaking and writing can also create a sense of urgent need. An exigence produces rhetoric, and rhetoric produces an exigence. It's a bit of a chicken-and-egg relationship, really.

Bitzer also talks about *constraints*, "which influence the rhetor [speaker or writer] and can be brought to bear upon the audience" (1999, 220). Constraints limit what can be said, decided, or done in a particular situation. We might think of these as reality checks: people, rules, events, physical objects or laws, attitudes, or anything else that binds the rhetorical act to the here and now.

At minimum, a rhetorical situation entails the following components (see Figure 3.1):

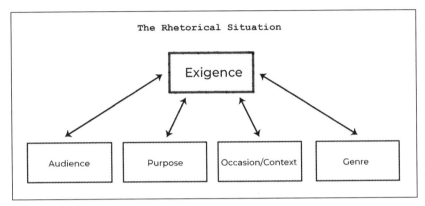

FIGURE 3.1
The Rhetorical Situation

Animating all these components and the dynamic relationships between them is that sense of exigence, filtered through the rhetor's perspective.

The Council of Writing Program Administrators' *Outcomes Statement for First-Year Composition (3.0)* offers a helpful description of how students develop the knowledge that enables them to respond appropriately to diverse rhetorical situations: "Writers develop rhetorical knowledge by negotiating purpose, audience, context, and conventions as they compose a variety of texts for different situations" (2014, 1). This includes writing in different disciplines and genres.

To be sure, students also develop this knowledge by reading a variety of texts, and literary works make particularly good candidates for rhetorical analysis. In the sections to follow, I share how I use literature to teach students how to assess and respond to diverse rhetorical situations.

Assessing Rhetorical Situations in Literature

One of the advantages of using literary texts to teach how to assess rhetorical situations is that students can learn from the approaches taken by fictional characters. How do characters in novels, plays, and short stories size up an audience? How do they negotiate rhetorical pitfalls? Which characters are most adept at choosing the right words at the right time? Learning from the effective (and ineffective)

Rhetorical situation as a distinct term doesn't show up in the argument and rhetoric books on my shelf published before the 1970s. It wasn't until Bitzer's landmark 1968 essay "The Rhetorical Situation" that this term even became a common feature of rhetorical theory and practice. However, the idea of assessing the situation—of being aware of the audience's needs and expectations, the rhetor's purpose, and the immediate social context—dates back millennia. See Aristotle's *Rhetoric* (1984) for the classical view on this subject.

communication strategies of fictional characters helps students become more attuned to the varied ways humans respond to situational demands.

William Shakespeare's play *Romeo and Juliet* gives students ample opportunities to examine the ways different characters approach daunting rhetorical situations. For a look at a character who feels ill at ease with the persuasive task she's obligated to perform, there's the scene in which Juliet's mother discusses Paris's offer of marriage with her young daughter (act 1, scene 3)—a task Lady Capulet stumbles through ineffectually with no little reliance on the nurse for backup support. The difficulty here is Lady Capulet's relationship with her audience. Juliet clearly shares a closer bond with her nurse than with her mother, which is why Lady Capulet has second thoughts about speaking to her daughter alone. "Nurse, give leave awhile, / We must talk in secret," Lady Capulet commands and then does an about-face: "Nurse, come back again; I have remember'd me, thou's hear our counsel" (act 1, scene 3, lines 9–11).

Lack of understanding or rapport between speaker and audience makes this mother-daughter conversation one of the play's more awkward moments. Lady Capulet also has difficulty negotiating the occasion for her speech: Should she speak to Juliet alone? With the nurse's help? Ultimately, the extent to which Lady Capulet achieves her purpose (i.e., persuading her daughter to marry) is unclear since Juliet is noncommittal in her response. The most Juliet will say is this:

> I'll look to like, if looking liking move:
> But no more deep will I endart mine eye
> Than your consent gives strength to make it fly. (act 1, scene 3, lines 97–99)

For an example of more effective rhetoric under pressure, how about the famous balcony scene in act 2? When Juliet appears above at a window ("But soft! What light is this?"), Romeo recognizes he has a special opportunity and some critical decisions to make. How best to declare his love under the given circumstances? They've only just met that evening, and now Juliet is alone and unaware of Romeo's presence below in her father's orchard. In the following lines, Shakespeare shows us Romeo's desire to make himself and his feelings known, as well as the challenge he faces in choosing his timing:

> It is my lady, O, it is my love!
> O, that she knew she were!
> She speaks yet she says nothing: what of that?
> Her eye discourses; I will answer it.
> I am too bold, 'tis not to me she speaks: (act 2, scene 2, lines 10–14)

He decides to listen for a while longer in silence, alert to the right moment to make his move. A few lines later, he thinks he sees his opening. Juliet, unburdening her soul to the night, makes her own feelings clear:

O Romeo, Romeo! wherefore art thou Romeo?
Deny thy father and refuse thy name;
Or, if thou wilt not, be but sworn my love,
And I'll no longer be a Capulet. (act 2, scene 2, lines 33–36)

Romeo is on the brink of speaking: "Shall I hear more, or shall I speak at this?" (act 2, scene 2, line 37). But he decides to let the moment fully develop—and Juliet fully commit herself—before he responds. When he does finally speak, telling Juliet, "I take thee at thy word" in response to her soliloquized "Take all myself," the tide has turned entirely in his favor, and there's no turning back for the two young lovers. Having chosen the right moment, Romeo now has to choose the right words, and he's empowered to do so by his astute reading of his audience. He reassures Juliet that his love is true and his intentions honorable. See the rest of this scene for a full display of Romeo's rhetorical skill.

If you read *Romeo and Juliet* with your students, have them examine how both Romeo and Juliet negotiate "purpose, audience, context, and conventions" (WPA 2014, 1) by asking them to answer the following kinds of questions. It might help to have students write their responses first before discussing their answers in pairs or small groups.

Directions to Students: Carefully read act 2, scene 2 of William Shakespeare's play *Romeo and Juliet* before responding to these questions:

- What factors influence how and when Romeo declares his love to Juliet in this scene?
- What does he know about Juliet, his audience, that helps him make this decision?
- When Juliet asks, "Art thou not Romeo and a Montague?" (act 2, scene 2, line 60), why doesn't he give her a direct answer?
- What kind of things does Romeo say when Juliet asks if he loves her? Do you think this is what Juliet wants to hear?
- How does she respond?
- Is his choice of strategies effective?
- What constraints, or rhetorical difficulties, does Romeo face? What constraints does Juliet face? Why does she say, "I should have been more strange, I must confess, / But that thou overheard't, ere I was ware" (act 2, scene 2, lines 102–103)?
- Why is this particular occasion important? What opportunity does Romeo have now that he might not have another time? What else is special about this moment and place? How does the occasion limit what the characters are able to say and do? (Hints: Consider Juliet's age and unmarried status, the roles and conditions of women at this time, the dangers of seduction, the significance of marriage, the feud, the threat of being caught, etc.)

- What's Romeo's purpose? To what extent is Romeo motivated by an urgent sense of need? Is his purpose the same as Juliet's? How do you know?

- Is there a problem the characters must solve? Is something "other than it should be"?

Exploring these kinds of questions will take students a good way toward understanding the constraints, challenges, and desires that shape the rhetorical situation Shakespeare's title characters face in this quintessential love scene. By the way, you might have noticed the difference between these rhetoric-based questions and typical study-guide questions. A nice benefit of a rhetorical approach is that it compels students to read the original text closely and critically. You can't do a rhetorical analysis of *Romeo and Juliet* if you've only watched the movie or read an online plot summary.

PAPA SQUARE ANALYSIS

An additional strategy that can help students develop their ability to assess rhetorical situations is a PAPA Square Analysis, a technique I write about in *Teaching Arguments* (2015). Based on the work of composition scholar Maxine Hairston, this activity also goes by the name "rhetorical square" (1986, 78), but I like the name PAPA Square because it reminds students of key components of effective communication: the writer's or speaker's Purpose, Argument, Persona, and Audience. Students can use the PAPA Square graphic organizer with literary or informational texts to describe different aspects of a rhetorical situation, along with the rhetorical strategies and methods a writer or speaker uses to meet the demands of that situation.

Using a PAPA Square Analysis with a literary work gives us some interesting options. For the section on *argument*, we can choose to identify what a character is saying (in a situation in which a character makes either direct or indirect claims about a topic), or we can choose to identify what the writer is saying (in other words, the theme). See Figure 3.2 for an example of what the first option can look like; in this case, the character making an argument is Mustafa Mond from Aldous Huxley's *Brave New World* ([1932] 2006).

For the section on *persona*, we can again choose either to analyze the narrator's ethos or the writer's ethos, an especially sophisticated task for novels such as Mark Twain's *The Adventures of Huckleberry Finn* ([1884] 1995) that have unreliable first-person narrators. Detecting Twain's singular persona behind Huck Finn's iconic voice demands tremendous powers of observation. But it's there, awaiting discovery like a galaxy hidden by stars.

When I used to ask my students to identify the point of view of a story, I'd receive a single phrase as an answer: "first-person," "third-person limited," or "third-person omniscient." Now when I ask students to describe the persona of either the narrator or the writer, I often receive a full paragraph or more of analysis.

Thinking about the rhetorical situation a literary text evokes or embodies, instead of just the text's setting, point of view, or even theme, takes readers beyond a static identification of

PAPA Square

Title and author of text: Chapter 17 of *Brave New World* by Aldous Huxley

PURPOSE: To explain to John "Savage" why the World State has sacrificed art, science, and religion for the happiness of its citizens.

AUDIENCE:
John—a free-thinking, free-willed, Shakespeare-loving "savage" who has not been conditioned in the ideology of the World State; John sees struggle, suffering, and passion as necessary to a rich and full human experience, and he's repelled by what he sees as the degrading comforts and ease of "civilized" life; an outsider.

Rhetorical devices and strategies:
- Logic (logos): " 'You can only be independent of God while you've got youth and prosperity; independence won't take you safely to the end.' Well, we've now got youth and prosperity right up to the end. What follows? Evidently, that we can be independent of God" (Huxley 233).
- Allusions to classic works of philosophy and literature familiar to John, his audience
- Cause and effect relationships
- If/then statements
- Deductive reasoning:
  - "But chastity means passion, chastity means neurasthenia. And passion and neurasthenia mean instability. And instability means the end of civilization" (Huxley 237).
  - "Where there are wars, where there are divided allegiances, where there are temptations to be resisted, objects of love to be fought for or defended—there, obviously, nobility and heroism have some sense. But there aren't any wars nowadays [...] Anybody can be virtuous now" (237-238).

ARGUMENT:
People in the World State are happy because they are conditioned to be "hard-working, goods-consuming" (Huxley 236) citizens who can gratify their natural impulses in a totally stable and controlled society. Great art, true religion, and true science lead to and grow from passion, instability, and discontent.

PERSONA (ETHOS): Mustapha Mond, the Controller of the World State—polite, pleasant, well-read, considers other possibilities, listens and responds to other viewpoints but is firm and authoritative in his own convictions; totally and confidently committed to the position he has chosen.

FIGURE 3.2
PAPA Square Analysis of Mustafa Mond's argument in *Brave New World*

literary elements toward a dynamic analysis of a text's communicative functions. In a rhetorical approach, the focus is on what writers and speakers are trying to say to an audience and the choices they make to accomplish their aims.

RHETORICAL PRÉCIS + (FOR LITERARY TEXTS)

Like Descriptive Plot Outlining and Say, Mean, Matter, Do—two strategies I write about in Chapter 2—Rhetorical Précis + is my value-added modification of a tried-and-true literacy strategy. I've used the rhetorical précis to help my students write an analytical paragraph about a text's rhetorical situation ever since I learned about this method in John C. Bean, Virginia

A. Chappell, and Alice M. Gillam's *Reading Rhetorically* (2014). Mastering the précis takes a good bit of practice and coaching, but the payoff in improved analytical reading skills is worth it. Recently, I discovered a way to make this strategy work even better with literary texts.

First, for my readers unfamiliar with the original rhetorical précis, here are the steps, as outlined by Bean, Chappel, and Gillam:

> ## How to Structure a Rhetorical Précis
> Sentence 1: Name of author, genre, and title of work, date in parentheses; a rhetorically accurate verb; and a "that" clause containing the major assertion or thesis statement in the work.
> Sentence 2: An explanation of how the author develops and supports the thesis, usually in chronological order.
> Sentence 3: A statement of the author's apparent purpose, followed by an "in order to" phrase.
> Sentence 4: A description of the intended audience and/or the relationship the author establishes with the audience. (2014, 63)

See, for instance, the sample rhetorical précis I wrote for Shakespeare's "Sonnet 18" that I share with students when I introduce this strategy:

> In "Sonnet 18," William Shakespeare asserts that although earthly beauty is ephemeral, the poet's art endures, granting a type of immortality to the subject of his poetry. Shakespeare develops this idea first through a critique of conventional metaphors in love poems (e.g., comparing the beauty of the beloved to a summer's day) and then through an assertion of the transcendent power of his poetry. Shakespeare elevates the status of a great poet above the subject of his poetry in order to illustrate the latter's dependence on the former for perpetual fame. Shakespeare's audience would have included the subject of his sonnet, patrons of literature, and fellow poets.

I'd been using this technique with both informational and literary texts, with the latter often to help students analyze a speech made by a fictional character. For example, when I taught *The Merchant of Venice*, I'd ask students to write a rhetorical précis of Shylock's speech that begins "Hath not a Jew eyes?" in act 3, scene 1 or of Portia's speech about the quality of mercy in the same play.

But then Jonathan, one of my students, asked some genius questions about my activity directions: "Are we supposed to be paraphrasing Shylock's claim or Shakespeare's claim? And do you want us to identify Shylock's purpose or Shakespeare's purpose?" Uh, right. Why hadn't I thought of this before?

After thanking Jonathan for his brilliance, I amended the rhetorical précis I used for literary texts to include one more direction and renamed the new five-sentence rhetorical précis the Rhetorical Précis +. Here are my revised directions, followed by a student example (see Figure 3.3):

> Sentence 1: Name of author, genre, and title of work, date in parentheses; statement identifying the character and context and paraphrasing the character's central claim (i.e., what the character is saying).
> Sentence 2: An explanation of how the character develops and supports the claim.
> Sentence 3: A statement of the character's apparent purpose, followed by an "in order to" phrase.
> Sentence 4: A description of the character's intended audience and/or the relationship the character establishes with that audience.
> Sentence 5: A statement interpreting what the author is saying (i.e., a theme) through the character's words and actions, as well as the impact of the author's choices on the reader.

1) The poem, "On Staying Behind," by Diana Garcia is written in the point of view of a mother. A mother that is faced with the reality that her daughter is leaving to another country in order to have a better life and the type of challenges she will be faced with. She also talks about her life staying at home. 2) "The journey is harsh, more than two weeks if she's lucky" is one of the the mothers statements. This supports one of the claims, that is, the types of obstacles the daughter will be faced with 3) The purpose to this poem in my belief, is to inform. To inform in order to have people be aware of the types of challenges a lot of people face in coming to another country for a better life. The intended audience would have to be anyone that is faced or has gone through or even have family members in this situation. I think that the relationship that she builds withe the audience is to empathize with them. So that the audience knows that they've not the only ones. The author wants to send out the message that sometimes harsh times lead to desperate measure Also to elaborate on the types of difficulties faced on any type of journey like this.

FIGURE 3.3

Student example of a Rhetorical Précis + for the poem "On Staying Behind" by Diana Garcia

Think of how the "+" statement boosts the analytical wattage of this strategy when applied to a passage such as Caliban's speech in William Shakespeare's *The Tempest*:

> I must eat my dinner.
> This island's mine, by Sycorax my mother,
> Which thou takest from me. When thou camest first,
> Thou strokedst me and madest much of me, wouldst give me
> Water with berries in't, and teach me how
> To name the bigger light, and how the less,
> That burn by day and night: and then I loved thee
> And show'd thee all the qualities o' the isle,
> The fresh springs, brine-pits, barren place and fertile:
> Cursed be I that did so! All the charms
> Of Sycorax, toads, beetles, bats, light on you!
> For I am all the subjects that you have,
> Which first was mine own king: and here you sty me
> In this hard rock, whiles you do keep from me
> The rest o' the island. (act 1, scene 2, lines 333–347)

What *is* Shakespeare saying through Caliban in this scene? Is he sympathetic to Caliban? Repelled by him? To what extent does Shakespeare uphold and/or subvert the worldviews of his time? Does he see Caliban as a product of the Old World (i.e., Europe) or the New World (i.e., the Americas)? What does the textual evidence suggest? How do Caliban's words and actions make the reader or playgoer feel? See Appendix 12 for a student example of a rhetorical précis of Caliban's speech.

Fostering a Deeper Understanding of Exigence: "On Leaving | On Staying Behind" by Diana Garcia

Integrating literary knowledge with rhetorical knowledge gives students twice the interpretive power. Thus, when we combine a rhetorical concept like *exigence* with literary concepts like *conflict* or *setting*, we significantly increase students' analytical bandwidth. Remember, according to Bitzer, an exigence is a critical problem or need that can be changed by rhetoric. Later scholars have also noted the way rhetoric creates an exigence (think of the urgent demand for social change generated by *Uncle Tom's Cabin*).

Literature's ability to respond to and create an urgent need and purpose is stunningly apparent in the two poems that follow by American Book Award–winner Diana Garcia. Having already written a series of poems about the young men who were part of the Bracero Program—the guest worker program that brought millions of Mexican men to the United States on short-term labor contracts—Garcia turned her attention to the experiences of young women impacted by war and poverty, particularly those who emigrate to the United States alone. Her paired poems, "On Leaving | On Staying Behind" (2014), powerfully illustrate the limitations of approaches to literary analysis that fail to consider the rhetorical situation and real-life exigencies of the writer and speaker.

On Leaving

*I can run five times around the village, my dog beside me. I have tested
myself against her speed, my younger cousins' endurance. I win.
My cousins go with me this morning, their dark hair glossy, so young
their shoulders. Their mothers tell me to watch over them.
I have said goodbye to all who remain, grayed village elders,
wooden statues of saints in our small church, my mother.
I go with the blessings of my mother and her sisters. I am the youngest
of the girl cousins, no great beauty, no wealth to keep me here.
I wear only what I have. I carry a blouse one aunt gave me,
a friend's old sandals for days when heat persists into the night.
My cousins who have made the journey send this advice: travel early
in the morning and at night. When you reach the trains, gain a space
in the middle; don't move. Don't let anyone steal your space. When we
reach Mexico, we are to look for coyotes wearing yellow bandanas,
not red or green. Those wearing yellow come from our region,
they speak our language, they are known to our village.
If no one waits at the border wearing yellow, we wait or take
our chances. I have waited two years for this chance. No more.
If the coyotes separate me from my two cousins, mis primas
instruct me to let them take what they will, but not my life, never my life.
They think I don't know what they mean. I know what a man
can take from a woman. I know my younger cousins' pride.
I will protect them from their pride, our family honor. I will scream
or fight if I can. I will run if I can. I know now how fast I can run.*

On Staying Behind

*She thinks I don't know why she runs. Not to catch the trains
or escape la migra or outrun packs of wild dogs. I listened
to the advice her cousins sent, the older girl cousins, married,
hard-working girls who left our village with their husbands.
The journey is harsh, more than two weeks if she's lucky.
So many dangers, only two younger male cousins to protect her.
My daughter has no husband. She cannot stay with me. I will
not have her stay with me to starve. She leaves with no wealth.
She and her cousins are their own wealth. I see the strength
in their arms and shoulders, blood that pumps through heart and lungs.
No water, no beans or corn. Today, the woman studying our village,
una profe de los estados unidos, spilled our pot of beans.
This woman has never known hunger. I saw her shock when I sifted
beans from dirt, placed beans, dirt, the bit of water I had planned to use
for grinding the last dried corn. What is a little dirt, I thought, the same dirt
in which I grew these beans. A child should not see a mother starve to death.
A mother should not hear that her last daughter has disappeared.
I bless this last child, daughter of my heart, the one I hoped
would wrap my body in a serape and lay me next to her father
at the edge of the church yard. I bless her journey, wishing
her safe passage, fleet journey. I have said my prayers
to the village saints. I have eaten my small meal. I will lay
myself alongside her dog tonight. Perhaps tomorrow, more food
will come my way. Again, I stay behind. I will wait and hope.*

If you take a rhetorical approach to analyzing these poems, what kind of things might you consider? Try making a quick list in your head of what you'd notice or look for. Your list probably includes some of the following considerations:

- The audience, purpose, and occasion of the poems
- The wider social and historical contexts of the poems
- The differences and similarities between the two speakers' situations and perspectives
- The differences and similarities between the speakers' voices and identities
- The exigencies motivating the speakers' words and actions
- The awareness of self and other in each poem
- The constraints on choice and expression imposed by the situation

A full rhetorical reading of these poems, with all the accompanying discussion and writing, can take a couple of hours. In my classroom, we move from a silent reading of the poems to get the gist of Garcia's message to an oral reading to fully experience Garcia's poetry. Textual analysis and annotation move from whole class, to small group, to individual, with each student noting and sharing one word or phrase that seems especially important.

I then ask my students to further respond to "On Leaving | On Staying" by freewriting about any of the following prompts.

1. What are the risks and sacrifices of leaving? Of staying? Do you think one experience is more difficult or painful than the other?

2. What does the daughter understand about her mother? About herself? What does the mother understand about her daughter? About herself?

3. What choices does the daughter have? What constraints does she face? How about the mother? Do you think one character is more limited and/or empowered by her situation? Why or why not?

4. What do you think is important about these poems?

I like to time my students' responses to the writing prompts to structure this activity and extend their thinking. The timer helps them to keep going when they get stuck because I tell them to keep their pen moving (or keep typing) until the timer goes off. If they can't think of anything more to write, they can repeat their last word over and over or write about how they can't think of anything until a new idea occurs to them. This approach often helps students brainstorm new insights beyond their first impression. I also use the same verbal cue each time I set students up for a quick-write: "Take a moment to think about the prompt, and when you're ready, begin writing." Then I push the start button on the timer and stand still for about twenty seconds until all my writers are under way.

Here is a sampling of my students' responses to Garcia's poems:

- The risks and sacrifices of leaving are not seeing your loved ones anymore and missing family time. The risks of staying are starving and being poor for the rest of their lives. They are both painful experiences because with both you still are separated from your loved ones.

- The daughter understands that her mother can no longer take care of her, that they are living in an extreme poverty situation where the daughter is more likely to succeed if she leaves home in hopes of a better future. The daughter knows she is strong and capable of achieving this goal.

- The risks of her leaving are getting raped, death, or losing her cousins. But if she stays she will suffer more by seeing her mother die slowly due to starvation. I think it might be more painful for the mother because she might feel she failed her daughter and that's why she had to leave, and she really cannot do anything to change it even if she wanted to.

- I think they really emphasize the struggles and hardships people are faced with when they leave their home country. It really puts into perspective how different people view the journey and what their worries are. The reasons why people decide to leave. How hard it can be for not only the person leaving but also for their families and friends. How it affects everyone.

Knowing that Garcia is also a teacher of writing who stresses the importance of attending to audience, purpose, and craft with her own students, I asked her a few questions about the rhetorical situations she engages through these poems. Here's our conversation:

Me: What inspired you to write "On Leaving | On Staying"? What problems or needs did you hope to address?

Garcia: Early ideas for "On Leaving" came to me as I prepared comments for a panel presentation titled "The Road Most Traveled," a symposium at San Diego's Museum of Photographic Arts in October 2006 on children refugees fleeing poverty and violence in Central America. Photographs of young Salvadoran refugees, mostly boys and young men, captured their harrowing journey piled on top of trains headed north to Mexico and the US. The photos haunted me, especially those few photos depicting young girls. The girls appeared to be partnered with young males. I imagined them as siblings and cousins, girls forced to flee because they had no one else to protect them or care for them in their home villages. My initial impulse, then, for writing these poems was in response to the images of the girls depicted in the photographs.

Throughout the early 2000s, I had grown more and more horrified at the discovery of hundreds of bodies of murdered young women in the Juarez/El Paso region. Determined to find work and help support families back home, the young women took advantage of better-paying jobs in the maquiladoras, or factories, in Juarez. Traveling and living alone, no families waited for them. They become easy prey for whoever continues to torture and murder these young women to the present time.

I know that part of my impulse to write "On Leaving" was to imagine survival strategies for young women who travel alone in search of a better life. At the same time, I recognized how any young man coming to help a girl under attack might result in both their murders, hence, the focus on running and fighting but hoping to protect a young male companion from their own macho instincts. Odd, even now, that I imagined the nurturing, protective (maternal?) instinct of the young girl as stronger than the male macho instinct to protect the females in the family.

The second poem, "On Staying Behind," depicts what every mother faces when her children leave home. In this case, however, the dangers for both mother and daughter are grounded in poverty, violence, starvation, and death, and the mother's determination that the daughter will survive. Like most mothers, I imagine this mother unwilling to place her daughter in the terrible position of having to bury her mother.

Hope is a powerful catalyst, and hope drives both mother and daughter to take extreme risks.

Me: What did you imagine as the wider context for these poems?

Garcia: The poems are intended to focus on the continuing and growing global pandemics of war, poverty, and violence and the concomitant victimization of young women as one of the more glaring manifestations of social and geopolitical conflict.

Me: A writer's message is often different from what their characters are saying. Is that the case in these poems? Can your characters say things you cannot? Can you say things your characters cannot?

Garcia: I would offer that our messages are the same. The difference is the degree to which I as both a mother and daughter witnessed and experienced poverty and victimization, especially as a single mother in my early twenties. I know the hopes and fears my own mother had for me. Even though I didn't go to them for help (after all, when I got pregnant my father told me, "You're on your own now") I knew that in a life-or-death struggle, they would come to my aid. I know how difficult it was to survive my early and midtwenties never knowing if I would be able to pay the rent, buy food and clothes for my son, enough gas for our car so that I could get us to school and work and back. I also know I was proud and strong and stubborn. These are qualities that I hope come through in the poems.

> Another example of a literary text that both produces and responds to an exigence is Angie Thomas's important young adult novel *The Hate U Give* (2017). After reading the novel's depiction of racism and police brutality, my daughter asked me in shock, "This is happening *now*?"

Garcia's attention to exigence—and to all the contingencies of her rhetorical situation—exemplifies the way creative writers effectively use communication to address social issues.

The Take-Away

I've learned that sometimes a single approach to poetry isn't enough to help students get at the good stuff. For instance, I've often used the popular TPCASTT method of poetic analysis I learned as a new AP English literature teacher twenty years ago. In this method, students work to understand a poem through the following steps:

1. Consider the meaning of the Title.
2. Paraphrase the poem.
3. Analyze word Connotations.
4. Identify the speaker's Attitude or tone.
5. Note any Shifts.

6. Reconsider the <u>T</u>itle.

7. Articulate the <u>T</u>heme.

But TPCASTT will only get a reader so far. This process typically treats a poem as a self-contained work of art, not a socially situated act of communication. In the case of poems like Garcia's "On Leaving | On Staying Behind," TPCASTT fails to do justice to the significance of the poems' context and purpose, to the lived exigencies of real human beings contending with the push-and-pull forces of migration and the contingencies of loss. It also doesn't offer an apparatus for analyzing the dialogic exchange between the two poems. For that, readers need an understanding of speaker and audience, of ethos and pathos. As in the case of *Fables You Shouldn't Pay Any Attention To* (Heide and Van Clief 1978), which I discuss in Chapter 2, it takes a rhetorical reading of Garcia's poems to bring out their full weight and complexity.

Considering Constraints

Teaching students to recognize the constraints faced by literary characters in particular situations is a good way to prepare them to deal with constraints in their own writing. Constraints can be productive as well as limiting. Like the audience expectations and style conventions that go along with writing in a particular genre, rhetorical constraints both restrict and generate acts of communication. When the ghost of Hamlet's father tries to convince his son to avenge his murder in act 1 of Shakespeare's play, what the ghost can say and do is shaped by a number of important factors: the limited time he has to make his appeal, the prohibitions against revealing details of his punishment, the challenge of inciting Hamlet against Claudius but not Gertrude, and the dodgy reputation of ghosts in general, to name a few.

Think of all the limits on what can be said or done in each of the following examples:

- The constraints faced by Mustafa Mond in speaking to John "Savage" in *Brave New World*
- The constraints faced by Juror 8 in *Twelve Angry Men*
- The constraints faced by Junior in *The Absolutely True Diary of a Part-Time Indian* when he tells his best friend, Rowdy, he's leaving the reservation high school

In each scenario, abundant reality checks make the task of persuasion a tricky business. Time, place, relationships, opportunity, available resources, and both written and unwritten rules of conduct (what ghosts/jurors/best friends can or cannot do) all impose restrictions on these acts of communication and largely determine the outcomes in each case. Constraints powerfully shape our ends, rough-hew them how we will.

Let's look at some extended examples. Mark Haddon's novel *The Curious Incident of the Dog in the Night-Time* (2003) offers a fascinating glimpse of how constraints shape rhetorical acts because the main character, fifteen-year-old math genius Christopher Boone, has been explicitly forbidden by his father from asking the neighbors questions about the mysterious death of a dog. Unwilling to give up his "detective game," Christopher nevertheless finds a way to comply with his father's commands while still obtaining the information he seeks. What's more, Christopher's own unique disposition and needs (Haddon suggests Christopher is on the autism spectrum) make the kind of communication Christopher must engage in to get the desired information particularly challenging for him—another constraint he has to negotiate in the following scene. Notice how Christopher makes the most of his opportunity and resources when he serendipitously meets his neighbor, Mrs. Alexander, outside of a shop:

> I wasn't going to say anything because I didn't want to get into trouble. Then I thought this was a **Super Good Day** and something special hadn't happened yet, so it was possible for talking to Mrs. Alexander was the special thing that is going to happen. And I thought that she might tell me something about Wellington [the dog] or about Mr. Shears [a suspect] without me asking her, so that wouldn't be breaking my promise. . . . And if you are a detective you have to take risks, and this was a super good day, which meant it was a good day for taking risks, so I said, "Do you know Mr. Shears?" (2003, 57; boldface in original)

If you read this novel with your students, you might ask the following kinds of questions about this scene:

- What's Christopher's exigence for speaking to Mrs. Alexander? What does he want?
- What special opportunity does Christopher take advantage of? How does he decide that this is the right moment to achieve his purpose? Why is this important? What does it show about his character?
- What constraints does he face? How does he negotiate them?
- What communication choices does he make? What role does he play?
- What other options does Christopher have in this scene?

Later in the novel, Christopher's father faces a rhetorical situation in which the stakes and constraints nearly overpower him. Faced with having to make a shocking confession to his son that could destroy their relationship (spoiler alert: if you haven't read the novel, you may want to skip this bit), Ed Boone struggles to get his words out:

> "Look, maybe I shouldn't say this, but . . . I want you to know that you can trust me. And . . . OK, maybe I don't tell the truth all the time. God knows,

I try, Christopher, God knows I do, but . . . Life is difficult, you know. It's bloody hard telling the truth all the time. Sometimes it's impossible. And I want you to know that I'm trying, I really am. And perhaps this is not a very good time to say this, and I know you're not going to like it, but . . . you have to know that I'm going to tell you the truth from now on. About everything. Because . . . if you don't tell the truth now, and later on . . . later on it hurts even more. So . . . I killed Wellington, Christopher." (2003, 120)

Christopher's and Ed's behavior in these scenes illustrates a key point made by Bitzer: "The situation controls the rhetorical response" (1999, 220). This knowledge can change how students read and write. Rather than seeing writing assignment requirements or time limits or audience expectations as stifling creativity, students who understand how various constraints shape *all* communicative acts can negotiate these constraints as they work to meet the demands of a particular rhetorical situation.

Extended practice with analyzing and responding to diverse rhetorical situations helps students develop transferable literacy skills. As Michael W. Smith, Deborah Appleman, and Jeffrey D. Wilhelm note in *Uncommon Core: Where the Authors of the Standards Go Wrong About Instruction—and How You Can Get It Right*, "What research on transfer teaches us is that students must have conscious control over what they will transfer and plenty of practice doing so" (2014, 106).

Purposes of Literary Texts

Once my students have bought into the idea that we can read literature rhetorically, I then propose that literature itself is a type of rhetoric. In Aristotle's classic description of rhetorical ends and means, he describes three primary purposes of rhetoric. They are deliberative, forensic, and epideictic (1984; Book I, Chapter iii). The three types of rhetoric relate to different kinds of rhetorical situations.

In *Teaching Arguments* (2015), I share ways to use these three categories to help students develop sophisticated understandings of the purposes of expository texts.

But I want to note here that these categories also work for literary texts. We encounter forensic, or legal, rhetoric in the courthouse scenes in *To Kill a Mockingbird* (Lee 1960), *The Crucible* (Miller 1953), and *Twelve Angry Men* (Rose 1954), for example, and deliberative, or advisory, rhetoric is present whenever characters have to make a decision about a future course of action ("We've got to decide about being rescued," says Jack in *Lord of the Flies* [Golding 1954]).

> **We can help students apply their understanding of rhetorical constraints by asking them to consider the following kinds of questions about writing tasks:**
>
> 1. **What are the limits on my time and resources?**
>
> 2. **Are there any special circumstances I have to pay careful attention to?**
>
> 3. **What do I absolutely have to do in this writing situation?**
>
> 4. **Does anything need to be handled with extra sensitivity?**

Imaginative literature, moreover, is itself a special form of rhetoric. It's epideictic rhetoric, the kind of ceremonial rhetoric that helps communities articulate and affirm or challenge their shared beliefs.

When we practice epideictic rhetoric, we take stock of where we've been and where we're going. Identity-shaping speeches such as a State of the Union Address are epideictic in nature. According to James Crosswhite, epideictic rhetoric "provides a rhetorical way of understanding issues which have broad importance in the study of discourse" (1996, 106). Rhetorician George Kennedy explains that epideictic rhetoric is "any discourse that does not aim at a specific action but is intended to influence the values and beliefs of the audience" (1994, 4).

When we think of what literature does to the hearts and minds of readers, these descriptions of epideictic rhetoric make excellent sense. Literature influences our values and beliefs; it is open ended in purpose and broad in appeal. This is not to say that epideictic rhetoric, or literature as epideictic rhetoric, needs to be didactic. Far from it. See what F. Scott Fitzgerald's unforgettable final lines of *The Great Gatsby* (1925) have to say about our shared sense of identity and values:

> And as I sat there brooding on the old, unknown world, I thought of Gatsby's wonder when he first picked out the green light at the end of Daisy's dock. He had come a long way to this blue lawn, and his dream must have seemed so close that he could hardly fail to grasp it. He did not know that it was already behind him, somewhere back in that vast obscurity beyond the city, where the dark fields of the republic rolled on under the night. Gatsby believed in the green light, the orgastic future that year by year recedes before us. It eluded us then, but that's no matter—to-morrow we will run faster, stretch out our arms farther . . . and one fine morning—
>
> So we beat on, boats against the current, borne back ceaselessly into the past. (182)

"This is who we are; this is what we do," says epideictic rhetoric, expressing our collective desires and disappointments. Crosswhite explains that ". . . epideictic is often necessary in order to reason with audiences whose adherence to particular ideas must be strengthened before an argument will have the intended effect" (1996, 108). We certainly can see this function in works like Henrik Ibsen's *A Doll's House* (1879) or Kate Chopin's *The Awakening* (1899). In its literary form, epideictic discourse often goes ahead to prepare the way for deliberative or forensic arguments.

Whether you choose to teach the term *epideictic rhetoric* or not, it's important for students to know that literature has a purpose. Literature, too, is part of the conversation.

Fostering a Deeper Understanding of Audience

While I'll have more to say about responding to audience need and interest in Chapter 7, "Communicating with Self and Others in Mind," I want to say here that, of course, an understanding of audience is an essential part of the ability to assess rhetorical situations. We can even say that, to a large extent, it's the audience's expectations, attitudes, and values that determine the rhetorical situation. In "Why Study Rhetoric? Or, What Freestyle Rap Teaches Us About Writing," Kyle D. Stedman defines rhetoric as "the art of making a connection with an audience" (2012). And to connect with a particular audience so that audience sees things from our point of view, we need to be mindful of how what counts as effective communication changes from one context to the next.

As an introduction to audience preferences (again, look for depth in Chapter 7), you might try the following activity.

ANALYZING READING AUDIENCES: GOODREADS BOOK REVIEWS

Directions to Students: Use the social network www.goodreads.com to see what fellow readers have to say about one of your favorite books. Choose a book that has at least ten reviews. After reading at least ten reviews, answer the following questions about the kind of audience that book attracts in the Goodreads community. Keep in mind that the ratings and recommendations reflect the collective views of this particular audience but may not represent the tastes and interests of the book's readers worldwide.

- What do the readers seem to care about? What kind of information seems to be valuable to the website's users?

- How do you decide whether a review is helpful? What's the typical length and writing style of the reviews? What kind of review would probably not be considered helpful on Goodreads?

- What else are these readers reading?

It might help to show your students some examples of books with interesting reviews on Goodreads first. The following are all great choices:

- *Persepolis*
- *The Crossover*
- *Brown Girl Dreaming*
- *American Born Chinese*
- *Zack Delacruz*

When we ask students *Who is the text's intended audience?* we want them to have lots of strategies for answering this question. Analyzing reader reviews is a good starting place.

Going Deeper into the Occasion

The idea of "the occasion" is a threshold concept—that is, a transformative, often counterin-tuitive concept that can be difficult to fully grasp.[1] Understanding the occasion for an act of communication requires expanded powers of observation and imagination. Students need to be able to see beyond the four corners of the text, to reconstruct the social worlds and conversations that mark a text like traces of invisible ink.

Think of it this way: It's like venturing out on a boat for the first time and watching the familiar landscape recede across an expanse of water. As you venture farther out, the port you left behind becomes just a small part of the wider shore. This new perspective forever changes your mental map of the terrain.

Crossing a learning threshold is like taking the boat trip; it irrevocably expands our un-derstanding of the known world. You can't unsee the broader view. It's that broader, more complex view of "the occasion" I'm after in teaching my students about *kairos*.

Building Rhetorical Knowledge Using *Kairos*

When it comes to seize-the-day responsiveness, nothing compares to the Greek concept of *kairos* for activating students' rhetorical sensitivity. *Kairos* is the notion of "situational time," a special kind of time distinct from calendar or clock time. It refers both to the opportune moment for persuasion and to the knowledge of what is appropriate, or fitting, for a particular occasion. "To think *kairotically*," write composition scholars John D. Ramage, John C. Bean, and June Johnson, "is to be attuned to the total context of a situation in order to act in the right way at the right moment" (2012, 117; italics in original).

Literary texts are bundles of potential *kairotic* energy; they carry the flame of revelatory opportunity. *Kairotic* moments often cluster around the climax of a short story or novel or within the third act of a five-act play. These are the turning points, the make-or-break de-cisions, and the now-or-never moments we encounter in a literary text. An understanding of *kairos* enriches literary analyses by drawing attention to the immediacy of characters' relationships and choices, as well as to the way rhetorical situations can shift in an instant. Romeo presses his advantage once he senses Juliet's ardent return of his love. Ed Boone, in the earlier example from *The Curious Incident of the Dog in the Night-Time*, fumbles to regroup and retreat after his confession goes disastrously awry. There's a good bit of make-it-up-as-you-go-along strategizing that comes with attending to *kairos*—something that helps students be more adaptive thinkers and communicators.

I think of the sensation of *kairos* as sort of like J. K. Rowling's description of the lucky potion, Felix Felicis, in *Harry Potter and the Half-Blood Prince*: "an exhilarating sense of infinite opportunity" (2005, 477). After consuming the magic potion known as "liquid luck," Harry develops an intuitive sense of the right thing to do in a series of rapidly changing challenges.

----

1.   *For a full discussion of the threshold concept, see Meyer, Land, and Baillie 2010.*

While *kairos* is more about opportunity than luck, *kairotic* awareness can be that quickened pulse and heightened readiness that tell you now is the time to act.

I was once in a meeting with a well-known writer that I'd long wanted to invite to our campus but was feeling self-conscious and hesitant about making this request. Then a voice inside my head said, "She's sitting right next to you—ask her now!" That was *kairos*, tugging at my indecision.

> In rhetorical situations, *kairotic* knowledge helps writers or speakers know what to say when.

A sense of situational time can enrich students' reading of literary texts. The notion that time can be about more than just chronology—that there are different flavors and qualities of time—helps readers to better understand the social and emotional atmosphere of a text. Shakespeare's gloomy Prince of Denmark, for instance, is consumed by a sense of temporal imbalance and impropriety. When Hamlet laments, "The time is out of joint—O cursèd spite, / That ever I was born to set it right!" (act 1, scene 4, line 90) he's complaining about situational time gone wrong, just as he does when he says that "something is rotten in the State of Denmark"—*state* here meaning both the nation and its state of being or condition. The whole political and personal moment feels off.

Much of Hamlet's tortuous indecision arises from his inability to see his *kairos*. In his obsession to find the supreme moment for revenge, Hamlet makes himself almost incapable of action, turning from "Now might I do it pat!" to "Up, sword; and know thou a more horrid hent" (act 3, scene 3, lines 77–100) in the blink of an eye. Hamlet's bad timing and situational confusion persist until he finally resigns himself to the unpredictability of *kairos* by recognizing, "If it be now, 'tis not to come. If it be not to come, it will be now. If it be not now, yet it will come—the readiness is all" (act 5, scene 2, lines 234–237). (In contrast, the super *kairos*-savvy Mark Antony in Shakespeare's *Julius Caesar* knows exactly how the terrain has shifted and what he should do about it).

Students who study *kairos* learn to ask "Where are we at this moment?" and "What doors of opportunity are open?" when assessing new rhetorical situations.

Literary texts are also helpful for drawing attention to another side of *kairos*—the side relating to decorum, propriety, or fitness for the occasion. In Jane Austen's *Pride and Prejudice* ([1813] 1985), Mr. Collins's cringeworthy marriage proposal to Elizabeth Bennet relies for its humor on Collins's idiotic neglect of *kairos*. As Austenites will recall, Mr. Collins is the gormless clergyman cousin to the Bennet sisters who is the heir to their family's entailed estate.

Mr. Collins thinks he's got the *kairos* of a marriage proposal nailed: "Having resolved to [propose to Elizabeth] without loss of time, as his leave of absence extended only to the following Saturday, and having no feelings of diffidence to make it distressing to himself even at the moment, [Mr. Collins] set about it in a very orderly manner, with all the observances which he supposed a regular part of the business" (146). But his reading of the situation is disastrously and hilariously off. He starts with a hyperrational explanation of why clergymen in general should marry: "My reasons for marrying are, first, that I think it a right thing for every clergyman in easy circumstances (like myself) to set the example of matrimony in his parish" (147). Collins then proceeds to go from bad to worse by spending the rest of his proposal to Elizabeth talking about the merits and influence of another woman—his patroness Lady Catherine de Bourgh—and offers Elizabeth his connection to Lady Catherine as a compelling reason for marrying him:

> Allow me, by the way, to observe, my fair cousin, that I do not reckon the notice and kindness of Lady Catherine de Bourgh as among the least of the advantages in my power to offer. You will find her manners beyond any thing I can describe; and your wit and vivacity I think must be acceptable to her, especially when tempered with the silence and respect which her rank will inevitably excite. (147–48)

His clear privileging of his patroness over his intended wife combined with the implied insult to Elizabeth's "wit and vivacity" results in an absurdly arrogant and ignorant performance—a feat Collins caps off with a callous reference to Elizabeth's poverty.

Classroom Activity

I show the video clip of this scene from the BBC's production of *Pride and Prejudice* (1995) before discussing the following questions about *kairos* with my students:

- What do women expect from a marriage proposal?
- What does this particular woman expect or value?
- What are "the regular parts of this business"? What are men supposed to do?
- What kind of behavior would surprise or disappoint a woman?
- Do you think the form of a marriage proposal has changed much over the years?
- Do you think Mr. Collins chose the right moment to propose marriage?
- Do you think Mr. Collins understood the decorum required by a proposal?
- Do you think Mr. Collins chose the right strategies for proposing marriage?

We then evaluate the effectiveness of Collins's argument.

Directions to Students: Analyze the scene from *Pride and Prejudice* with your group, discussing Mr. Collins's purpose, argument, strategies, and persona and identifying the occasion. Then, as a group, decide whether you believe all these elements add up to an effective act of persuasion. Try using the formula that follows to make your decision:

Message/Argument + Means by Which Message Is Expressed + *Kairos* = Persuasion

It's easy to see that the means and the *kairos* don't contribute to persuasion in this case, but there's something else we want students to notice. As a colleague noted, no persuasive strategy would have compelled Elizabeth to marry Mr. Collins because the main problem in terms of persuasion is his ethos. What Collins's neglect of *kairos* does, however, is to make the passage funny. It's not really about Collins reaching Elizabeth but about Austen reaching us.

Not for nothing does Wayne C. Booth call Austen "one of the unquestionable masters of the rhetoric of narration" (1961, 244).

The *Kairos* Analysis graphic organizer can help students dig deeper into the occasion for acts of communication. See Appendix 13 and the student sample in Figure 3.4.

Promoting Transfer of Learning

In *Writing in the Real World: Making the Transition from School to Work*, Anne Beaufort asks a question that I keep mulling over in my head: "How can transfer of learning be fostered to give writers flexibility and versatility in handling a variety of occasions for writing?" (1999, 2). One way to do this is to teach literature rhetorically so that the skills and knowledge students develop in their English language arts classes transfer to their future lives.

Transfer of learning and rhetoric have this in common: both involve making the most of a good opportunity. Students who develop a spirit of transfer have what skilled rhetoricians also possess in abundance—an ability to analyze and evaluate the particularities of each new situation and respond appropriately. Learners searching for transfer opportunities are looking for similarities and differences between the new context and familiar ones while rhetoricians assess the audience and issue, but both approach novelty with the expectation that they're going to have to adapt.

This mind-set is what helps students carry their learning beyond their English language arts classes into other contexts.

Kairos also helps us to situate ourselves as teachers. I recently found myself brought up short during one of those "that was then, this is now" moments during a student conference. I was writing comments on a student's paper when she asked, "Could you print, please? I never learned to read cursive." I must have done a double take because when she saw my startled expression, the student quickly said, "Oh, I know—you're from a different era." I surely am. Today's students and teachers were born in different centuries from one another.

Reading and Writing Across Contexts

My students had just finished reading Gene Luen Yang's graphic novel *American Born Chinese* (2008) and were getting ready to write an interpretive essay on the book. Maya came up to me with a question: "I've been reading about stereotype threat in another class. Can I use that in this essay?"

That's exactly the kind of question I want students to ask when they read and write across contexts. Do I already have something I can use here? Is what I know and can do valued in this new context? Do I need to adapt or recontextualize my knowledge for this different setting? And if I don't know the answers to these questions, is there a way I can find out? This is how we go about assessing a new rhetorical situation. It's also how we transfer our learning. In Maya's case, since she didn't know if it was appropriate to make the kind of text-to-text and class-to-class connections she was interested in making, she asked me. Good for her.

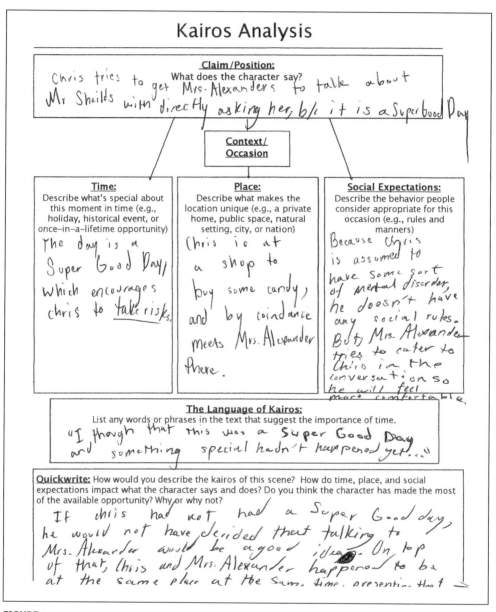

FIGURE 3.4

Student *Kairos* Analysis for *The Curious Incident of the Dog in the Night-Time*

Reading and writing across contexts successfully demands a high level of self-efficacy. We have to believe that we can figure out how to communicate in different settings, even if we're at first unsure about the appropriate discourse and genre conventions to use. We have to trust ourselves as troubleshooters.

In one of the clearest explanations I've found of what it means to teach students how to assess rhetorical situations in disciplinary contexts, the *WPA Outcomes Statement for First-Year Composition* advises faculty in "all programs and departments" to help students learn how to discern the following:

- The expectations of readers in their fields
- The main features of genres in their fields
- The main purposes of composing [or communicating] in their fields. (Council of Writing Program Administrators 2014, 2)

Transitioning from one literacy site to the next requires an ability to adapt and recontextualize our learning. I must here repeat a quotation from the National Research Council I cited in this book's introduction: "A major goal of schooling is to prepare students for flexible adaptation to new problems and settings" (2000, 235).

As students move from class to class and eventually transition from high school to college and from school to work, the abilities to compare and contrast contexts (including the people and places involved) and adjust their problem-solving skills and communication strategies as needed and *appropriate* will be essential to their success.

All this responsiveness can ultimately help students feel more at ease in their academic and professional lives. As my son's baseball coach put it, "If a player pays attention and understands the situation, he'll have fun. If he's struggling and doesn't know what's going on, he won't have fun."

Conclusion

Learning to assess a rhetorical situation requires that students think differentially about literacy tasks and contexts. That is, students have to assume that reading and writing in one setting could be different from reading and writing in another setting. As John T. Gage notes, "No two pieces of writing arise from the same situations or need to satisfy the same conditions" (2005, 6). In a rhetorical approach, one size does not fit all.

Let's imagine now that Tony, the student I described in the opening of this chapter, brought a wealth of rhetorical knowledge and transferable literacy skills with him to his first college writing assignment. Let's say one of those skills was the ability to assess unfamiliar rhetorical situations. Instead of feeling overwhelmed and underprepared when confronted with a new task, Tony would be able to ask himself the following questions:

- What am I being asked to do? What are my options for responding?

- Where can I find help?

- What's my purpose? What need, problem, or question am I being asked to address?

- Who's my audience? What does my audience care about? What does my audience need to know to understand my position?

- What's special or important about this writing situation? What do I need to pay attention to?

- Are there any limits on what I can say or how I can say it?

Starting with this kind of creative problem solving, instead of someone else's rules or formulas, is what real college and career readiness looks like.

CHAPTER FOUR

Analyzing Genres

*As writers respond to rhetorical situations by adapting content, structure, and style to different purposes and audiences, they must also adapt to the conventions of a text's **genre**, a term that refers to a recurring category or type of writing based on identifiable features.*

—JOHN C. BEAN, VIRGINIA A. CHAPPELL, AND ALICE M. GILLAM

Genres provide a powerful exigence for transfer.

—REBECCA S. NOWACEK

For the newcomer to a conversation who's unsure of how to act or where to begin, the ability to analyze genre conventions is an essential skill. Genres are loaded with information about audience, purpose, and context; they offer critical insights into how and why people in particular settings communicate with one another in the ways that they do. By teaching the concept of genre rhetorically—not as the rigid classification of fixed types but as the study of living forms—we prepare students to successfully negotiate the rhetorical demands of a changing world.

More than just a category of writing, a genre is a means to an end. "Genres are ways of doing things" says Charles Bazerman (2013, 24) in *A Rhetoric of Literate Action*. A sonnet, for example, can be a way of expressing love for an object of affection or disdain for rival poets, whereas a lab report is a way of sharing research findings with a scientific community.

And a "bro country" song is apparently a way of getting rich and famous. Here's where I wish all my readers could click on a hyperlink, so I can show you the video I use to introduce my students to genre analysis. If you have the print copy of this book and don't mind taking a quick break from the reading, go to YouTube.com to watch "Sir Mashalot: Mind-Blowing

SIX Country Song Mashup" (2014; www.youtube.com/watch?v=FY8SwIvxj8o). Let me explain why I'm asking you to do this.

In January 2015, NPR ran a story about what happened when songwriter Greg Todd noticed that several top-charting country songs sounded remarkably similar. The songs included Florida Georgia Line's "This Is How We Roll" (2014) and Blake Shelton's "Sure Be Cool If You Did" (2013), both huge hits in the subgenre of bro country. Curious to see how closely such chart-toppers followed the same conventions, Todd experimented with blending six of these songs using sound-editing software. The result was his "Six Song Country Mashup"—the video I use as my hook for my introductory lesson on genre awareness and analysis. Todd described what these bro country songs have in common in an interview with Melissa Block for NPR's *All Things Considered*:

> Well, right off the bat, the melodies and music bits I noticed were all strikingly similar. But it was only when I started really listening to the lyrics that I noticed five out of the six—I think six out of the six songs talked about either moonlight or the sun going down or the sunset. All six had to do with picking up a girl who wasn't yet their girlfriend or the love of their life or something like that. It was just more of a summer thing and almost all of them had a girl who was either in the truck or who was going to be in the truck at some point. (2015)

To create his seamless mash-up, Todd first analyzed the generic conventions of the popular country songs, their stock moves, predictable patterns, and identifying characteristics. The resulting frankentune is a distillation of the features of this category of music, a sort of superformula, the phenotype of the genre. It also exemplifies rhetoricians Anis S. Bawarshi and Mary Jo Reif's explanation of genres as "typified rhetorical ways of interacting within recurring situations" (2010, 3), perhaps *too* typified in this case. More on this later.

Before my students and I watch the video the first time, I tell them their purpose is to identify the major characteristics shared by the six songs. I begin a cluster on Genre Features in "Six Song Country Mashup" on the whiteboard with just two branches to get us started: lyrics and subject matter. Then we watch the video. Now we're ready to start adding to our cluster.

"What did you notice?" I ask.

"They all have the same rhythm."

"Same chords."

"Trucks."

"Same kind of guitar solo."

"They're all singing about girls."

We add these observations to the cluster, building out new categories as appropriate. Then we watch the video a second time, this time adding to the cluster while we watch. I coach students to capture specific words and phrases as examples of the lyrics and subject matter. After we share observations from the second viewing, I ask more focused questions about generic features: "How would you describe the style of language used? What do you notice about the songs' structure?" An expanded cluster created by one of my classes shows my students' responses (see Figure 4.1):

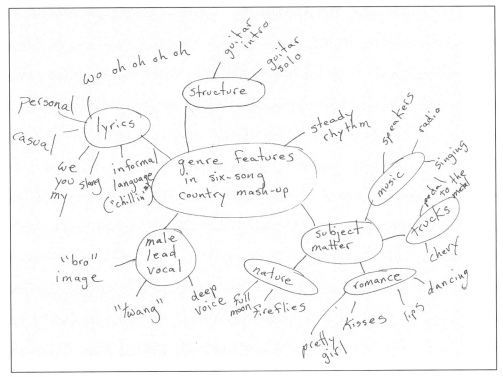

FIGURE 4.1

Genre features shared by "bro country" songs in Sir Mashalot's "Six Song Country Mashup"

Of course, what stands out from our discussion is how similarly each of the six songs responds to the same exigence: the need to produce a top-charting hit.

Learning from the Choices of Other Writers

I use "Six Song Country Mashup" to prepare students to conduct genre analyses of written texts. One of the units I teach—a unit developed by Nelson Graff (2010), my colleague at California State University, Monterey Bay—invites students to compare the features of different literacy narratives written by famous writers in preparation for composing their own communication autobiography. Students read several texts for this assignment, including

Amy Tan's essay "Mother Tongue," Sherman Alexie's "Superman and Me," and an excerpt from *The Narrative of the Life of Frederick Douglass*. By studying the organizational patterns, recurring moves, and stylistic choices common to this genre, students begin to develop *procedural knowledge* of literacy narratives, that is, knowledge of *how* to write this kind of text.

After practicing with "Six Song Country Mashup," my students are prepped to look for common characteristics in texts of the same genre. Although the literary nonfiction I use for this activity is in no way formulaic (in contrast to the country songs we heard), there are still regular features shared across the narratives we read. We were frankly surprised by the similarity of some of the writers' moves, given their different identities, experiences, and historical contexts. These similarities illustrate a point rhetorician Rebecca S. Nowacek makes about genres: that they are responses to reoccurring exigencies, or needs (2011, 128). In the following excerpts from these texts, I've highlighted in bold the special features that caught our attention:

EXCERPT 1: FROM SHERMAN ALEXIE'S "SUPERMAN AND ME"

I can **remember** picking up my father's books **before** I could read. The words themselves were mostly foreign, but I **still remember** the **exact moment** when I first understood, with a **sudden clarity**, the purpose of a paragraph. I didn't have the vocabulary to say "paragraph," but I **realized** that a paragraph was a fence that held words. The words inside a paragraph worked together for a common purpose. They had some specific reason for being inside the same fence. This knowledge **delighted** me. I **began** to think of everything in terms of paragraphs. Our reservation was a small paragraph within the United States. My family's house was a paragraph, distinct from the other paragraphs of the LeBrets to the north, the Fords to our south and the Tribal School to the west. Inside our house, each family member existed as a separate paragraph but still had genetics and common experiences to link us. **Now**, using this logic, **I can see** my changed family as an essay of seven paragraphs: mother, father, older brother, the deceased sister, my younger twin sisters and our adopted little brother. (1998, 54; emphasis added)

EXCERPT 2: FROM AMY TAN'S "MOTHER TONGUE"

Recently, I was made **keenly aware** of the different Englishes I do use. **I was giving a talk** to a large group of people, the same talk I had already given to half a dozen other groups. The nature of the talk was about my writing, my life, and my book, *The Joy Luck Club*. The talk was going along well enough, **until I remembered** one major difference that made the whole talk sound **wrong**. My mother was in the room. And it was perhaps **the first time** she had heard me give a lengthy speech—using the kind of English I have never used with her. I was saying things like, "The intersection of memory upon imagination" and "There is an aspect of my fiction that relates to thus-and-thus"—a speech filled with carefully wrought grammatical phrases, **burdened**, it suddenly seemed to me, with nominalized forms, past perfect tenses, conditional phrases—all the forms of standard English that I had learned in school and through books, the forms of English I did not use at home with my mother. (1990, 7–8; emphasis added)

EXCERPT 3: FROM FREDERICK DOUGLASS'S *NARRATIVE*

Very **soon after** I went to live with Mr. and Mrs. Auld, she very kindly **commenced** to teach me the A, B, C. **After** I had learned this, she assisted me in learning to spell words of three or four letters. **Just at this point** of my progress, Mr. Auld found out what was going on, and **at once** forbade Mrs. Auld to instruct me further, telling her, among other things, that it was unlawful, as well as unsafe, to teach a slave to read. . . . **These words sank deep into my heart**, stirred up sentiments within that lay slumbering, and called into existence **an entirely new train of thought**. It was **a new and special revelation**, explaining dark and mysterious things, with which my youthful understanding had struggled, but struggled in vain. I **now understood** what had been to me a most perplexing difficulty—to wit, the white man's power to enslave the black man. It was a **grand achievement**, and I **prized it highly. From that moment**, I understood the pathway from slavery to freedom. It was **just what I wanted**, and I got it **at a time** when I the least expected it. Whilst I was **saddened** by the thought of losing the aid of my kind mistress, I was **gladdened** by the **invaluable** instruction which, by the **merest accident**, I had gained from my master. (1845; emphasis added)

By annotating and descriptively outlining the full texts of "Mother Tongue," "Superman and Me," and *Narrative of the Life* (see Chapter 2, "Reading Closely and Critically," for activity directions for descriptive outlining), we were able to see that all three narratives shared these common characteristics:

- A strong personal voice
- A recollection of a significant autobiographical incident
- An important realization that accompanied this incident
- A reflection on the lasting impact of this experience
- Time markers that indicate a special moment ("now," "first," "recently," "suddenly," "never," etc.)
- Language expressing the writer's emotions ("loved," "fascinated," "saddened," "delighted," etc.)

We also looked at how these features performed similar rhetorical functions; for instance, the strong personal voice and emotional language deepen the reader's interest in the writer's experience in each case, while the time markers emphasize the exceptional and transformative nature of the autobiographical incident the writer describes. The shared moves accomplish shared communicative purposes.

My students used the comparison chart in Figure 4.2 to track these moves across the texts they read. Then, when it was time for them to write their own literacy narratives, they could apply what they'd learned from the mentor texts. Jordi did this brilliantly, deploying the same strategy he'd seen in two of the readings in his own paper: an opening statement about what the writer was *not*. Here is Tan's original opening: "I am not a scholar of English or literature. I cannot give you much more than personal opinions on the English language and its variations in this country or others" (1990, 7). And here's Jordi's own take on starting with a negative: "I am clearly not a writer. I am not a skimmer. I am not a thinker who likes to brainstorm on paper." When I shared an article later in the course that opened with this same move (this time, it was an excerpt from Julien C. Mirivel's autobiography), I heard Jordi quietly say, "Huh, interesting" when he read the first lines: it was an I-see-what-you-did-there nod to a fellow writer.

"Comparing and Learning from Communication Autobiographies" developed by Dr. Nelson Graff

Author Add the names of those you talk to about that narrative under the author's name.	Problems or Conflicts List problems or conflicts that arose about literacy in the narrative.	Solutions or Resolutions List what the authors did to meet their challenges.	Ideas About Communication List insights the narrative offered you about effective communication.	Reflection List one or two sentences that clearly show reflection in the narrative.	Qualities List characteristics of the narrative that made it effective.
Sherman Alexie					
Amy Tan					
Frederick Douglass					

FIGURE 4.2

Comparing and Learning from Communication Autobiographies

Genre analysis is the study of these kinds of signature moves in mentor texts. Students who can recognize these moves in the works of literary writers such as Alexie and Tan can transfer this ability to their reading of informational texts.

Finding Your Own How-To Guide

Genre, as I noted in Chapter 3, "Assessing the Rhetorical Situation," is one of the things we consider when assessing a new rhetorical situation. So it's also one of the means of support we can offer the struggling writer who says, "I have no idea what to do." Assigned a writing task but unsure of where to start? Begin by learning more about the genre.

This is exactly what award-winning writer and critic Elizabeth Hand did the first time she attempted to write a film novelization—a genre, by the way, that didn't exist when my grandmother was born. Although Hand was already a prolific fiction writer when she took on the task of adapting the 1995 movie *12 Monkeys* into a novel, she had the same question any writer has when facing a new rhetorical situation: *How do I do this?*

In an interview with *On the Media*, Hand talked about how she turned to an expert in the genre for help:

> Elizabeth Hand: And then I said, [to my friend and fellow novelizer, Terry Bison], what do I do, how do I do this? You know, I'm looking at this screenplay and there's just—there's n– there's not a lot there, there's just a little dialogue. And he said, "Well"—he has this great Kentucky drawl—he said, "Well, the first thing you gotta know is that when somebody walks into a room and sits in a chair, if that's what the stage direction says, he doesn't just walk in the room and sit in the chair, he ambles slowly across the Oriental rugs that are covering the polished hardwood floors, and with a sigh he sank deeply into the beautifully-upholstered velvet wing chair." . . . And I said, okay, well, I guess I can do that. (2016)

Being a novice heightens our genre awareness. Bazerman says, "We become more consciously aware of genres when we meet new ones, and we need some orientation to what is going on" (2013, 23). Faced with her own inexperience, Hand did what we hope all our students will learn to do: when in doubt about a genre's conventions, find a mentor. She eventually went on to write several successful novelizations of films, including *X-Files: Fight for the Future* and *Catwoman*.

What other kinds of newbie questions can a genre analysis answer? Here are some examples:

How should I write the introduction (or conclusion)?

Can I use humor? Can I use the first person?

How should I organize my ideas?

What style of sentences should I write?

What kind of language should I use?

When my students conduct a genre analysis of a mentor text, I encourage them to pay particular attention to the writer's language choices, including vocabulary and grammar, and to the way the text is organized. We use the Genre Feature Analysis Matrix to record our observations (see Figure 4.3). You can try leaving some of the

> Genre analysis helps students understand *why* members of particular discourse communities write the way they do.

boxes for genre features blank so that students can add characteristics they'd like to look for. The matrix then becomes a kind of do-it-yourself guide to writing in this genre.

This is the switch I want to flip in students' brains: Instead of asking a teacher what to say or do, I want students to ask mentor texts how they can communicate in a new genre. What can mentor texts tell writers about their choices?

Genre Feature Analysis Matrix
Name of Genre:_____.

Directions to Students: Create a list of 4-6 titles of mentor texts that are examples of the genre you are analyzing. Write the titles of these texts in the far left column. Then, for each mentor text, place a check mark in the box for each genre feature that is a characteristic of that text. Mark all that apply.

Mentor Texts	Rhetorical and Literary Devices									Language Choices								Organization							Special Features							Context and Community					Medium
	figurative language	imagery	rhyme scheme	scholarly evidence	personal anecdotes	fictional characters	symbolism	plot	setting	simple sentences	complex sentences	formal diction	casual diction	academic English	specialized vocabulary	first-person "I"	headings	chapters	stanzas	cause and effect text structure	compare and contrast text structure	narrative text structure	dialogue	charts or tables	visuals	footnotes or endnotes	citations	index	stage directions	discipline-specific	specialized	broad	time-sensitive	age-specific	oral communication	written communication	visual rhetoric

FIGURE 4.3

Genre Feature Analysis Matrix

A modification of the Genre Feature Analysis Matrix is to have *no* preidentified features and, instead, to let students come up with the genre features themselves. This can be an especially good idea if your students will be writing in the genre they're analyzing and they've been asking you lots of questions about what they can or cannot say and do. Tell them to put these questions into the feature boxes in the matrix. It's the mentor texts and discourse community that can best answer their questions.

Genre Awareness and Rhetorical Flexibility

These activities raise students' genre awareness—that attention to textual and contextual cues that enables us to choose the right genre for a particular rhetorical situation. Genre awareness also entails the recognition that there *are* genres and that these genres matter to the discourse communities from which the genres emerge. I'm guessing you've cringed more than a few times in your life as an English teacher to hear a play like *Romeo and Juliet* or a poem like "The Rime of the Ancient Mariner" described as a "novel." Students will even call nonfiction texts, such as *The Last Lecture*, novels. Why do they do this?

I think it's because many students see the words *book* and *novel* as synonymous, an indication that they haven't yet joined the community that uses and values distinctions in literary genres. Genre knowledge is a kind of badge of membership. When we teach students to investigate and negotiate different types of writing, we foster their sense of belonging in academic communities. As Vijay Bhatia explains in *Worlds of Written Discourse: A Genre-Based View*, "It is through genres that professional objectives are achieved, and it is through shared generic knowledge that professional solidarity is maintained" (2014, 25).

Ann Johns, Professor Emerita of Linguistics and Writing Studies at San Diego State University in California, says genre awareness education "prepare[s] students for the academic challenges that lie ahead" (2008, 239). According to Johns, many first-year college students struggle when they are confronted with different types of reading and writing assignments in their classes because they've been trained for specific tasks rather than educated for an unpredictable future; for example, they might try to use the five-paragraph essay structure they learned in high school in situations in which this formula doesn't work.

The ability to adapt to changing conditions is essential for success. Some days we face rhetorical situations akin to those crazy cooking show challenges, and we're scrambling to "make it work!" with the limited ingredients and tools we have on hand. Johns (2008) sees this kind of rhetorical adaptability as one of the benefits of genre knowledge. Figuring out what we have to work with and what's expected of us gives us a far better chance of responding appropriately. She recommends that students consider the following questions as they prepare to write, revise, and edit an academic writing task (see Johns [2008] for a complete list of questions):

1. GENRE NAME: What is this text called (its genre name)? What do you already think you know about what a text from this genre looks and "sounds" like? For example, how should the text be organized? What kind of language do you need to use?

2. PURPOSE: What are you supposed to DO as a writer when completing this task? Are you asked to make an argument? To inform? To describe or list?

3. CONTEXT: If you are writing this task in, or for, a classroom, what do you know about the context? What does the discipline require for a text? Under what conditions will you be writing? For example, are you writing a timed, in-class response?

4. WRITER'S ROLE: Who are you supposed to BE in this prompt? A knowledgeable student? Someone else?

5. AUDIENCE: Is your audience specified? If it is your instructor, what are his or her expectations and interests? What goals for students does the instructor have? (2008, 237—252)

> **Knowledge of form without an understanding of function isn't enough to help students repurpose their learning in new settings.**

Working through these questions can help students avoid the rookie mistake of submitting a book review when a teacher asks for a literary analysis. These are the papers that talk about the "brilliant," "wonderful," and "excellent" strategies a writer uses instead of specifying how these strategies create meaning. Understanding that an evaluative essay (i.e., an essay that judges or critiques the quality of a writer's work) is a different English class genre from an analytical essay (i.e., an essay that describes how distinct parts of a text work together to form a thematic whole) can help students respond appropriately to writing tasks.

Teaching for Transfer

Sometimes our traditional literature curriculum reinforces the idea that genres are locked categories. Does this yearlong course outline look familiar to you?

First Quarter: Short Stories

Second Quarter: Novel

Third Quarter: Drama

Fourth Quarter: Poetry

If students experience genres only as premade labels for dividing up the curriculum, it's not likely that they're going to ask questions about how and why the genres came about or how they can change. The terms *short story, novel, drama,* and *poetry* become just mile markers on the march through the literature anthology, extra words to add to the weekly spelling list. Genre knowledge is treated as something acquired by memorization, not by analysis and application. No wonder, then, that it seems, to many students, that all the choices about genre have already been made.

Teaching genre for transfer, on the other hand, engages the notion of genre as a dynamic and responsive component of rhetorical situations. Like the related concepts of audience, purpose, and occasion, genre is a threshold concept in rhetoric: a transformative idea that can change how students read and write. Threshold concepts "are certain concepts, or certain

FIGURE 4.4
Genre as a conceptual gateway into the rhetorical situation

learning experiences, which resemble passing through a portal, from which a new perspective opens up" (Meyer, Land, and Baillie 2010, ix). Without the kind of transformative learning that comes with a threshold crossing, students cannot progress to the next level of understanding (Meyer, Land, and Baillie 2010, ix). Threshold concepts go hand-in-hand with deeper learner, and deeper learning is a precondition for transfer (see Figure 4.4).

Here's why: If we only see the surface appearance of something, but we don't know why it's that way or how it works, we don't have the under-the-hood knowledge needed to adapt in changing circumstances. Then when change happens—for instance, to the form of a business letter or the conventions of a research paper—we get frustrated and think, *Why do they keep changing the rules?* as if some omnipotent, anonymous force makes these decisions for us.

The revelatory insight that forever changed my own understanding of genre is this: It's not just that genres have distinct forms but that these forms perform specific functions that are important to the discourse communities from which they emerge. For me, the shift from seeing genres as the predetermined framework for organizing literary studies to seeing genres as flexible and evolving responses to recurring rhetorical situations—that I, too, could help shape—was a radical reorientation in my thinking. A threshold crossing of this kind "results in a reformulation of the learners' frame of meaning" (Meyer, Land, and Baillie 2010, ix). In other words, mind = blown.

Bhatia, a professor in the Department of English and Communication at the City University of Hong Kong, notes, for instance, how the introductory sections in academic texts follow the same purposeful pattern, a pattern that matters to fellow academics:

1. A Preface *explaining* the general purpose and scope of the book

2. A Foreword written by someone else *promoting* the importance of the book

3. An Acknowledgement *expressing gratitude* to everyone who helped with the book

4. An Introduction *explaining* what the rest of the book is about (2014, 78–79; emphasis added)

Awareness of the purposes behind the patterns is what helps us to communicate successfully in new rhetorical situations. In the previous example, the genre choices show that members of academic communities care about paying their intellectual debts and establishing the importance of their own contributions to a field. Students need this kind of insider knowledge to make effective choices about genre. As Nowacek cautions, "Without experiencing the exigencies that give form and meaning to genres, students will not develop writing knowledge that can effectively transfer to other contexts" (2011, 128).

Teaching *how* to analyze genres is thus not quite the same as teaching genres. We can train students to replicate the features and strategies of recognizable forms of writing, such as an op-ed piece or a personal statement, but this doesn't necessarily prepare them to communicate in genres that haven't been invented yet. Loads of today's genres didn't exist when I was a kid: the pithy tweet, the graphic novel, the mash-up, to name a few. Rather than forearm students with everything they need to know about a particular genre, teaching for transfer means we help students develop the investigative skills necessary to communicate effectively in any form or medium.

By teaching for transfer, we're pursuing a moving target. In *Thinking Through Genre: Units of Study in Reading and Writing Workshops* 4–12, Heather Lattimer (2003) notes that it would be impossible to instruct students in all the potential text forms they might encounter in their lives. "However, by teaching students to engage in an inquiry-based approach to genre, Latimer writes, "I hope to prepare them to navigate their own way through unfamiliar text forms in the future" (5). Mastery of genre inquiry skills is characterized by an internalized, reflective practice. It's a disposition for discovery.

That disposition for discovery is what helps students negotiate the literacy tasks they'll encounter in what Bhatia describes as "the real world of discourse" a world that is "complex, dynamic, versatile, and unpredictable, and often appears confusing and chaotic" (2014, xv). Bhatia sees a problem in the "wide gap between genre analysis of texts in published literature, emphasizing the integrity and purity of individual genres, and the variety of complex and dynamic instances of hybridized genres that one tends to find in the real world" (2014, xv).

The unpredictability of real-world discourse[1] and the hybridity of real-world genres are good reasons for not dismissing literary genres as only pertinent to future English majors. Instead of denigrating the teaching of poetic forms such as haiku as irrelevant in the real world, we can teach haiku with an eye for the transferable literacy skills students are developing. The question for students and teachers to keep in mind during any lesson is, *What's the transfer opportunity here?* The disciplined restraint fostered by *writing* a haiku

----

1. *Bhatia defines* discourse *as "language use in institutional, professional or more general social contexts" (2014, 3).*

and the appreciation for economy of language fostered by *reading* a haiku are valuable literacy skills that have cross-context applications. Indeed, clarity and concision are traits haikus share with business memos. When mined for transfer potential, the study of literary genres is no less suitable to students' preparation for the workplace than the study of informational texts.

Genre Awareness and Reading Comprehension

As many literacy researchers have noted, genre study can also help with reading comprehension because when students know what to expect of a certain kind of text, they can predict the moves the text is likely to make. Closely reading a set of model texts in a genre develops students' knowledge of the strategies and processes that characterize the genre and can help students write their own texts of this kind. Rebecca Nowacek observes that prior genre knowledge activates "a range of knowledge domains, ways of knowing, identity, and goals appropriate to the new situation" (2011, 82)—knowledge that can be accessed and reassessed whenever a student encounters the genre.

> Generic expectations activate a schema and prompt a particular kind of response.

Understanding generic conventions aids in reading comprehension because it helps readers anticipate writers' moves. If we know, for instance, that the third or fourth paragraph in an op-ed piece in the *New York Times*, the *Wall Street Journal*, or the *Washington Post* often begins with the word *but*, we read the opening paragraphs on our guard for a rhetorical shift.

THE GENRE ANALYSIS GRAPHIC ORGANIZER

The Genre Analysis Graphic Organizer is another tool that can help students learn how genres work (see Figure 4.5). The student sample in Figure 4.6 identifies common features of digital articles. Try having small groups of students collaboratively analyze a mentor text using this graphic organizer as preparation for writing in a genre themselves.

Playing with Genre Conventions

A fun way to increase students' genre awareness is to have them create a mock version of a well-known type of writing. This is what Alexander Pope did in 1712 when he published "The Rape of the Lock," his mock epic poem imitating the conventions of the heroic narrative. And it's what Rowan Jacobsen (2016) did when he published a mock obituary for the Great Barrier Reef. Rowan's astute redeployment of the stock features of this genre intensify the emotional impact of the environmental catastrophe he describes. His opening lines combine the somber tone of an obituary with the irony of the mock genre: "The Great Barrier Reef of Australia passed away in 2016 after a long illness. It was 25 million years old" (2016). Working within the conventions of this genre, Rowan chronicles the birth and early years of the Great Barrier Reef ("seemingly happy ones") and notes that "the reef was an extremely active member of its community" (2016).

Genre Analysis

Genre Name: _____

Mentor Texts:
List the titles of several texts that exemplify the key characteristics of this genre.

Purpose:

Organization:
How are texts in this genre generally structured (e.g., chronological order, compare and contrast, etc.)? Are there paragraphs, stanzas, dialogue, chapters, lists, headings, etc.? Do texts usually have a certain kind of beginning or end?

Language Choices:
Describe the kinds of words and sentences commonly used in this genre. Is the language typically formal or casual, simple or complex?

Writer's Ethos:
How do writers generally present themselves in this genre? What kind of "voice" do they typically use? Do you get to know the writer personally?

Special Features:
List any other conventions or stylistic choices that characterize this genre, including features like documentation style (e.g., MLA), figurative language, pictures, and rhetorical moves.

Context and Audience: In what situations is this type of writing typically used? Who typically reads this genre?

FIGURE 4.5

Genre Analysis Graphic Organizer (see Appendix 15 for a blank graphic organizer)

Genre Analysis: *Digital Article*

Mentor Texts:
List the titles of several texts that exemplify the key characteristics of this genre.

"Finding Floating Forests" by Laura Rocchi

Purpose:

To educate the importance of kelp Forest.

Organization:
How are texts in this genre generally structured (e.g., chronological order, compare and contrast, etc.)? Are there paragraphs, stanzas, dialogue, chapters, lists, headings, etc.? Do texts usually have a certain kind of beginning or end?

Paragraphs with a few pictures in between

Language Choices:
Describe the kinds of words and sentences commonly used in this genre. Is the language typically formal or casual, simple or complex?

Formal complex writing. as an article attempting to be as formal, mature as possible

Writer's Ethos:
How do writers generally present themselves in this genre? What kind of "voice" do they typically use? Do you get to know the writer personally?

Article authors usually present themselves as educated, formal writers. Having evidence to back up their claims.

Special Features:
List any other conventions or stylistic choices that characterize this genre, including features like documentation style (e.g., MLA), figurative language, pictures, and rhetorical moves.

Title not much bigger than the actual writing
The author and designer's names are on the side written in a lighter color, along with the date
pictures and maps in between writing to keep the readers attention
References in the back

Context and Audience: In what situations is this type of writing typically used? Who typically reads this genre? environmentalist, that go to NASA's website, educated adults.

FIGURE 4.6

Student example of Genre Analysis Graphic Organizer

Or how about this mock rubric published in *McSweeney's*? You'll figure out the context when you read it (see Figure 4.7).

NOVEMBER 11, 2016
POST-ELECTION COLLEGE PAPER GRADING RUBRIC
DAVEENA TAUBER

	WINNER / YUGE / TREMENDOUS	MEH	LOSER
Argumentation	High-level repetition of simplified point or slogan. Advanced use of the red herring. Arguments are untainted by facts or evidence. Blames professor, classmates, and everyone else. Insists that if the paper does not receive an "A" the rubric was rigged and the professor, department chair, and president of the university will be sued.	Inadequate repetition of slogans. Negligently slips in some evidence to justify arguments. Blames professor, failing to blame large structure. Mentions lawsuit only in footnotes.	Feels compelled to justify argument with evidence and cited material. Utterly neglects repetition of slogans. Fails to mention lawsuit altogether.
Syntax and punctuation	Shows high-level mastery of the sentence fragment. The best sentences are short and great. They are the best. Excellent use of ellipses to elide concluding sentence clauses. Exclusively uses exclamation points. Uses underline, bold, italics, and highlighting simultaneously to great effect.	Sentences may run into multiple clauses, leaving the reader struggling to keep up. Use of multiple types of punctuation is likewise disorienting and potentially subversive.	Flagrantly tries to show off sentences with interior clauses. Uses elitist punctuation like the semicolon. Sentence length and complexity show blatant disregard for the reader's attention span.
Organization, coherence, and use of course texts	Advanced bloviation. Admirable lack of organizational structure gives paper an inspiringly off-the-cuff air. Successfully addresses the subject without reference to the course texts. Displays absolute rhetorical flexibility and is unshackled by internal consistency. Appropriately addresses audience through pandering. Manages to avoid the highly structured, thought-out sequencing that makes the losing paper so ponderous and hard to read.	Negligently references the course text rather than producing original material, betraying lack of imagination. Inadequate attempt to move past the stultifying laws of introduction, body, conclusion. Totally lacks rhetorical insouciance. Ignores audience need to feel catered to. Hampered by attempts at internal coherence.	Slavish reliance on cited material. Dangerous attempts at persuasion on the basis of textual evidence. Cannot muster even a single shred of filler or blather. Fails audience pandering altogether. Organization into intro, body, and conclusion betrays utter lack of vision. Knee-jerk dependence on internal consistency makes the paper unreadable.

FIGURE 4.7
2016 Post-election writing rubric
SOURCE: TAUBER (2016).

The generic function of a rubric as a statement of shared values and expectations illuminates the satire at work in this example.

Some possible mock genres for your students to try:

- Mock adventure story (First date? First day of school? Drivers' training?)
- Mock horror story (Substitute teacher? Final exam? Babysitter?)
- Mock obituary (Trends and fads? Technology? Fashion?)
- Mock diary (Household object? Pet? Classroom?)
- Mock Facebook or Twitter page (Historical event? Abstract concept? Academic subject?)

Before your students write their mock version of a genre, you might want to help them find several mentor texts they can use as guides.

Note: A twist on this activity is "genre conversion"—translating a text from one genre to another, the way a weekly *Enterprise-Tocsin* newspaper based in Indianola, Mississippi, has done by turning police reports into haiku (Dwyer 2017):

> *Three shotguns stolen*
> *Owner not smiling one bit*
> *But ducks can relax*

The tweet-friendly poems are part of an effort "to reach the new era of digital-savvy, poetry-loving millennials," the newspaper explained in a tweet, illustrating the link between genre and audience (Dwyer 2017).

> **We need to tell students *why* we study genre features and how this will help them in their future lives.**

See the student directions for my Logic Haiku in Chapter 6 for another way to play with these genre conventions.

Genre play of this kind makes the point that readers bring expectations about genre conventions with them to their reading experiences. As Peter J. Rabinowitz observes in *Before Reading*, "No matter how much a writer wishes to play with conventions, however, he or she can do so only if the readers share those conventions to begin with" (1987, 57–58). Genre and audience are interdependent components of rhetorical situations.

Learning from Other Writers: Style Analysis and Imitation

Listening to a text and paying careful attention to the moves other writers make, including how they organize and present their ideas, is reconnaissance work for our own essays. Frankly, we're looking for moves we can steal. Not content—no, that would be plagiarism. But style and structure are fair game when writers are in apprentice mode (which is always) and searching for ways to improve their craft. I tell students it's OK to try out that tricky lead-in to a counterargument that so-and-so finesses in an article we read. I sure "borrowed" plenty of language from my peers and mentors when I was a struggling graduate student trying to learn how to communicate in my field, especially at conferences. I noticed that most scholars phrased their questions the same way: "Thank you for that really fascinating discussion of X. I was interested in your claim that _____ and am wondering if you could say more about _____." Even the critical responses seemed to follow this same acknowledgment/paraphrase/question structure, only the question would be a dig at the speaker's stunning neglect of a key issue: "Have you considered _____?" or "How do you reconcile/contend with/account for _____?" or "Are you familiar with _____?"

Style imitation is a great way to find moves we can use in our own writing. It also helps with reading comprehension. Here are my directions for guiding students through a style analysis and imitation of a passage. See the sample that follows from *The Left Hand of Darkness* ([1969] 1976), Ursula Le Guin's brilliant science-fiction novel about ambisexual extraterrestrials. Students can also do this with passages of accessible literary criticism, such as an excerpt from Toni Morrison's *Playing in the Dark* (1992) or Elaine Showalter's *Sister's Choice* (1991).

Directions to Students: Your task is to analyze the style of a passage from your selected text in preparation for writing a style imitation. Your imitation will keep the same kind of sentences, word choices, tone, and literary or rhetorical strategies as the original passage but will change the topic. A close study of the writer's syntax and diction will help you be successful.

Part 1

Step 1: Count the number of words in each sentence of the passage and write these numbers in a column in the margin. Put an "S" for "short" by numbers under 10. Put an "M" for "medium" by numbers between 10 and 18. Put an "L" for "long" by numbers over 18. Notice the pattern of short, medium, and long sentences.

Step 2: Underline the start of each sentence in this passage. Notice the way the writer varies the syntax.

Step 3: Circle signal words or phrases like "but," "next," "however," "then," "although," "yet," "thus," and "as a result." Notice when and how the writer transitions between ideas.

Step 4: Find the subject and verb in each sentence and write an "S" over the subject and a "V" over the verb. Notice where the subjects and verbs are located in each sentence.

Step 5: Annotate any figures of speech (e.g., simile, metaphor, personification) or rhetorical devices (e.g., parallelism, loaded language, analogy) you find.

Step 6: Circle all the punctuation marks.

Step 7: Notice the formality level of the writer's word choices. Is the diction academic, casual, professional, or mixed?

Part 2: Now it's your turn! Write a passage imitating the style of the text you analyzed but changing the subject matter. Your style imitation can be about anything you want (e.g., getting ready for school, taking a test, washing a dog), but you need to closely follow the grammar, organization, devices, mechanics, and vocabulary level of the original passage. If the original starts with a four-word sentence, you should start with a four-word sentence. Include important signature moves from the original, too.

> We had stopped in the gateway of the walled garden. Outside, the Palace grounds and roofs loomed in a dark snowy jumble lit here and there at various heights by the faint gold slits of windows. Standing under the narrow arch I glanced up, wondering if that keystone too was mortared with bone and blood. Estraven took leave of me and turned away; he was never fulsome in his greetings and farewells. I went off through the silent courts and alleys of the Palace, my boots crunching on the thin moonlit snow, and homeward through the deep streets of the city. I was cold, unconfident, obsessed by perfidy, and solitude, and fear. (Le Guin ([1969] 1976, 21)

Here's how one of my students responded to this task:

> **My dog walked in the store of the big plaza. Indoors, the store was cold because of the air conditioning and bright from the fluorescent lights dangling from the high ceiling of the pet store. Together on the cold, vinyl flooring, my dog and my brother headed towards the back to the pet groomer. Haircuts and nail filings are this groomer's expertise; she is loving in her kind manner. I trust her with my dog and so does my brother, my heart never racing in fear, and I always tip for her gentle and nurturing care. I was happy, confident, excited by anticipation, and calm, and grateful.**

In addition to helping students understand important features of texts and improve their own writing, style imitations can also increase students' enjoyment of reading. One of my students didn't like *The Left Hand of Darkness* at all until she got down into the weeds with Le Guin's language choices. While this student loved poetry, she told me she couldn't stand science fiction, and she doggedly resisted reading the novel until we conducted a style analysis of the preceding passage in class. "All right," she grudgingly told me after class, "there's something I can learn here."

> When we know a genre, Bazerman says, "We not only know the genre, we know what we can say through the genre, and how the genre can be made to work" (2013, 32).

Classroom Activity: Character Style Sheets

Students can heighten their awareness of the impact of different writer's choices by creating a style sheet for a fictional character, noting how the character's language use reveals important aspects of his or her identity.

Directions to Students: **Create a style sheet for a character in a work of literature. Make a list of characteristic dialogue, including quotations, phrases, and sentences that best represent the character's style of speaking, along with any other verbal traits you notice. Then respond to the following quick-write:**

Quick-Write Prompt: How do these rhetorical choices impact the characters' relationships with other characters? How does the way the character speaks reflect his or her social status? What does the character care about?

Moves Like Chaucer: Analyzing Stylistic Choices

We teach awareness of writers' moves as part of genre analysis so that students have a deeper understanding of the choices they have as meaning-makers when they communicate in different forms and contexts, especially when these forms and contexts are new to them.

I've found that giving students lists of rhetorical devices doesn't help students describe *how* writers create meaning. What does help is analyzing writers' moves in language they can understand. As Wilhelm, Smith, and Fredricksen (2012) note in *Get It Done!*, metacognition and student ownership are essential for transfer of learning. "[If] a student is not yet capable of articulating what has been learned, and is not yet able to transfer what has been learned in flexible ways to future tasks, then we would have a hard time supporting the notion that anything substantive has been taught or learned" (2012, 43).

The three moves I explore in this next section are common features of literary writing. I'm calling these moves the Monty Python, the Reversal, and the Twofer, but you may know them by other names. The ability to recognize, evaluate, and deploy these moves enhances students' practice as readers and writers. The ability to recall their classical names probably does not. Try having your students invent their own name for each writerly maneuver (à la figure skating jumps or skateboarding tricks) to give them a greater sense of ownership and understanding.

> **Genre analysis is the study of writers' moves in mentor texts.**

I want to note that these are moves readers aren't likely to encounter in many nonliterary genres, including technical writing (at least right now). Understanding that moves are associated with specific forms and functions is an important part of genre awareness. Remember: Genre analysis starts with genre awareness. That's why so many of my analytical reading activities open with the *What did you notice?* question. If we don't *see* the special features of texts, we can't analyze their function and effect. The purpose of showing lots of examples is to make the moves visible.

Let's take a closer look at each of these special stylistic devices.

UNDERSTATEMENT

In my head, I think of this move as the Monty Python—that figurative understatement that calls attention to something by downplaying it. This is a dry, acidic device that pairs well with snarky humor. Remember that scene in *Monty Python and the Holy Grail* when the Black Knight's arm has been lopped off, and he says, "'Tis but a scratch"? Or in *The Meaning of Life* when the army officer wakes up with a leg missing and says of his bleeding stump that it "stings a bit"?

Understatement is another one of those devices that invites readers to go below the surface of the text. Like irony, understatement creates the experience of shared identification between writer and reader; the writer assumes the reader can handle the inside joke, that the two can understand each other without having to spell things out. One of the effects of this move is that it gives the audience a special job to do: filling in what's implied but unsaid.

Understatement is the flip side of hyperbole. Although our students tend to be familiar with figurative exaggerations of the I'm-so-hungry-I-could-eat-a-horse variety, they're less attuned to the ways nonliteral understatements impact tone and ethos.

Here's Chaucer's narrator in *The Canterbury Tales*, for instance, using understatement to describe the character of the Clerk:

> There was also a Clerk of Oxford,
> who had long since devoted himself to the course of logic.
> His horse was as lean as a rake,
> and he himself **was not exactly fat**, I assure you (Chaucer [1387–1400] 1985,
> 15; emphasis added)

And here's the grim humor of the *Beowulf* poet, dryly noting the effect of Grendel's reign of terror on Hrothgar's warriors:

> *Then it was easy to find a **few men***
> *Who [sought] rest elsewhere, at some **slight distance*** (1977, lines 138–139;
> emphasis added)

When we encounter understatement like this, we respond with a mental guffaw and "I should think so! A few men? At a slight distance? How about a whole bunch of men at as far a distance away as possible?" The reader is invited to provide the scale and intensity that the understatement omits. This kind of understatement is a figure of speech precisely because it amplifies, rather than minimizes, the experiences or feelings it understates. That shoulder-shrugging, no-big-deal attitude often conveys exactly the opposite meaning of what is said. This is true in *Beowulf* when the poet speaks of "small pleasure" in deadly "sword-feast" (line 562) when he means instead that there was great pain or when he says that a famous meeting between leaders "is scarcely a secret" (lines 2000–2001).

Beowulf himself describes his father's death in language that both downplays and underscores the impact of loss and change: "He outlasted many a long winter/ and **went on his way**" (1977, line 19; emphasis added). The understatement is a check on sentimentality, even as it acknowledges the deepest mysteries of human experience.

Students who learn to appreciate figurative understatement in literary texts can transfer their knowledge to informational reading. In a 2014 article on Alaskan civilians trained as secret "stay-behind agents" during the Cold War, for example, the dark humor of understatement emphasizes the mortal danger faced by the civilians and the callous attitude of those who endangered them:

> To compensate for expected casualties, a reserve pool of agents was to be held
> outside of Alaska and inserted by air later as short-term replacements. This
> assignment was seen as an easier sell to potential recruits because "some agents
> **might not be too enthusiastic** about being left behind in enemy-occupied
> areas for an indefinite period of time," one planning document noted dryly.
> (Burns 2014; emphasis added)

The understatement here offers a doorway into analyzing the narrative strategies used in report writing.

Understatement can also function as a means of expressing thoughts that lie too deep for words. In the following example from an article on NASA's unmanned Orion spacecraft, the first of its kind for the postshuttle age, a spare and compact understatement contains a dense emotional center:

> Michael Hawes, a former NASA official who now leads the Orion program
> for prime contractor Lockheed Martin Corp., choked up as he recalled the
> preshuttle days.
>
> "We started with all the Apollo guys still there. So we've
> kind of now finally done something for the first time for
> our generation," he said, pausing for composure. "**It's a good
> thing**." (Dunn 2014; emphasis added)

Students often miss moves like understatement and reversal in their initial reading of a text. Many need help recognizing special features of a text before they can explain their effects and functions.

When you encounter figurative understatement with your students, encourage them to consider these questions: *What's the rhetorical effect? Who uses it? What does it show about the person or the moment?*

Another name for this move is *litotes*.

REVERSAL

With reversal, too, it's not the label that's important; it's the move. One of the first places adolescent learners are likely to encounter the device of grammatical reversal is in song lyrics. I share several examples with my students and then ask them to come up with their own definition of reversal based on what they notice about the structure and effect of this strategy:

> The hand you hold is the hand that holds you down. —*Everclear*

> With my mind on my money and my money on my mind. —*Snoop Dogg*

> Make the money, don't let the money make you. —*Macklemore*

Some of my students have described this move as "The Flip Flop," "The Mirror Image," or "Opposites." One student generated this terrific definition: "When you use a set of words, then rearrange them to give them a different meaning to show differences in two related ideas."

To help students dig into the effects of this move, I share additional examples of reversal I've encountered in my own reading, such as the following line from Robert E. Probst's *Response and Analysis: Teaching Literature in Secondary School*: "We have to bring those texts to bear upon our lives, and our lives to bear upon the texts" (2004, vii). We talk about the work this move accomplishes, how Probst's reversal underscores the reciprocal relationship between texts and contexts in acts of meaning-making.

In an explanatory note to *Rhetoric and Rome*, historian Garry Wills notes the many different names this move has been given: "What the Greeks called antimetabole ('reverse interchange') or khiasmos ('khi-ing'), some Romans called commutatio ('interchange'), regressio ('step back,' going from a-b to b-a), or chiasmus" (2011, 163). Whatever it's called, the reversal can be a shift in thought, a turning back, a balancing of contraries. This grammatical turn is particularly poignant when the language shift reflects a reversal in meaning, as with a September 4, 2016, *San Francisco Chronicle* headline: "The War on Terror Is Now Terror's War on the World." The total and striking inversion of realities often signals irrevocable change in relationships or circumstances.

Another name for the reversal is *chiasmus*.

THE TWOFER

With a twofer, you get two different meanings linked to one pivotal word. Notice how each of the following sentences does what only a twofer can do so nicely, how one word stands in a different relationship to two other words, creating a clever twist in meaning:

- From Gerald Graff's "Hidden Intellectualism": "The hoods would turn on you if they sensed you were putting on airs over them: 'Who you lookin' at, smart ass?' as a leather jacketed youth once said to me as he **relieved me of my pocket change along with my self-respect**" (2014, 246; emphasis added).

- From a newspaper article on Amazon pioneer Joy Covey: "She was the only member of her Harvard cohort to arrive with bragging rights **over bagging both groceries and high school**" (Newman and Owens 2013; emphasis added).

- From a TV commercial for a credit card company featuring a barbecue pit master: "**He smoked 40 pounds of ribs and the competition.**" (2014, emphasis added) Bank of America.

What it means to be "relieved" of your pocket change (i.e., robbed) is different from what it means to be relieved of your self-respect (i.e., humiliated). The same word *relieved* applies to "pocket change" and "self-respect" in different senses. That's a twofer. In this case, the turn between the two senses upgrades Graff's loss from a material to a personal injury.

This same raising of the stakes occurs in Chaucer's "The Wife of Bath's Prologue" when she tells her co-pilgrims how she gained mastery over her last husband:

> *He gave the bridle completely into my hand*
> *to have* **control** *of* **house** *and* **land**,
> *and also of his* **tongue** *and* **hand**; ([1387–1400] 1985, 219; emphasis added)

Chaucer's double-decker twofer—the turn from "house and land" to "tongue and hand"— reveals the Wife of Bath's multitiered ascendancy over her husband; she achieves not just material control but also psychosocial control. The takeaway value of teaching the twofer is that it helps students stop and notice important moments like this.

Another name for this device is *zeugma*. I used to make fun of the term *zeugma* when I taught AP English Literature. I really did. It was my favorite example of an abstruse literary term that would never show up as the correct answer on a multiple-choice item but that might occasionally appear as a distractor. I thought this because I hadn't yet internalized this move myself and wasn't aware of all the zeugmas I was encountering in my everyday life. Once my zeugma radar was turned on, however, it was impossible not to see this powerful strategy in all kinds of literary and nonliterary texts. Collecting real-world examples of this figure of speech helped me to make the move more visible to my students.

> Our enthusiasm for genre analysis should be contagious. I geek out over stylistic devices like litotes, chiasmus, or zeugma because they do interesting work. Engaging students in an analysis of this work helps them develop their own passion for inquiry.

Forget the Names but Remember the Moves

Litotes, chiasmus, and *zeugma*: the obscure Greek names are reason enough for most students to forget these devices before they've even learned to recognize them, and, frankly, I don't care if students never use this terminology. But I do want them to be alert to these moves and what they do. An excited "Oh! There's that thing again!" during a reading is good enough for me.

The names of things can sometimes get in the way of our understanding, especially when it comes to the arcane Greek terminology associated with classical rhetoric. Students see "zeugma" or "chiasmus" and think, *Yeah, that's not for me*. And teachers may see these terms and think, *Yeah, those aren't for my non-AP kids*. But the moves of poets, journalists, and rappers certainly are for all of our students; we just need to help students understand what these moves do.

To help students better understand the effect of these moves, try flipping back to the writer's perspective. Most writers probably don't think *I'm going to use a zeugma now* as they're composing a text. Instead, they've been working toward some kind of interesting relationship between two things when they find the moment is right for making the kind of striking grammatical turn and connection a zeugma performs. Same with litotes (or understatement). Effective writers don't ornament their texts with litotes like decorations on a Christmas tree. Rather, they've been developing a certain kind of relationship with their reader and attitude toward their subject, and litotes is the result.

As with the teaching of specific literary forms, the teaching of stylistic devices such as zeugma, litotes, chiasmus, parallelism, or any other technique most benefits students when they are mined for transfer opportunities. The ability to analyze stylistic choices is an important part of genre awareness—a highly portable intellectual capacity. Students need to know that stylistics aren't just for poets. As Anne Beaufort says in *Writing in the Real World: Making the Transition from School to Work*, "For writing to be effective, composers have to learn to adapt, quickly and effectively, the *style*, length, and content of their texts, and they must do so in less than optimal working conditions" (1999, 2; emphasis added).

Recognizing what is—and is not—a common move in the forms of communication used by particular discourse communities is an essential competency for postsecondary success. If you use litotes in technical writing, for example, where everything is supposed to be taken literally, you will confuse your reader. Zeugmas are often half-literal and half-figurative, making them likewise an unlikely choice for technical writers. Even something like the grammatical reversal effected by a chiasmus is typically considered too fancy or flowery for most genres in business communication. So finding something like a zeugma, a chiasmus, or a litotes in a text tells us we're in the world of creative and persuasive genres. This is important information our students need to be able to access on their own.

Noticing Language

Genre analysts pay close attention to language. The CSU Expository Reading and Writing Course (ERWC), a rhetoric-based curriculum I've been involved with for many years in California, invites students to practice this aspect of genre analysis by asking them to notice "how particular language features are used in written texts so they will be better able to both comprehend them and subsequently incorporate these features into their own writing"

(2013). As the ERWC makes clear, students can develop their linguistic awareness in the following ways:

- Mark words, phrases, or sentences that may still be confusing, writing down brief notes explaining what about them is confusing.

- Identify grammatical patterns, such as verb tenses, time markers (last week, since, tomorrow), modal verbs (can, could, must, might, should), or singular and plural noun forms.

- Analyze the logical relationships between the parts of sentences. (California State University 2013)

The Common Core State Standards similarly call for students to take note of language features, such as transition words, coordination and subordination, and parallel structures. One Grade 9 and 10 Standard for "Knowledge of Language," for instance, requires students to "apply knowledge of language to understand how language functions in different contexts, to make effective choices for meaning or style, and to comprehend more fully when reading or listening" (CCSS. ELA-Literacy.L.9-10.3). Another requires students to "write and edit work so that it conforms to the guidelines in a style manual . . . appropriate for the discipline and writing type" (CCSS. ELA-LITERACY.L.9-10.3). Competence in both standards depends on genre awareness.

Obasan, Joy Kogawa's deeply moving 1981 novel about the persecution and internment of Japanese Canadians during World War II, provides abundant opportunities for analyzing language choices. In one scene, the narrator—Naomi Nakane—discovers a letter from the Canadian government indicating that her mother, a Canadian citizen who was in Japan when the atom bombs were dropped, survived the war and sought readmission to Canada.

The generic conventions of the letter, especially its verbs and transitions, reveal a great deal about the forces that displaced and divided Naomi's family. Note how features like text organization, verb tense, word choice, and tone construct the Canadian government's ethos and purpose, as well as its attitude toward Mrs. Nakane. In the following excerpt, I've highlighted language features of the letter I think are particularly important.

> *Dear Miss Kato,*
>
> **This refers to your letter of April 18** *concerning your application for readmission to Canada of your sister, Mrs. Tadashi Nakane, Canadian-born, also for the admission of her four-year-old adopted daughter and niece.*
>
> *The status of Mrs. Nakane* **has been carefully reviewed** *and* **it has been decided that** *she has retained her Canadian citizenship and* **therefore** *would be readmissable to Canada.* **However,** *the child is a national of Japan and* **as such** *is inadmissible under* **existing** *immigration regulations.* **It is regretted** *that the Department is* **unable** *to extend any facilities for admission of the child at the present time.* **It is assumed** *that Mrs. Nakane would not desire to come forward alone, leaving the child in Japan, and* **therefore** *it can* **only be suggested** *that the matter of her return be left in abeyance*

until such time in the future as there *may be a change* in the regulations respecting admission of Japanese nationals which **would enable** the Department to deal with the application of the child. (1981, 255; emphasis added)

We read the letter within the context of the novel and then create a mini-descriptive outline of its signature moves, keeping in mind these questions: *What is the letter saying? What is it doing? What is it a way of doing?*

Students share their initial response by completing the following statement:

The letter from the Canadian government is a way of _____.

Students further analyze the letter in small groups, using my questions to guide their discussion:

- What do you notice about the letter's greeting? How does the letter open? How does it close?
- What is significant about the words and phrases highlighted in bold?
- What is the rhetorical effect of the use of passive voice in this letter (e.g., "has been carefully reviewed," "it has been decided," "it is regretted," "it can only be suggested")?
- What does the word "carefully" in the first sentence of the second paragraph suggest?
- What is assumed about Mrs. Nakane? Why is this important?
- Why does the letter repeat the logical transition "therefore"? What's the effect of this?
- How is being "unable" to do something different from being "unwilling" to do something?
- What is significant about the words "only" and "suggested"?
- Why does the letter conclude with conditional language about possible future changes in regulations ("may be a change . . . which would enable")?
- How would you describe the ethos of the letter writer? What's the letter's purpose?
- How does this genre, an official government letter, enact social identities and relationships in ways that might be different from a personal letter or a face-to-face conversation? What does an official government letter do?

If your students have extensive experience with rhetorical analysis, you might want to skip the highlighting and let them find their own interesting textual bits to talk about.

You might also decide that this example merits a mini-lesson on the rhetorical functions of a particular language choice, like passive voice. To answer some of my questions, students will need to know what passive voice is and does, how the phrase "it has been decided" deflects responsibility from real human individuals onto a faceless government entity. Students who understand the rhetorical effects of different verb choices understand that the passive voice—in which a form of "be" is used with another verb with an -ed or -en ending, as in "has been decided"—can be used intentionally by writers who want to avoid assigning responsibility for an action. A little direct instruction in the form and function of the passive voice could go a long way here.

> Analyzing an excerpt from a genre doesn't take the place of reading and enjoying whole works of literature. The rhetorical moves of the excerpt make the most sense when considered in relation to the full text.

Noticing Structure: The Sonnet Mash-Up

When I want students to play with the organizational patterns that characterize a particular genre, I have them make a genre flip-book—my version of the mash-up. You know those children's picture books where you can combine the head of a robot with the torso of a clown and the legs of a ballerina? It's the same idea, only, in this case, students are manipulating distinct chunks of literary texts in order to better understand their rhetorical functions. This activity works best with genres such as Shakespearean sonnets that have consistent and purposeful structures. My students create their sonnet mash-ups from three thematically related sonnets by William Shakespeare: "Sonnet 17," "Sonnet 18," and "Sonnet 19."

Directions to Students: Work in groups to create a flip-book for William Shakespeare's "Sonnet 17," "Sonnet 18," and "Sonnet 19" by stapling copies of these sonnets together in book form. Each sonnet needs to be on its own page and carefully aligned to the other pages so that the quatrains and ending couplets of each sonnet are all in the same place. Then, cut the pages between each quatrain and the final couplet (but not all the way through the paper!) to fold back the flaps to create different combinations of the sonnet sections.

Experiment with different mash-ups of the three sonnets. For instance, use the first quatrain from "Sonnet 19" with the second quatrain from "Sonnet 17" and the third quatrain from "Sonnet 18" before ending with the couplet from "Sonnet 19." Read your sonnet mash-ups aloud with your group.

After the groups have had time to play with the different structural features of these sonnets, I ask the students to say "Thank you" and "Goodbye" to their group members and return to their seats for a reflective quick-write.

These are the questions they respond to:

Quick-Write Prompt: Do any of your mash-ups work as a cohesive poem? Why or why not? What features do all four sonnets have in common? What do you notice about the common rhetorical function or purpose of each of the following sections in the sonnets?

First quatrain

Second quatrain

Third quatrain

Heroic couplet

Here's what one student wrote:

> Our group mash-up worked well. I enjoyed the end product. I thought it was interesting because when we looked at each sonnet as a whole, it was hard to see how they would mesh, but when we broke them up quatrain by quatrain and started looking at them as individual pieces it was easier to see that they flowed. Having the end in mind made it is easy to find quatrains that worked in our mash-up, as well. I think dissecting the sonnets in this way showed me that the genre features play a key role in what the genre is, that if you can mash up these features you can create something new.

Another student wrote:

> When we did our sonnet mash-up, some of it did work, but not as fully as the original. In order for it to work and fit quatrains from different sonnets together, we had to bend the meanings and highlight different points of emphasis. We were able to make a functional sonnet, but not as complete as Shakespeare's original. This demonstrates the consistent formula used in making sonnets, how they all have the same outline, just different content.

This activity targets the same instructional goal as descriptive outlining; it's another way for students to distinguish functional chunks of text. In both cases, the focus is on how the organizational structure creates meaning. (See Figure 4.8.)

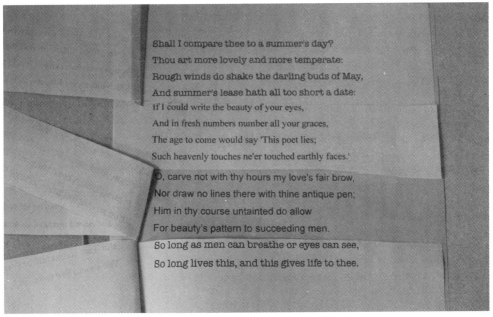

FIGURE 4.8
Sonnet mash-up flip-book

Reading and Writing Across Contexts

In *Future Wise*, David Perkins recommends that teachers target "learning that promises payoffs in diverse circumstances" (2014, 229). Genre awareness is an aspect of rhetorical knowledge that is particularly useful for negotiating the different disciplinary discourses students encounter in their academic lives. Understanding, for instance, that "the very forms of texts that students read, along with their central purposes, differ across domains" (Jetton and Dole 2004, 16) is part of students' cross-context competence. This is learning that pays off in diverse circumstances.

By teaching genre awareness and analysis rhetorically, we help students understand that "'good writing' looks different in different contexts" as Kathleen Blake Yancey, Liane Robertson, and Kara Taczak say in *Writing Across Contexts* (2014, 6). They caution against a one-size-fits-all approach to writing instruction:

> If writers learn to write one thing or in one way, and they practice just that one thing or way over and over, they might think all writing is like the writing they do, and they might not recognize that good writing looks different and happens differently across different contexts. (6)

A helpful activity for promoting genre awareness of academic assignments, including an understanding of what constitutes "good writing" in this particular discourse community, is a prompt or syllabus analysis.

> Ultimately, the ability to analyze a genre in depth depends on reading volume and fluency. Students need abundant exposure to a particular form of writing and its function and variants within a discourse community (e.g., a position announcement in a job search website) in order to internalize and appropriately adapt and apply the how-to guide for this genre.

Classroom Activity: Syllabus Analysis as Genre Analysis

Directions to Students: As you work on your assignments for this class, consider what our course syllabus tells you about the academic community and conversations you are joining. Take a few minutes to study the syllabus before answering the following questions:

- What does my audience (in this case, my instructor and peers) seem to value?

- How can the other course readings serve as mentor texts? What do they suggest about the style of writing appropriate to an academic setting? What do they suggest about the conventions of academic writing? What do they suggest about the interests and expectations of my instructor?

- What does my instructor's syllabus or course description suggest about the diction, syntax, and tone of academic writing? What kind of voice or image does my instructor create for herself or himself in the syllabus? What kind of voice and image do I want to create for myself if I'm writing to this person?

Avoiding Generic Writing

A final point worth repeating: Genre awareness works best when paired with creativity. There are many rhetorical situations in which an effective response depends on a writer's ability to stand out from the crowd.

Take the letter of recommendation. Like many teachers, I spend a good chunk of my working life writing well-deserved letters of support for my students. While I might study the signature moves of this genre to see what's appropriate for particular occasions and purposes, particularly if I'm stuck in a rut or writing to an unfamiliar institution, the last thing I want is for one of my letters to be generic. Run-of-the-mill form letters aren't going to help make my students' educational or professional dreams come true. To be effective, I have to write original, heartfelt letters that will set my students apart.

Ultimately, facility with genres is about negotiating the fine line between creativity and convention. We need to be careful that the study of forms doesn't turn into training in formulas. Instead, we can teach for transfer by helping students leverage their knowledge of familiar genres to learn how new genres work.

Conclusion

The first step toward helping students communicate effectively in diverse genres is raising genre awareness through guided study of model texts. As students become more attuned to the ways forms of expression change across contexts, they become more active and independent genre analysts, intuitively searching texts for clues to the writerly choices most valued by particular discourse communities at a given moment. They come to understand that a genre is a way of doing things, that forms of writing emerge from distinct rhetorical functions, and that as those functions change, the forms will, too.

CHAPTER FIVE

Negotiating Voices and Meaning

*The novel can be defined as a diversity of social speech types
(sometimes even diversity of languages) and a diversity
of individual voices, artistically organized.*

—M. M. BAKHTIN

*Elaborate inferences are always required when
reading what we call literature.*

—WAYNE C. BOOTH

his chapter explores ways to help students productively engage academic conversations about literature: to navigate among different textual voices as readers and to direct conversational traffic as writers. While I offer practical support for teaching students how to quote, paraphrase, summarize, and synthesize the words of other writers, this chapter is about more than just the conventions of reading-based writing; it's about helping students genuinely care about what other human beings have to say.

The Value of Literature

Literary reading helps us care about the experiences and perspectives of people different from ourselves. Literature also speaks to our own experiences, deepening our understanding of our individual identities. This is what literacy scholar Katie Egan Cunningham means when she describes literary texts' capacity to function as both "mirrors and windows" (2015,

6)—tools for enhanced self-knowledge and greater empathy for others. We lose ourselves and find ourselves in literature, explains Leila Christenbury (2000).

Mary Shelley offers a powerful depiction of how this works in her prescient novel *Frankenstein* ([1818] 1983). When Victor Frankenstein's parahuman creation discovers a collection of books in the woods, including John Milton's *Paradise Lost*, Plutarch's *Lives*, and Johann Wolfgang von Goethe's *The Sorrows of Werther*, he gains access to a wide range of human experiences beyond his limited personal circumstances. He describes how the books deepened his understanding of himself, noting how he "applied much personally to my own feelings" ([1818] 1983, 123), while expanding his knowledge of his world:

> I learned from Werther's imaginations despondency and gloom, but Plutarch
> taught me high thoughts; he elevated me above the wretched sphere of my
> own reflections, to admire and love the heroes of past ages. Many things
> I read surpassed my understanding and experience. . . . The cottage of my
> protectors had been the only school in which I had studied human nature, but
> this book developed new and mightier scenes of action. ([1818] 1983, 123)

His new reading life also gives the creature insights into the humans close at hand: the cottagers who have unwittingly been living side by side with Victor's science experiment. Of these the creature says that Goethe's novel "accorded well with my experience among my protectors [the cottagers] and with the wants which were forever alive in my own bosom" ([1818] 1983, 123).

But it is Milton's epic poem *Paradise Lost* that most powerfully draws the being whose creator refuses to give him a name other than the oft-repeated epithet of "wretch." The creature experiences a profound sense of shared identification with Milton's Lucifer, a fallen angel left to beweep his outcast state alone. Yet not entirely alone either, as Victor's rejected creation is quick to note: "Satan had his companions, fellow devils, to admire and encourage him, but I am solitary and abhorred" ([1818] 1983, 125). Literature reveals us to ourselves and calls us to bear witness to the joy and pain of others.

Research supports this claim. Liz Bury's 2013 article, for instance, describes a study that found that reading literary fiction measurably improves empathy, the capacity to feel what others feel. An excerpt from the article suggests the work we do as literature teachers has far-reaching social benefits:

> Have you ever felt that reading a good book makes you better able to connect
> with your fellow human beings? If so, the results of a new scientific study
> back you up, but only if your reading material is literary fiction—pulp fiction
> or non-fiction will not do.
>
> Psychologists David Comer Kidd and Emanuele Castano, at the New
> School for Social Research in New York, have proved that reading literary

fiction enhances the ability to detect and understand other people's emotions, a crucial skill in navigating complex social relationships. (Bury 2013)

How do literary texts build empathy in readers? Philip Davies, a professor of psychological sciences at Liverpool University, explains, using an example from Charles Dickens's novel *Great Expectations*:

> In *Great Expectations*, Pip is embarrassed by Joe, because he's crude and Pip is on the way up. Reading it, you ask yourself, what is it like to be Pip and what's it like to be Joe? Would I behave better than Pip in his situation? It's the spaces which emerge between the two characters where empathy occurs. (Bury 2013)

Empathy is a transferable competency with important real-world applications, including the ability to navigate complex social roles and relationships. Transfer of learning happens, psychologist David Comer Kidd says, because "the same psychological processes are used to navigate fiction and real relationships." He adds, "Fiction is not just a simulator of a social experience, it is a social experience" (Bury 2013). Louise Rosenblatt's landmark *Literature as Exploration* praises this benefit of literary reading in memorable language, calling "the capacity to sympathize or to identify with the experiences of others" a "most precious human attribute" ([1938] 1995, 37).

This benefit, however, isn't conferred automatically. Literature *can* enhance our ability to detect and understand other people's emotions provided we frame our instruction or reading experiences with this intention. We have to make listening with the purpose of understanding our first priority.

Listening to the Conversation

During a workshop I gave in Salinas, California, I heard one teacher describe the teacherly eavesdropping she does to monitor student comprehension as "ear hustling." This struck me as a perfect description of what we want students to do when they're sizing up a rhetorical situation, literary or otherwise. We want them to ear hustle, that is, listen to the conversation in a way that prepares them to make an informed contribution. This listening for significant chatter is not unlike the reconnaissance work a detective performs to identify meaningful patterns or trends. We "hear" the audience's implied voice through counterarguments, concessions, and commonplaces;[1] the demands of the subject matter through attention to accuracy and appropriateness; and the constraints and opportunities of the situation. What

----

1. *Commonplaces are aphorisms or clichés that represent the shared, or common, knowledge of a community. "You can't buy happiness" is a commonplace that is familiar to most high school students. When writers use these common phrases of advice, they're drawing on this shared knowledge with their readers, which is why a commonplace marks a text with the audience's "voice."*

we're especially listening for, rhetoricians would say, is a sense of exigence—that critical need or problem that makes the topic of discussion timely and important.

When we analyze literary texts, we engage in conversations that are not merely ongoing, but that indeed may last "so long as men can breathe, or eyes can see," as Shakespeare says of his own writing in "Sonnet 18." These enduring conversations occur within and across literary and critical texts and sociohistorical contexts, and involve numerous voices: writers, narrators and speakers, characters, scholars, critics, teachers, students, and other readers. That's a lot of ear hustling to do.

Listening to Literary Texts

Trying to detect and understand writers' themes is an important part of listening to literary texts. Themes are the "they say" of literature: the writers' comments or observations about life or human nature. When I teach the concept of *theme* to my students, I explain that literary themes tend to be more descriptive than prescriptive; that is, they describe some aspect of human experience rather than prescribe or dictate how we should live. (I'm pretty safe saying this since we read works by writers like Robert Louis Stevenson, Virginia Woolf, Toni Morrison, Kazuo Ishiguro, Louise Erdrich, and Rudolfo Anaya; I might have to modify my explanation if I started teaching *Aesop's Fables*.) I also tell students there isn't just one right interpretation of what a literary text means. Literary texts offer multiple and sometimes conflicting messages. Developing a nuanced understanding of theme helps students engage diverse perspectives with an open mind.

> New learning happens when we listen nondefensively. If we listen defensively (or not at all), we remain unchanged by the academic conversation.

UNDERSTANDING THEME: CHORAL READING

Using a kind of call-and-response structure, in which a second student finishes a sentence started by the first, we explore the concept of theme together as a class. Students can partner up and read the statements depicted in Figure 5.1 in pairs or the entire class can be divided into two groups, with readers alternating between the two sides. You could even have your whole class form two lines facing each other, à la English country dancing, and have each "couple" read their sentence aloud together when they move to the head of the lines.

READER 1	READER 2
A theme is …	an underlying meaning of a literary work.
A theme is the author's comment …	about an aspect of human experience.
A theme offers insight …	into the writer's perspective on life.
A theme is **not** necessarily …	a lesson the writer is trying to teach.
A theme has value …	outside the literary text.
Themes gives the text …	its purpose.
A writer usually has …	a point to make.
Novelists make their points …	through the story and its characters.
Poets make their points …	through their language choices.
The theme is the reason …	for the plot.
A theme is **not** …	the same as a plot summary.
A theme does **not** have to …	have a moral.
A theme is a response …	to a question at issue.
A theme can be expressed …	by a complete thought.
A theme is more …	than just the topic.
A text can have …	multiple themes.
A theme is usually **not** …	just a cliché.
A text can even have …	themes that contradict one another.
There isn't just one "right" interpretation …	of what a literary text means.
Remember, a theme is …	a writer's message or argument.

FIGURE 5.1

Promoting tolerance of ambiguity through an understanding of theme

Students can then practice writing thematic statements for specific works of literature using broad, qualified language:

Life can be …

Human nature is …

People are often …

A broad and nuanced understanding of theme builds students' capacity for tolerating ambiguity and postponing judgment. It also helps students know it's OK if they don't see a theme in a text that "everybody else" in the class sees. There are many approaches to meaning.

Literary reading is an important, but not necessarily an automatic, pathway to greater empathy and tolerance. Those habits of mind require active cultivation.

Figuring Out Who's Saying What

Negotiating the different voices in a conversation starts with figuring out who is saying what. Has the English teacher in you ever bristled to see a mug, T-shirt, or magnet with the following quotation and attribution?

"To thine own self be true." —**William Shakespeare**

Hey, you think, *Shakespeare didn't say that, Polonius did, and Polonius is an annoying know-it-all. I don't want a Polonius magnet on my refrigerator.* But for many of our students, the difference between what the writer says and what the literary character says isn't so clear. Discerning what a writer says *through* his or her characters and over the characters' heads takes a highly developed capacity for inference making. Students have to not only read between the lines but also listen to multiple voices simultaneously and discern who has the greatest say in shaping a text's meaning.

This ability takes practice and coaching. When students are newer to literary analysis, they often confuse the narrator's perspective with the writer's perspective, as one of my students did when writing about Jonathan Swift's satirical novel *Gulliver's Travels* ([1726] 2004). Her paper opened with this sentence: "Throughout this story the author gives some of his own personal account about himself and his family." Swift's narrator, Lemuel Gulliver, does this, but Swift himself does not. Like the student who calls any book, including works of nonfiction, a "novel," the student who confuses a writer with a fictional character hasn't yet developed insider knowledge about how literary writing works.

As students become more skilled readers of literary texts, they're better able to discern the unique qualities of different textual voices. Heather, another one of my students, picked up on some of Gulliver's quirks as a narrator. She noticed that Gulliver "appears to be very interactive with the reader" and explains "his reasoning for writing and apologizes for taking so long to describe something."

Students who can bring a novelist like Swift and a narrator like Gulliver into dialogue with each other demonstrate additional sophistication in negotiating voices. Annalise insightfully argued that "Gulliver is used as Swift's pawn so he can make satirical points about the human experience during his lifetime," thereby linking Swift's purpose and message to his literary technique. Edgar took this one step further; his analysis noted the convergence and divergence of writer's and narrator's voices at various points in *Gulliver's Travels*, arguing that "Gulliver's and Swift's views begin to align and Swift's voice becomes more and more pronounced as the story continues."

This ability to negotiate voices is essential to reading comprehension, especially when what a character or narrator says is the opposite of what a writer implies, as is so often the case with works of literature. Mark Twain's *The Adventures of Huckleberry Finn* ([1884] 1995) famously requires this kind of inferential or reverse reading. When Huck says of the dinner ritual at the Widow Douglas's that "when you got to the table you couldn't go right to eating, but you had to wait for the widow to tuck down her head and grumble a little over the victuals, though there warn't really anything the matter with them" (12), we understand what Huck doesn't: that the widow is praying, not complaining or apologizing. And we hear *Twain* saying Huck is utterly (and perhaps blessedly) unschooled in the social graces so familiar to the "sivilized" characters in the novel. We apply this same layered reading strategy to Huck's comment that the widow "called me a poor lost lamb, and she called me a lot of other names, too, but she never meant no harm by it" (11), hearing both what Huck says and what Twain implies.

In the case of Huck's villainous father, Pap, we have to flat-out take the opposite of what he says if we want to get at Twain's meaning. Irony pervades all references to Pap, the "fond parent" who tries to murder his son and who says he would boycott an election if he "warn't too drunk to get there" ([1884] 1995, 35). When Pap rants against the outrages of the "govment," including granting voting rights to free African Americans, Twain's readers are prepared to distance themselves as far as possible from Pap's views. Twain makes it mighty uncomfortable for readers to identify with the racist reprobate who cruelly kidnaps and beats the novel's amiable protagonist. As the instrument of Twain's satire, Pap is the mouthpiece for social views Twain suggests are as morally reprehensible as they are absurd. When Pap says it's outrageous that a free African American college professor can't be enslaved in Missouri until he's been in the state six months, Twain says it's outrageous that such a man could be enslaved. And lest we have any doubt about how we should receive Pap's words, Twain cuts him off in the midst of his tirade, by launching him "head over heels over the tub of salt pork" (36). Pap's ignominious death caps his narrative punishment, making redemption—and sympathetic identification—impossible.

How do we help students learn how to do this kind of multivalent reading? By helping them to listen to the multiplicity of voices in a text, including what characters say about themselves, what other characters say about them, how we're positioned to read the character (favorably or unfavorably), and what the plot outcome implies about the narrative judgment. Writer/Character T-Graphs and Conversation Sketches are two strategies I use to help students discern different layers of voices in literary texts.

Classroom Activities: Writer/Character T-Graph and Conversation Sketch

The Writer/Character T-Graph invites students to distinguish between what a literary character is saying and what a writer is saying through the character's words. While we can grab a character's words right off the page, I explain that we have to make an inference about the writer's meaning. Learning to paraphrase what is unsaid but implied is an essential aspect of literary analysis.

I start by sharing one of my own examples, for *Huck Finn* (see Figure 5.2).

CHARACTER SAYS	WRITER MEANS
Huck: "When you got to the table you couldn't go right to eating, but you had to wait for the widow to tuck down her head and grumble a little over the victuals, though there warn't really anything the matter with them."	Twain: Huck doesn't realize the widow is saying grace because he's never lived in a home where this was a custom before.

FIGURE 5.2
Writer/Character T-Graph

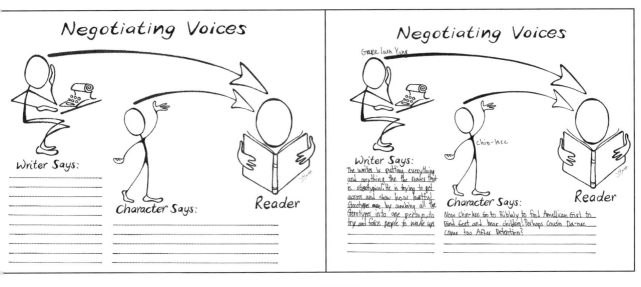

FIGURE 5.3
Distinguishing between what a writer says and what a character says

FIGURE 5.4
Student sample for Gene Luen Yang's graphic novel *American Born Chinese*

To help students visualize how these different voices must be negotiated by a text's reader, I also ask students to compare writer and character messages through a diagram (see Figures 5.3 and 5.4).

Both of these activities treat literary texts as acts of communication.

Ethos Analysis for Narrators

A Narrator Ethos Analysis is another strategy for helping students to develop a more nuanced understanding of the textual voices in a novel or short story. Narrators come in all varieties: first person, third person, omniscient, limited, named, unnamed. Some we like, some we detest. Some tell us how to judge the situations they describe, others stand back and let us do our own thinking (or at least, their approach is so subtle, we're not aware of their influence). Asking students to unpack the qualities that make a narrator tick is a way of examining how a narrative works.

See the student sample for this activity in Figure 5.5.

Directions to Students: **Complete the Ethos Analysis for Narrators based on your close and critical study of the text. Use your annotations and notes from class discussions to inform your analysis. Remember: the word *ethos* refers to the narrator's image, persona, and credibility.**

The quick-write at the bottom of the graphic organizer asks students' to deepen their thinking about the distinctions between narrators' and writers' voices. Writers step in and out of their own books. Jonathan Swift is in his book and out of it. Charles Dickens does the same. There are moments when they call attention to their authorial presence and moments when they slip behind their narrator's persona. A student who can argue *when* and *why* these shifts happen has developed an advanced ability to negotiate textual voices.

The Rhetoric of Irony

In his landmark work *The Rhetoric of Irony*, Wayne C. Booth states that "every good reader must be, among other things, sensitive in detecting and reconstructing ironic meanings" (1974, 1). Negotiating different voices and meanings in literary texts often depends on this ability. If students can't detect the irony in Mark Twain's *The Adventures of Huckleberry Finn*, for instance, they won't be able to make defensible inferences about the novel's meaning. The struggle to sort out who is saying what becomes exponentially more challenging when what a writer *seems* to be saying is not supported by the other clues in the text and context.

As a teacher who works with students who often struggle to access complex texts, what especially concerns me is how irony affects our students' understanding of what different textual voices have to say. In literary texts, irony often takes the form of characters or narrators saying one thing and meaning another. This means that students have to read and interpret the text at least twice: once for the surface meaning and once for the implied meaning. I find that most students have to work hard just to access the literal meaning of a text like Jonathan Swift's *A Modest Proposal*. To then reconstruct a second meaning according to Swift's ironic intentions can be a tall order, especially for English language learners. Irony forces readers to do double the work. No wonder, then, that less experienced readers tend to get stuck in the starting blocks.

But if students don't get to the second meaning, their understanding of the text's message will be off; that is, it won't be a responsive and responsible interpretation that takes into full account the text's communication strategies and context. Context can be an especially important clue to recognizing and understanding irony. The rhetorical situation, including what the audience is already expected to know, is key to reversing the literal meaning of texts such as *A Modest Proposal*.

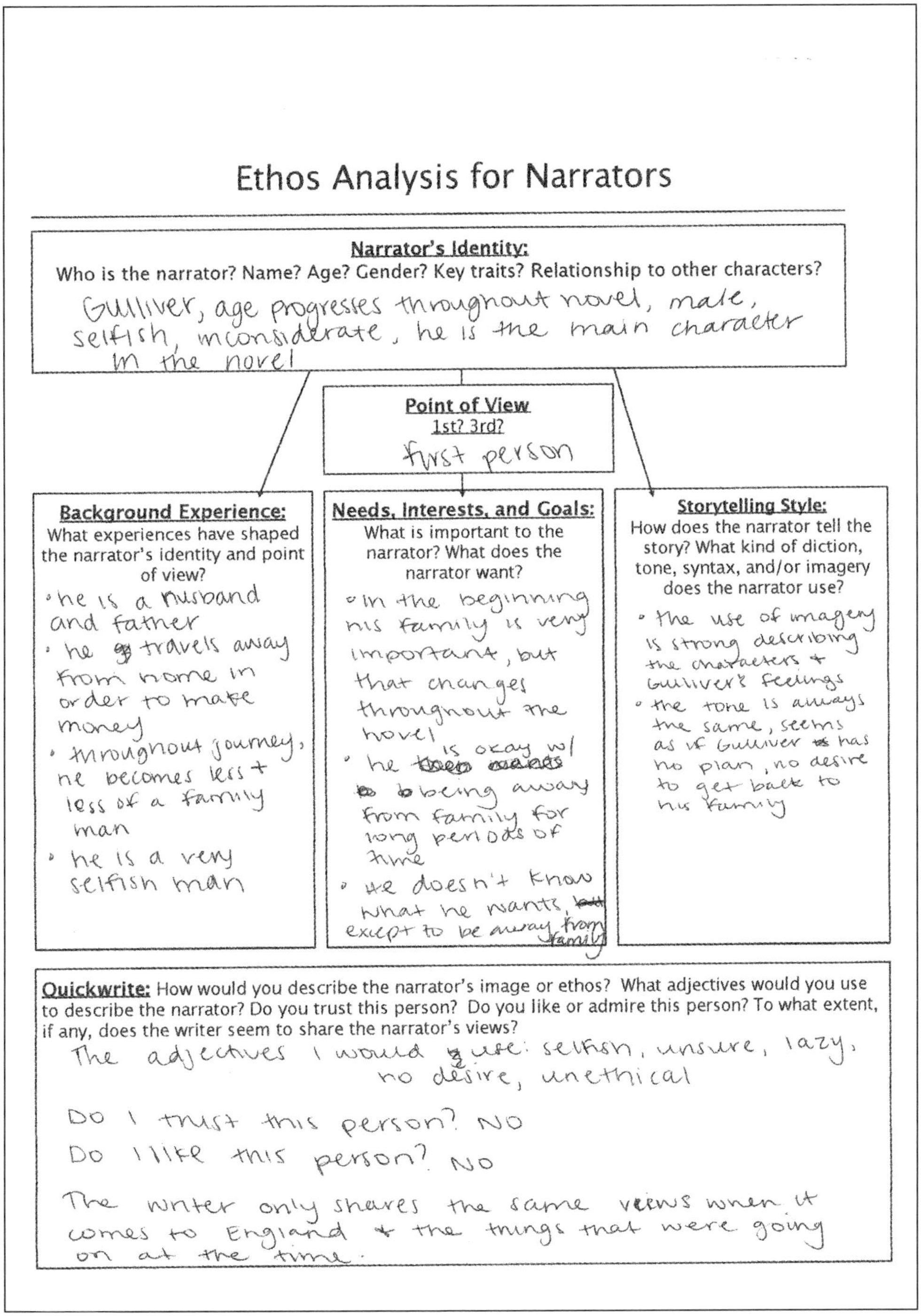

Ethos Analysis for Narrators

Narrator's Identity:
Who is the narrator? Name? Age? Gender? Key traits? Relationship to other characters?

Gulliver, age progresses throughout novel, male, selfish, inconsiderate, he is the main character in the novel

Point of View
1st? 3rd?
first person

Background Experience:
What experiences have shaped the narrator's identity and point of view?
• he is a husband and father
• he travels away from home in order to make money
• throughout journey, he becomes less + less of a family man
• he is a very selfish man

Needs, Interests, and Goals:
What is important to the narrator? What does the narrator want?
• In the beginning his family is very important, but that changes throughout the novel
• he is okay w/ being away from family for long periods of time
• he doesn't know what he wants, except to be away from family

Storytelling Style:
How does the narrator tell the story? What kind of diction, tone, syntax, and/or imagery does the narrator use?
• the use of imagery is strong describing the characters + Gulliver's feelings
• the tone is always the same, seems as if Gulliver has no plan, no desire to get back to his family

Quickwrite: How would you describe the narrator's image or ethos? What adjectives would you use to describe the narrator? Do you trust this person? Do you like or admire this person? To what extent, if any, does the writer seem to share the narrator's views?

The adjectives I would use: selfish, unsure, lazy, no desire, unethical

Do I trust this person? No

Do I like this person? No

The writer only shares the same views when it comes to England + the things that were going on at the time.

FIGURE 5.5

Student sample of a Narrator Ethos Analysis for *Gulliver's Travels*

Booth further suggests the interesting notion that we can violate a writer's intended meaning by reading a text ironically if we're not meant to do so (1974). Reading a "straight" passage like Brutus's funeral oration in Shakespeare's play *Julius Caesar* as meaning something radically different from what Brutus says would be an example of this kind of violation. Of course, this very idea gets at a notion that makes some literary critics (and perhaps the framers of the Common Core) uncomfortable: that writers intend particular meanings.[2]

Speaking from a rhetorical perspective, I'll say this: meaning-making is a collaborative enterprise. And irony requires a whole lot of collaboration. To study irony rhetorically, Booth says, is to examine "how authors and readers achieve it together" (1974, xiv). Irony doesn't just invite audience participation; it demands it. The construction of a hidden meaning that is not apparent on the surface of a literary text is a creative act that happens in the reader's mind. As Booth notes, irony is a game that must be played by two.

He offers readers a helpful four-step process for reconstructing meaning from ironic texts:

1. Reject the literal meaning.
2. Try out an alternative explanation.
3. Make a decision about the writer's beliefs based on available information.
4. Choose a new meaning you can defend with evidence. (1974, 11–12)

Booth's process gives students a concrete way to test out their thinking. It also makes clear why going beyond the four corners of the text into the rhetorical situation gives us a bigger data pool. To make a decision about a writer's beliefs—and, yes, intentions—we have to consider the writer's social, political, and cultural contexts and personal experiences and identity. Engaging the broader rhetorical situation allows us to say that, according to the available evidence and our best analytical efforts, we think this is what the writer is saying.

Often, the challenge for me as a teacher is to coach students back to Booth's Step 2: to explore alternate meanings. I try to get students to test out other interpretations to see how they stack up to the body of evidence, including the work as a whole, the writer's biography, the historical period, and any other data points they think are relevant.

Other times, it's Step 1 that needs more attention: the rejection of the surface meaning. I was surprised when one of my twelfth graders read Aldous Huxley's *Brave New World* as an endorsement of sexual freedom and personal empowerment. This student took the World State's slogan that "every one belongs to every one else" ([1932] 2006, 43) as a straightforward statement of theme; she even cited Fanny's encouragement of Lenina's promiscuity as evidence for her interpretation. While a defensible argument perhaps could be made in support of this

- - - - - - - - - - - - - - - - - -

2. *In* Before Reading: Narrative Conventions and the Politics of Interpretation, *Peter J. Rabinowitz explains that we can see a reader who attempts to interpret the text as the author intends as joining "a particular social/interpretive community." In this view, "intention" is a matter of "social convention" (1987, 22).*

reading (although I'm not sure how), I at least wanted this student to conduct the thought experiment of interpreting the World State's slogans ironically. If Huxley wasn't saying that everyone belongs to everyone one else, what might he be saying instead? That's the brainwork I want students to do.

Let's look at how this works with Gene Luen Yang's graphic novel *American Born Chinese* (2008). In Figure 5.6, an exchange occurs between two characters, neither of whom is who he appears to be. Yang's use of racial stereotypes and slurs in the scenes with Chin-Kee trigger that kind of "Is he for real?" reader reaction that Booth describes as key to detecting irony. The first step, Booth says, in constructing the hidden ironic meaning is "to reject the literal meaning" (1974, 10). Something in our reading experience doesn't add up, and we think, *The writer can't really be saying that.*

As readers, we sense that Yang is frustrating our expectations. We know we're not supposed to be laughing at racial stereotypes, so what's going on here? Yang plants an important clue to help his readers reconstruct his meaning. The sections featuring Chin-Kee are literally framed differently from the other sections in the graphic novel; the panels are surrounded by the words of a TV sitcom laugh track. The fake "ha ha ha" forces us to see and react to racial stereotypes being treated as popular jokes.

FIGURE 5.6
Irony at work in Gene Luen Yang's *American Born Chinese*

For readers who might be used to thinking of these jokes as funny and harmless, that confrontation triggers what some scholars have called a "rupture in knowing" (Meyer, Land, and Baillie 2010)—a violation of expectations or assumptions that forces a person to recognize the limits of his or her knowledge. The rupture results from a gap between what is known and what needs to be understood (Meyer, Land, and Baillie 2010). Coaching students to be alert to this kind of discomfort or confusion helps them detect the presence of irony. I tell my students if they're reading something and they start to think *That's messed up!* they need to ask whether the writer's being ironic.

Sometimes, in reading ironic texts, we have to live with our uncertainty and discomfort for a while. Although we may have rejected the surface meaning, we may not be ready to try out an alternate interpretation or infer the writer's intentions until we have more data points. So, we start looking for more information:

Who is the writer? What else do we know about this person?

What other clues to the text's meaning does the writer provide?

What's the context?

Who is the intended audience? What does this audience expect? What does it care about?

What do other readers think?

In the case of *American Born Chinese*, we have the plot outcome to help inform our reading (spoiler alert). By the end of the graphic novel, Chin-Kee's head is cut off, and he's revealed as a disguise for the Monkey King, who has finally learned to accept himself as a monkey and a deity. The stereotypes Chin-Kee embodies are thus destroyed by the book's conclusion. Students can also find YouTube videos of Gene Luen Yang speaking about *American Born Chinese* that offer important insights into his choices and interests as a writer.

> We make decisions about what a text means based on the best available evidence. And we test the strength of these interpretations by applying them to the work as a whole and by putting them into dialogue with the thinking of other readers, critics, and scholars.

Irony, like all rhetorical moves, is about engaging other people. It creates particular roles and relationships, as well as meanings. Irony succeeds as effective communication by calling on the audience to supply what is unsaid, thereby making the audience an intimate collaborator in meaning.

The extra challenge irony poses to readers makes it even more important to remind students that literary analysis isn't a game we play just to show how clever we are. It's what we do in an earnest attempt to understand the cares and concerns of real human beings. To refuse to read the Chin-Kee scenes in *American Born Chinese* as ironic is to disregard literature's function as communication. Yang is saying something to us, and if we believe in ethical and effective communication, we're obligated to try to understand his meaning. Adding a rhetorical focus on communication saves literary analysis from being a rarified activity only useful to future English majors. All students need analytical tools for facilitating human communication.

Summary Writing

Summary writing is a matter of understanding what is said. I often think that summarizing a text is one of the most cognitively demanding tasks we ask students to perform because doing this successfully depends on close and critical reading skills, such as annotation and rhetorical analysis. That means that, when we're assessing summary writing, we're really assessing a whole constellation of academic literacy skills.

Moreover, in the case of literary works or literary criticism, a summary must often be a synthesis of what is not only said but also implied and even unsaid because silences carry additional meaning potential in literature.

The research on summarizing doesn't make this task sound any easier.

> The ability to summarize information requires readers to sift through large units of text, differentiate important from unimportant ideas, and then synthesize those ideas and create a new coherent text that stands for, by substantive criteria, the original. This sounds difficult, and the research demonstrates that, in fact, it is. (Dole et al. 1991, 244)

When we ask students to summarize what a writer says in a novel, for instance, we need to distinguish between plot and theme. Plot summary is fairly easy for students to do, but it doesn't match the description of Dole and her colleagues (1991). Retelling a story doesn't require developing substantive criteria, differentiating important from unimportant ideas, and creating a coherent synthesis.

We also need to distinguish between what a writer says and does. With nonfiction texts, I'm usually overjoyed if my students get to the "does" aspect of textual analysis. But with literature, I find that students sometimes get stuck on the "does"—i.e., the use of literary devices—because they're not sure what the writer is saying *through* these devices. See if the following student thesis statements from literary analyses look familiar to you:

- "In *Gulliver's Travels*, Swift uses a lot of satire as well as great imagery to hook the reader."
- "I analyzed act 2, scene 3 when Jessica is talking to Lancelot. In this scene Jessica is thanking Lancelot for being there when her household is a madhouse."
- "Anaya uses symbolism and diction to help tell his story."
- "In the story of *The Tempest*, seven people came from a wedding celebration on their way to Italy from Alonso's daughter Claribel's wedding to the prince of Tunis."

Some of these statements focus on plot and some on other literary devices, but all stop short of connecting the writers' choices to their themes. Summarizing a work of literature's message or messages involves figuring out what a writer is saying *through* choices like particular plot events or images. Again, we've got to sift through a lot of chatter if we want to hear the writer's voice.

Although the following student example refers to John Steinbeck's short novel *Of Mice and Men*, it could be about almost any work of literature: "The writer uses imagery that allows our imagination to paint a vivid picture and catches the reader's attention." When I read statements like these in students' papers, I'll write a few questions in the margin to nudge them closer to an analytical claim about the text's meaning: *Can you be more specific? What kind of imagery? What does it do besides draw the reader in? How does it relate to the text's message(s) or purpose?*

Lastly, we can help students summarize what literary texts say by teaching them to avoid what Gerald Graff and Cathy Birkenstein call "the closest cliché syndrome" (2014, 33), that is, substituting a familiar platitude in place of what the text actually expresses or suggests. Saying *The Great Gatsby* is about how money can't buy happiness or *Of Mice and Men* is about how a true friend will do anything for you are examples of the closest cliché syndrome. Graff and Birkenstein offer students this advice: "Whenever you enter a conversation with others in your writing, then, it is extremely important that you go back to what others have said, that you study it very closely, and that you do not collapse it to something you already believe" (2014, 33).

The test of a good summary, Graff says, is this: can you summarize the text's main ideas in a way the writer would recognize and affirm?

Models of published summary writing can help students understand the way real writers and scholars use this skill. Notice how the following description of Junot Díaz's critically acclaimed novel *The Brief Wondrous Life of Oscar Wao* (2007) from *Historical Dictionary of U.S. Latino Literature* (Urioste, Lomelí, and Villaseñor 2017) sifts through large units of text, differentiates important from unimportant ideas, and synthesizes those ideas to create a new coherent text (Dole et al. 1991). I share an annotated version of this summary with my students (see my comments in brackets), so they can see the moves Urioste, Lomelí, and Villaseñor make:

> *The Brief Wondrous Life of Oscar Wao* takes place in the Dominican Republic and in New Jersey, and **narrates the experiences of three generations** [condenses the three narrative threads into a concise statement] of the Cabral/de Léon family, including the title character, Oscar, a nerdy, overweight young man who is **obsessed with two things: science fiction and love.** As in *Drown* [situates the novel in relation to Diaz's other work], the narrator of *Oscar Wao* is Yunior, who in a signature description in the novel says that Oscar "wore his nerdiness like a Jedi wore his light saber." **A key feature of the novel is Díaz's use of footnotes,** included for the benefit of "those who missed their mandatory two seconds of Dominican history," **as**

Díaz writes in *Oscar Wao*. The footnotes include some of the fruits of the historical research conducted by Díaz in preparation for writing the novel, as well as witty asides, jokes, and explanations that **shed light on everything from Dominican culture to science fiction to comic books** [describes function of reoccurring device]. *Oscar Wao* **addresses the historical traumas of slavery, colonialism, and the more than 30-year dictatorship of Rafael Trujillo that began in 1930 in the Dominican Republic and how the legacies of these persist**. In discussing the intersections of the historical questions engaged by his work and the influence of different genres on *Oscar Wao* **in a 2010 interview, Díaz remarked:** "In comic books there is more of the New World than in the literary fiction, and so therefore, if I'm writing a book about the deep history of the Caribbean, I had to find its echoes where they reside, and I would argue that that would be in all of the marginal, hybrid forms like comics, science fiction, apocalyptic movies, and even role playing games." **Thus,** Díaz skillfully **weaves together these multiple strands** in order to tell a rich, multifaceted story about a Dominican family that illuminates some of the **larger concerns** of the Dominican **diaspora** [identifies writer's purpose; points to themes]. (2017, 104)

Studying mentor summaries in published works helps students learn from the choices of professional writers, including their strategies for introducing quotations, indicating main ideas, situating a work in context, and creating an academic voice. Models also make the point that summaries serve specific purposes for specific audiences. The audience for *Historical Dictionary*, for instance, includes students and scholars in the field of Chicanx Studies who are looking for a concise description of the key features, themes, and achievements of Diaz's novel. What a summary looks like changes across rhetorical contexts.

> We can't assess students' summary skills unless we've read what they're summarizing.

KEY-WORD SUMMARIES

I use the Key-Word Summary strategy to help students push past their first impression of a text and test their understandings against their classmates'. This activity also asks students to practice their synthesis skills.

Directions to Students:

Step 1: Identify five key words in the text you are summarizing that you believe are central to the writer's main idea. List words in your notes.

Step 2: Pair up with another student and compare your lists. Then synthesize your two lists into a new list of five words you both can agree are central to the text's main idea.

Step 3: Quad up with another pair to form a group of four. Discuss and compare your lists, and provide a justification of your choice of key words. Then come to a consensus as a group of four about the five words that best convey the text's main idea.

Step 4: Return to your seat and write a summary paragraph of the text, using the five words from your final synthesis.

QUESTIONS MATRIX

Another way of helping students understand what a literary text is saying is a Thematic Questions Matrix. We can think of a theme as a writer's response to some question(s) at issue. Writing a thematic statement thus is a way of summarizing a novelist's, playwright's, or poet's message about life or human nature or experience. The Thematic Questions Matrix (see Figure 5.7) invites students to track key questions at issue across several young adult texts they read in my class. Tracking questions in this manner helps students understand texts' themes and connect writers in the same conversation.

THEMATIC QUESTIONS MATRIX
Directions: In the left column, complete the list of questions on adolescent themes using your own ideas for three additional questions. Then place an "x" in the column under each YA text we've read that responds to each question.

THEMATIC QUESTIONS	FUNNY IN FARSI	BURIED ONIONS	ONE CRAZY SUMMER	AMERICAN BORN CHINESE	THE ABSOLUTELY TRUE DIARY OF A PART-TIME INDIAN	AM I BLUE?
Can there be a "good" betrayal?						
What's the connection between language and identity?						
When does childhood end?						
Does art transcend boundaries? If so, how?						
Is the past important? Why or why not?						
What does it mean to be "true" to ourselves?						

FIGURE 5.7
The Thematic Question Matrix

Seeing theme as an answer to a question (i.e., a claim) additionally can help students articulate themes as complete thoughts. If a student tells me the theme of a novel or poem is "friendship" or "revenge," I'm going to ask, "What *about* it? What is the writer *saying* about this topic?" Identifying potential questions texts ask gets students to do this brainwork.

Checking for Understanding: So I Hear You Saying . . .

When we practice active listening in face-to-face conversations, we often check our understanding by mirroring back what we've heard to the person we're talking to. Readers can similarly check their understanding of written texts by testing their interpretation against the original work. This is how we say to a poem or novel, "Let me see if I've got this right."

So when one of my classes said that Shakespeare's "Sonnet 138" was about how love is blind, I took us back to the text to see whether that paraphrase of Shakespeare's meaning made sense in the context of the whole poem. Here's how we checked our understanding:

Sonnet 138 by William Shakespeare: Is Shakespeare saying love is blind?

When my love swears that she is made of truth,

I do believe her, though I know she lies,   *[Is the speaker being blind? If so, what __kind__ of blindness?]*

That she might think me some untutored youth,

Unlearnèd in the world's false subtleties.   *[Is love blind here? If so, what doesn't the speaker or his love see? What do they see? What are they aware of?]*

Thus vainly thinking that she thinks me young,

Although she knows my days are past the best,   *[Is she blind to her lover's age?]*

Simply I credit her false-speaking tongue: *[Is he blind to her lies?]*

On both sides thus is simple truth suppressed.   *[Is blindness the same as deception?]*

But wherefore says she not she is unjust?

And wherefore say not I that I am old?   *[Are they blind to their own faults?]*

Oh, love's best habit is in seeming trust,   *[Does this mean love is blind? What does "seeming" mean?]*

And age in love loves not to have years told.

Therefore I lie with her and she with me,   *[Is Shakespeare's conclusion that love is blind? What does "therefore" suggest?]*

And in our faults by lies we flattered be.   *[Are they blindly flattered?]*

When we put our interpretation to the test, we found that the theme "love is blind" didn't fully capture all the nuances of Shakespeare's meaning. It was almost as if we said to

Shakespeare, "So I hear you saying 'Love is blind'—is that right?" and Shakespeare said back to us, "No, that's not what I'm saying."

A sound critical interpretation has integrity; it's solid enough to hold together under scrutiny. An unsound interpretation falls apart when put to the test.

Negotiating Meaning

The word *negotiating* in my chapter title acknowledges the give-and-take of academic reading and writing. To negotiate something means to manage it successfully, as when a skier negotiates the hazards of a particularly tricky slope. It also means facilitating a shared understanding or compromise, as when a real estate agent negotiates a deal between a buyer and a seller.

Jeff Zwiers and Marie Crawford, authors of *Academic Conversations: Classroom Talk That Fosters Critical Thinking and Content Understanding*, add this helpful explanation: "Negotiation means to modify your meaning in response to a partner's differing meaning on the same issue. . . . The object is not to win, but to understand and build stronger ideas that are less black and white" (2011, 81). Rhetoricians call this *dialectic*.

In teaching students to negotiate different voices and meanings, we're developing their comprehension skills as listeners (i.e., readers) and their management skills as conversation hosts (i.e., writers).

POLAR OPPOSITES GUIDE [BEAN AND BISHOP 1992]

This activity accomplishes the reverse of what its name suggests—rather than guide students to take polarized stands on an issue, the Polar Opposites Guide helps students to explore the gray areas between binary oppositions. It also helps students to see the array of views held by their classmates and to negotiate meaning through the give-and-take of classroom discussion.

The following example guides students through an analysis of the main characters in Kazuo Ishiguro's novel *The Remains of the Day* ([1989] 1993). See Appendix 20 for Polar Opposites Guide for Women in 19th Century Literature and Young Adult Literature.

Directions to Students: This Polar Opposites Guide invites you to explore your developing understanding of the three main characters in the novel *The Remains of the Day* by Kazuo Ishiguro. Feel free to use a dictionary for any unfamiliar vocabulary.

Step 1: Place a check mark closest to the adjective that best describes your understanding of each character. There are no right or wrong answers—just an opportunity to investigate some of the nuances of these complex characters and to make some initial comparisons between them.

Step 2: After you have completed your Polar Opposites Guide, share your responses with a partner or a small group. Notice where you have differences of opinion. Discuss your reasons for seeing the characters the way you do and be willing to change your mind if you hear a compelling argument from a peer.

Please complete this activity AFTER you have read through the end of "Day One, Evening: Salisbury."

Mr. Stevens is . . .

responsible	—	—	—	—	—	irresponsible
dignified	—	—	—	—	—	undignified
honest	—	—	—	—	—	dishonest
cold	—	—	—	—	—	warm
diligent	—	—	—	—	—	lazy
reliable	—	—	—	—	—	unreliable
self-aware	—	—	—	—	—	self-deceived
compassionate	—	—	—	—	—	selfish
sensitive	—	—	—	—	—	insensitive
confident	—	—	—	—	—	insecure
loyal	—	—	—	—	—	disloyal
foolish	—	—	—	—	—	wise
weak	—	—	—	—	—	strong
ethical	—	—	—	—	—	unethical
repressed	—	—	—	—	—	fulfilled
loving	—	—	—	—	—	heartless
funny	—	—	—	—	—	humorless
logical	—	—	—	—	—	illogical
guilty	—	—	—	—	—	innocent
naïve	—	—	—	—	—	knowledgeable
honorable	—	—	—	—	—	dishonorable
happy	—	—	—	—	—	sad
lonely	—	—	—	—	—	connected
frustrated	—	—	—	—	—	content
obsolete	—	—	—	—	—	relevant
exploited	—	—	—	—	—	respected

Miss Kenton is . . .

responsible	—	—	—	—	—	irresponsible
dignified	—	—	—	—	—	undignified
honest	—	—	—	—	—	dishonest
cold	—	—	—	—	—	warm
diligent	—	—	—	—	—	lazy
reliable	—	—	—	—	—	unreliable
self-aware	—	—	—	—	—	self-deceived
compassionate	—	—	—	—	—	selfish
sensitive	—	—	—	—	—	insensitive
confident	—	—	—	—	—	insecure
loyal	—	—	—	—	—	disloyal
foolish	—	—	—	—	—	wise
weak	—	—	—	—	—	strong
ethical	—	—	—	—	—	unethical
repressed	—	—	—	—	—	fulfilled
loving	—	—	—	—	—	heartless
funny	—	—	—	—	—	humorless
logical	—	—	—	—	—	illogical
guilty	—	—	—	—	—	innocent
naïve	—	—	—	—	—	knowledgeable
honorable	—	—	—	—	—	dishonorable
happy	—	—	—	—	—	sad
lonely	—	—	—	—	—	connected
frustrated	—	—	—	—	—	content
obsolete	—	—	—	—	—	relevant
exploited	—	—	—	—	—	respected

Lord Darlington is . . .

responsible	—	—	—	—	—	irresponsible
dignified	—	—	—	—	—	undignified
honest	—	—	—	—	—	dishonest
cold	—	—	—	—	—	warm
diligent	—	—	—	—	—	lazy
reliable	—	—	—	—	—	unreliable
self-aware	—	—	—	—	—	self-deceived
compassionate	—	—	—	—	—	selfish
sensitive	—	—	—	—	—	insensitive
confident	—	—	—	—	—	insecure
loyal	—	—	—	—	—	disloyal
foolish	—	—	—	—	—	wise
weak	—	—	—	—	—	strong
ethical	—	—	—	—	—	unethical
repressed	—	—	—	—	—	fulfilled
loving	—	—	—	—	—	heartless
funny	—	—	—	—	—	humorless
logical	—	—	—	—	—	illogical
guilty	—	—	—	—	—	innocent
naïve	—	—	—	—	—	knowledgeable
honorable	—	—	—	—	—	dishonorable
happy	—	—	—	—	—	sad
lonely	—	—	—	—	—	connected
frustrated	—	—	—	—	—	content
obsolete	—	—	—	—	—	relevant
exploited	—	—	—	—	—	respected

Working through a variety of interpretations makes clear why a rhetorical approach to literature is important. Booth says, "Many of the literary works we value cannot be interpreted unambiguously by any two readers, no matter how skilled they are" (1974, 16). Rhetoric, Aristotle reminds us, is useful in cases where the absolute truth cannot be known.

Hosting the Conversation

Hosting an academic conversation through writing is an act of synthesis that requires great skill and responsiveness. As writers, we are also directors: We direct conversational traffic in our texts, we direct the audience's focus, we direct the flow of ideas. We orient our readers toward our purpose and position through the choices we make as intertextual discussion facilitators.

The following activities develop students' ability to synthesize and situate their sources effectively.

HOSTING THE CONVERSATION [INCLUDE HANDOUT FROM APPENDIX 18]

Directions to Teachers: This activity asks students to think through the responsibilities of hosting a conversation, including how they will facilitate the exchange of different viewpoints. Remind students that every time they let another writer have some airtime in their paper, someone else's voice besides theirs is dominant for that moment. After the other writer has his or her say, we need to find a way to reclaim the direction and tone of our argument. We can tell students that using the words of other writers is like moderating a talk show; you may find you want to spotlight some voices while keeping others in the background. You also want to think about how your introduction of each voice can convey a favorable or unfavorable impression to your audience, while still showcasing your fairness and responsibility as the host. Your job as a writer is to help your audience read the evidence in a way that ethically and effectively supports your claims.

Directions to Students: Imagine you are the host of a talk show, and you have invited several of the writers you've been reading to be guests on your program. Choose a topic to discuss that all your guests are interested in and have written about. (See Figure 5.8.)

Take a few minutes to prepare for your show by planning how you will introduce each guest and what questions you will ask to keep the conversation going. Consider the following:

1. What topic will you discuss?

2. What does your audience need to know about each guest?

3. How do your guests feel about one another? With whom do they agree? With whom do they disagree?

4. What key points or questions do you want the discussion to include?

5. Will some guests get more airtime than others? If so, who?

6. How will you handle conflicts between guests?

Notes for Introductions:

Possible Interview Questions:

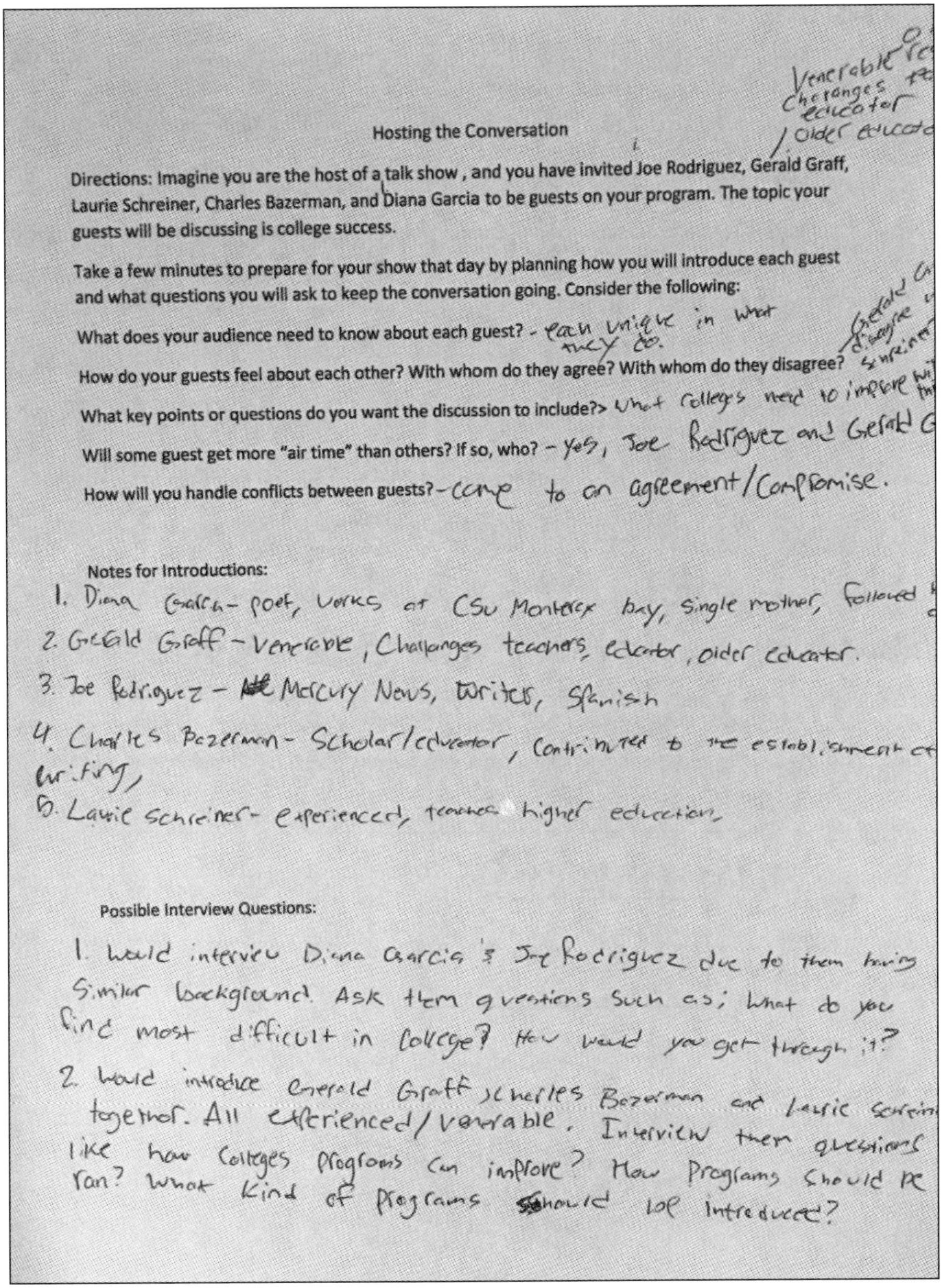

Hosting the Conversation

Directions: Imagine you are the host of a talk show, and you have invited Joe Rodriguez, Gerald Graff, Laurie Schreiner, Charles Bazerman, and Diana Garcia to be guests on your program. The topic your guests will be discussing is college success.

Take a few minutes to prepare for your show that day by planning how you will introduce each guest and what questions you will ask to keep the conversation going. Consider the following:

What does your audience need to know about each guest? - each unique in what they do.

How do your guests feel about each other? With whom do they agree? With whom do they disagree? Gerald Graff disagree Schreiner

What key points or questions do you want the discussion to include?> What colleges need to improve

Will some guest get more "air time" than others? If so, who? - Yes, Joe Rodriguez and Gerald G

How will you handle conflicts between guests? - come to an agreement/compromise.

[margin note:] Venerable educator Challenges to educator / older educator

Notes for Introductions:

1. Diana Garcia - poet, works at CSU Monterey bay, single mother, followed
2. Gerald Graff - Venerable, Challenges teachers, educator, older educator.
3. Joe Rodriguez - Mercury News, writer, Spanish
4. Charles Bazerman - Scholar/educator, contributed to the establishment of writing,
5. Laurie Schreiner - experienced, teaches higher education.

Possible Interview Questions:

1. Would interview Diana Garcia & Joe Rodriguez due to them having similar background. Ask them questions such as; what do you find most difficult in college? How would you get through it?

2. Would introduce Gerald Graff, Charles Bazerman and Laurie Schreiner together. All experienced/venerable. Interview them questions like how colleges programs can improve? How programs should be ran? What kind of programs should be introduced?

FIGURE 5.8
Hosting the Conversation Student Example

CONVERSATION SEATING PLAN

It's important for students to think about how their sources mix and mingle in their writing. On the days when students turn in a reading-based writing assignment, I've started to ask them to do a rather unusual activity: I ask them to draw a seating plan for the conversation they've hosted in their essay by inviting their different sources to speak on the issue. The image I want is not unlike a map of table assignments for a big wedding, a quinceañera, or a formal luncheon. Here's the catch: Their seating plan needs to match the way they actually facilitate conversation in their paper. (See Figures 5.9. and 5.10) Sources can only sit together if they "talk" to each other in the essay. Did they put all the people with similar interests at the same table? Or did they mix it up? Who's sitting together and who's all alone? If a student put several sources into dialogue with one another by noting points of agreement and disagreement, then they can all sit at the same table. But if a source isn't integrated into the discussion, that needs to be represented in the seating plan. And that may be just fine—perhaps the lone speaker is the person who gives a special toast before leaving the party early.

Synthesis is the act of making connections among these voices.

After students create their seating plans, I ask them to consider this question: Did you have a bunch of lonely people at your event, or did you host a lively exchange of ideas?

Introducing Sources

Knowing who is saying what (and why it matters) is an important reader need. Less experienced academic writers tend to skip the crucial step of introducing their sources to their readers. Doing a little more prep work as host can help writers avoid the confusion caused by unattributed quotations.

FIGURE 5.9

Seating Plan for
Sources in an Academic
Conversation

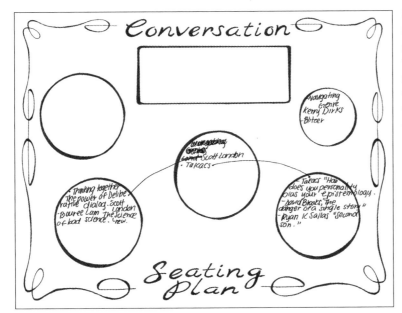

FIGURE 5.10

Ulises insightfully noticed a couple "floaters" in his conversation: writers who made the rounds to a few different tables.

AUTHOR FRIEND INTERVIEWS

To sharpen students' citation skills, I create low-stakes writing opportunities that mimic real-world writing occasions. Recently, I had the great pleasure of being interviewed by a local news crew about one of my outstanding students. I knew the reporter was looking for sound bites that would say a lot in just a few words. So I had to think carefully about what was most special about this young woman. What part of her story hadn't been told yet? What unique qualities made her stand out in a crowd? Why would I remember teaching her twenty years from now? This experience gave me the idea of using Author Friend Interviews as a strategy for helping students think through how they introduce sources in their writing.

Directions to Students: Imagine you are a close personal friend of the author whose book you just finished reading. Your friend the famous writer is being profiled for a big magazine story. As an intimate acquaintance of this writer, you are being interviewed for the article. This is your chance to tell the world what is special and memorable about your celebrity BFF. Keep in mind that while you want to make your friend look good, you don't want to just give empty praise that will easily be forgotten.

And remember the No. 1 rule in public relations: never talk to a reporter without taking a few moments to collect your thoughts. So, take another look at your friend's work before the interview. Skim the preface or back cover and jot down a few ideas. Ready for the reporter's questions? Here they are:

- How is your friend different from other writers?

- What special contribution does your friend make to the literary world?
- Why do your friend's books appeal to so many readers?
- What's the most important thing you think people should know about your friend?
- What do you think your friend will be remembered for most?

The answers to these questions are similar to the content of a literature review, one of the most scholarly genres students encounter in their academic lives. Although a magazine profile and a literature review may seem, on the surface, to be widely different writing tasks, they share some important functions: situating a writer in an ongoing conversation, identifying the text's key points or characteristics, and assessing the impact of a writer's work.

What's more, this is real-world, on-demand writing. When a reporter calls and says she wants to talk to you that day about a breaking story, you may have only minutes to pull your talking points together.

A twist on this activity (and another way to think about the exigence of a writer's work) is the Interview Gone Wrong.

INTERVIEW GONE WRONG

Directions to Students: Imagine you are interviewing one of your sources, and you find yourself asking all the wrong questions. Instead of lively, intriguing responses, you keep getting flat, boring answers to your questions. Your questions just aren't showcasing the best thinking of this individual. Write three to five examples of the wrong kinds of questions to ask this person. Then write one really great question that you hope will reveal what is most interesting about this person's point of view.

KEYNOTE SPEAKER INTRODUCTION

Writers are more effective conversation hosts when they can situate a source within the context of an academic conversation and discourse community.

Directions to Students: Imagine an author you've been reading will be giving the keynote address (i.e., the main speech) at a major event, and you have the task of introducing this author to the audience. Write an introduction for this author's keynote address. How would you situate this author within the discourse community? Why does his or her work matter? What does he or she try to accomplish through writing? Watch YouTube videos of author talks. What are the conventions of a speaker introduction? Watching the videos can also help give you a sense of the individuality of authors and the real audiences they address.

The image of President Obama awarding Luis Valdez the National Medal of Arts was used on a flyer announcing Valdez's speaking engagement at CSU Monterey Bay (Figure 5.11).

FIGURE 5.11

Image of President Obama awarding Luis Valdez the National Medal of Arts. The Keynote Speaker Introduction activity asks students to consider what they would say if they had the task of introducing someone like Valdez at this kind of event.

Synthesizing Sources and Integrative Thinking

The Association of American Colleges and Universities says integrative thinking involves "making simple connections among ideas and experiences" and "synthesizing and transferring learning to new, complex situations" (2009). This is what we're asking students to do when they synthesize sources. Newcomers to source-based writing are often unsure about what *synthesis* means. When I ask students why they didn't make a connection to a class reading that could provide additional support or context for their argument, I often hear "I didn't bring it in because I didn't think it was relevant" or "I didn't think I could use more than one source in a paragraph."

Synthesis requires students to go beyond summarizing to analyze and make connections among multiple sources. Here's how literary critic Jonathan Loesberg effects this move in an article on Oscar Wilde's 1889 novella *The Portrait of Mr. W. H.*:

> **It is not new, of course, to discuss** fictional theory about the identification of W. H. with the young man addressed by Shakespeare's sonnets as concerned with the literary, and as connecting the literary to the sexual. **But these earlier readings** connect the novella's theory about the content of the sonnets with a general concept of literariness, or with what aspect of a work makes it literary. **They do not engage** with the characters' arguments about the nature of interpretation. **As I agree with and build on these readings'** interest in the ways Wilde's novella looks at the duplicities of art, literary representation, and sexuality, **I also want to note** the way the novella explicitly parodies and extends a developing Victorian interest in what counts as a specifically literary interpretation or reading. (Loesberg 2015, 10; emphasis added)

Notice how Loesberg situates himself within this ongoing conversation on Wilde's novella; he first summarizes the views of previous scholars before articulating the way his own argument will go beyond what has been done before. His language choices clearly follow the "they say/I say" pattern common to academic writing that Gerald Graff and Cathy Birkenstein (2014) describe: **As I agree with and build on these readings' . . . /I also want to note . . . .**

This positioning of oneself within the conversation is a large part of what we're asking students to do when they synthesize sources.

LOST LUGGAGE

Lost Luggage works as a strategy for synthesizing different perspectives. In this activity, students are responsible for paraphrasing the views of other writers' views in relation to their own views. I use Lost Luggage to help students understand the positions of different writers who are addressing the same topic or issue. (Much thanks to Shirley Hargis at the Fresno County Office of Education for introducing me to this strategy.)

Directions to Teachers: Distribute the Lost Luggage handouts to your students with the key questions you'd like them to answer. Be sure they write their names on the handouts. After giving students some time to write their responses to the questions, instruct students to meet and greet another student and share their responses to the questions by exchanging papers and discussing their answers. Each paper then becomes "lost luggage"; that is, it is left behind with the student's partner. Students then carry the lost luggage into a new conversation with a second partner and will summarize both their own responses to the questions and the responses of the person whose luggage they're carrying. After exchanging luggage a few more times, instruct students to find the original owner of the luggage they've picked up and to check that their understanding of the owner's responses is correct.

Lost Luggage
Name:

Directions to Students: Answer each of the questions below. Then, when your teacher instructs you to do so, "meet and greet" another student and share your responses. After you share, you will lose your "luggage" by leaving your responses behind with your partner and taking your partner's responses instead. Meet and greet a new partner and share both your own responses to the questions and the responses on the lost luggage you're carrying.

1. Why did you write this piece?
2. What is the most important idea or issue you explore?

A twist on Lost Luggage is to have students role-play various authors they've read. The responses then become paraphrases of the authors' ideas.

ARCHETYPE/RESPONSE/SOURCE

Students practice integrative thinking when they compare and connect across multiple sources. This is the basis of any synthesis work. The next activity helps students make text-to-text connections by tracing the representation of character and plot archetypes (or universal models) across multiple texts, genres, and periods. Although the following example uses British literature and Greek mythology, this activity could be adapted for world literature and culture.

Directions to Students: This exercise is designed to help you explore the various ways plot and character archetypes are embodied, altered, and contested by diverse genres and periods. Using the readings from our class, trace the connections between the characteristics of classical archetypes, the Greek sources from which those archetypes emerged, and literary responses to those archetypes.

Step 1: Analyze the relationships between the archetype, the literary response, and the Greek source for each of the sets in the grid shown in Figure 5.11. Your analysis should include a description of the key features of the archetype, the extent to which the literary response stays true to (i.e., maintains fidelity) or resists the mythological source, and a brief summary of the archetype in the Greek source. Use the last set of "free choice" boxes to identify additional connections among an archetype, a literary work, and a Greek myth of your own choosing.

Step 2: Peer review one another's grids. Walk around the room and write your comments and questions in the margins around each student's grid. These could include points of agreement or disagreement or questions that ask for clarification. Your goal is to help one another deepen your understanding of the British writers' range of responses to the implicit values and assumptions of Western mythology.

Step 3: Return to your seat and read the questions and comments in the margins of your own grid. Then respond to the following questions in a quick-write: What do you notice about how these archetypes have been represented across different time periods and works of literature? Why is this important?

ARCHETYPE	RESPONSE	SOURCE
The Hero Characteristics:	*Beowulf* Extent of fidelity/resistance:	*The Odyssey* Summary:
The Hero Characteristics:	*Jane Eyre* Extent of fidelity/resistance:	*The Odyssey* Summary:

FIGURE 5.12
Making text-to-text connections by tracing archetypes across works of literature

The Siren Characteristics:	"The Wife of Bath's Tale" Extent of fidelity/resistance:	The Odyssey Summary:
The Hero's Journey Characteristics:	*Gulliver's Travels* Extent of fidelity/resistance:	*The Odyssey* Summary:
The Creator/Artist Characteristics:	*Pygmalion* Extent of fidelity/resistance:	"Pygmalion and Galatea" Summary:
The Creator/Artist Characteristics:	*Frankenstein* Extent of fidelity/resistance:	"Pygmalion and Galatea" and/or "Prometheus" Summary:
The Seer Characteristics:	*Orlando* Extent of fidelity/resistance:	"Oedipus" Summary:

FIGURE 5.12 (CONTINUED)

Making text-to-text connections by tracing archetypes across works of literature

The Hero's Journey Characteristics:	*The Remains of the Day* Extent of fidelity/resistance:	*The Odyssey* Summary:
The Monster Characteristics:	*Beowulf* Extent of fidelity/resistance:	*The Odyssey* and/or "**Perseus**" Summary:
The Monster Characteristics:	*Frankenstein* Extent of fidelity/resistance:	*The Odyssey* and/or "**Perseus**" Summary:
The Monster Characteristics:	*Dr. Jekyll, and Mr. Hyde* Extent of fidelity/resistance	*The Odyssey* and/or "**Theseus**" Summary:
Archetype: Free Choice	Literary Response: Free Choice	Mythological Source: Free Choice

FIGURE 5.12 (CONTINUED)

Making text-to-text connections by tracing archetypes across works of literature

Making text-to-text connections like this helps students understand that writers do not write in isolation. Instead, writers engage in ongoing conversations with other writers, a key rhetorical concept for academic success and transfer of learning.

Beyond literary analysis, the ability to trace the source of an idea and how that idea has developed over time has important applications in other contexts. This is what we do when we write a literature review for a research project in the sciences and social sciences. And it's what we do in argumentation when we examine the backing for a claim. In all these cases, the question we're asking is *Where does this way of thinking come from?*

Quote, Paraphrase, or Summarize[3]

Academic writing includes citations from other sources. Words and ideas from sources can be incorporated in three ways: (1) direct quotation, (2) paraphrase, and (3) summary. Each of these choices has a different rhetorical function.

1. *Quotation* showcases a source's language choices when those choices matter.

2. *Paraphrase* seamlessly integrates a source's content with a writer's argument.

3. *Summary* offers a big picture of a source's main ideas or importance.

When students decide to quote, paraphrase, or summarize, we want them to consider the following questions: What are you trying to do? Why are you trying to do this? What's the best choice in this situation? Different choices accomplish different ends. Social scientists, for instance, tend to use more paraphrase than direct quotation because their focus is on the content of their sources rather than on the writers' language choices.

When I teach Mark Haddon's novel *The Curious Incident of the Dog in the Night-Time* (2003), I use a writing prompt that asks students to apply ideas they've explored in nonfiction readings to an analysis of a literary text. This task requires students to integrate multiple sources and perspectives.

Here's my prompt:

> In "The Ways We Lie," Stephanie Ericsson challenges the assumption that, in some cases, the truth will cause more harm than a lie. She condemns white lies as an act of arrogance: "In effect, it is the liar deciding what is best for the lied to. Ultimately, it is a vote of no confidence. It is an act of subtle arrogance for anyone to decide what is best for someone else" (1991, 181). Write an argument essay in which you evaluate whether or not Christopher's father was justified in lying to his son in Mark Haddon's novel *The Curious Incident of the Dog in the Night-Time*. Consider Ericsson's criticism of white lies, and establish your own ethical criteria for making this judgment. For instance, do you

----

3. *The activities in this section are inspired by the CSU Expository Reading and Writing Curriculum (ERWC).*

believe the end justifies the means? Or do you think there are absolute ethical principles we must follow regardless of the outcome? In other words, are some things always right or always wrong? Include an analysis of Christopher's father's reason for lying about Christopher's mother. Support your position with evidence from the novel, our other course readings, and your personal observations and experiences as relevant.

Students have read numerous texts in preparation for joining this conversation. These include scholarly articles, the introduction to Ursula K. Le Guin's science fiction novel *The Left Hand of Darkness* ([1969] 1976), and an excerpt from Darrell Huff's popular book *How to Lie with Statistics* ([1954] 1993).

The following prewriting exercise helps students think through their citation choices.

QUOTE, PARAPHRASE, OR SUMMARIZE?

Directions to Students: For each of the following citations, decide whether the words of other writers should be quoted, paraphrased, or summarized. In cases in which you see direct quotation as the most rhetorically effective method, decide which words and phrases should be quoted and which should be paraphrased in your lead-in or commentary. Feel free to rewrite or eliminate the lead-ins that are provided. When considering multiple quotations from the same source, decide which quotations will best suit your purpose and how the quotations will work with one another. If one citation best expresses the idea you want to capture and can most efficiently do the work of supporting your claim or articulating a counterclaim, you may find that you do not need the other examples.

1. In Study 1, for instance, researchers found that "the majority of people [surveyed] report[ed] telling no lies during the past 24 hours and most of the reported lies [were] told by few people" (Serota, Levine, and Boster 2010, 8).

2. Serota, Levine, and Boster see humans as holding contradictory attitudes toward lying: "Humans are ambivalent about deception. On the one hand, virtually all human cultures have some prohibition against lying. On the other hand, the ability to deceive well may be essential for polite interaction and, at times, self-preservation" (2010, 2).

3. "In making arguments, writers filter numerical data through the screen of their own perspective or angle of vision—an interpretive process that, as we have seen, is characteristic of how evidence is used in all thesis-based prose. As a critical thinker, you need to be aware of how writers select and present numbers and how their choices support their own perspectives while de-emphasizing others" (Ramage and Bean 1998, 249).

4. "I think [a metaphor] should be called a lie because a pig is not like a day and people do not have skeletons in their cupboards" (Haddon 2003, 15).

5. "I do not tell lies" (Haddon 2003, 19).

6. "A lie is when you say something happened which didn't happen. But there is only ever one thing which happened at a particular time and particular place" (Haddon 2003, 19).

7. "People say that you always have to tell the truth. But they do not mean this because you are not allowed to tell old people that they are old and you are not allowed to tell people if they smell funny or if a grown-up has made a fart" (Haddon 2003, 46–47).

8. Ursula K. Le Guin claims that "a novelist's business is lying" ([1969] 1976, ii).

9. "The only truth I can understand or express is," Le Guin writes, "logically defined, a lie" ([1969] 1976, v).

10. "In reading a novel, we have to know perfectly well that the whole thing is nonsense, and then, while reading, believe every word of it" (Le Guin [1969] 1976, v).

11. Huff acknowledges that sometimes a strictly logical or informational approach to graphs may lack persuasive power, offering a sample of circumstances that might call for some enhanced images: "Suppose you wish to win an argument, shock a reader, move him into action, sell him something" ([1954] 1993, 64). Under those circumstances, Huff suggests, an unscrupulous graph designer can find several ways to manipulate the picture without spoiling "the illusion of objectivity" ([1954] 1993, 65).

A rhetorical approach doesn't treat these choices just as a mechanical set of citation skills but as strategies for facilitating the productive exchange of ideas.

Conclusion

Literary texts have a special ability to bring people together. As a form of epideictic (or ceremonial) rhetoric, imaginative literature explores our most cherished values and grievous faults. Rhetoric of this kind shapes our shared sense of identity as a human family, helping us to understand points of view different from our own and find common ground in our culture and communities. But in order for that to happen, readers need a deep understanding of what they're reading. A casual acquaintance with a poem or novel isn't enough to bridge social divisions.

We can make the most of the opportunities literary reading affords for bringing people together by teaching students to responsibly negotiate different textual voices and meaning. By paying careful attention to what writers, characters, narrators, and readers say and mean, students deepen their own and others' understanding of texts and prepare to make informed contributions to academic conversations.

CHAPTER SIX

Developing and Supporting a Line of Reasoning

The teaching of writing is nothing less than the teaching of reasoning.
—JAMES CROSSWHITE

Argumentation differs from other forms of dialogic communication in its emphasis on reasonableness.
—JOSINA MAKAU AND DEBIAN MARTY

Picture the following writing conference: A new student has come to see me about her first essay for my class. After reading her half-finished draft, I offer some advice about how she could further develop and support her argument. I suggest she start by rereading and analyzing her sources and pulling more quotations and paraphrases to use as evidence. "Think of how you want to situate these different voices in the conversation you're hosting," I tell her. "Whose perspective should be front and center? Whose will be more on the periphery? And which bits of evidence do you want to group together?" This isn't what she wants to hear.

Confused and looking for a familiar handhold, she asks what she really wants to know: "Should I plan for about five paragraphs then?"

I attempt to let her down easy. "Well, your essay is supposed to be three to four pages long," I say. "So you'll probably need more paragraphs than that. Try looking for different patterns or clusters of ideas in your evidence and then create your outline accordingly."

"So, I should write one paragraph on each source?" she says.

I'm prepared for this: "Not necessarily. Instead of thinking of what formula you're going to use to generate body paragraphs, think of the story your evidence tells. What conclusions can you draw? How does one idea relate to the next? There are lots of effective ways to develop and support an argument. Part of your assignment is to figure out the best way to arrange your ideas."

Silence. Then strained politeness as she asks, "What do you want these paragraphs to be about again?"

Knowing that what I'm about to say may well push this student over the edge, I do my best to make my response sound cheerful and encouraging: "So, as the writer, *you* get to make your own decisions about the order and content of your paragraphs based on the demands of the rhetorical situation. Look again at your assignment directions and at models of this type of writing. Think about the choices you see other writers making about structure and support."

The student looks back at me with weary eyes. I know this look. It's that pained expression that says, "Why are you doing this to me?" She smiles faintly and thanks me for my help, summarily ending our conversation.

Do I get that it's hard for students to see what I see in texts? I do. And I'm frustrated that I haven't found a pain-free way to help students cross the threshold from formulaic, school-based writing exercises to rhetorically effective real-world communication.

Asking me what *I* want the paragraphs to be about tells me the student hasn't figured out what *she* cares about saying, which also probably means she hasn't yet figured out what other writers have to say about this topic. Writing is still a compulsory, teacher-driven assignment to her, not a heartfelt act of communication.

What we have here is an invention problem. *Invention* is a concept from classical rhetoric that refers to two aspects of early-stage composing: (1) analyzing a particular case or situation to determine the issues that can be argued most effectively and (2) searching for the means of developing and supporting an argument (i.e., the proof; Brandt 1970, 14–15). We can thus think of invention as the search for meaning and means. Both involve critical thinking.

One of the best things we can do for all students, particularly our most vulnerable students, is to take their thinking seriously. And that means responding to the substance of their ideas, not just the form of their writing. Working out a chain of reasoning takes a great deal of thought and effort. It can be maddening to be faced with a messy collection of notes and evidence and not yet know how all this information is related or what story it tells. This is high-level, creative problem solving, the kind of portable competency that pays off in multiple contexts. It's also stressful and intimidating and can make students feel like the academic life just isn't for them. A commitment to educational equity requires that we give students extended encouragement and guidance for this challenging intellectual work.

In this chapter, I share ways to cultivate students' critical reasoning abilities through the study of literary arguments.

Developing a Line of Reasoning

As my opening vignette suggests, students and teachers often have different notions of what it means to develop an argument. For many students, "develop a position" means "make it long enough to meet the length requirement." But this interpretation falls far short of the brainwork we're actually asking students to do.

Development is a matter of discovery. It means doing the research and development work needed to discover new understandings (like scientists doing research and development, or R&D, to find a vaccine for the Zika virus). And it means discovering the best available means of persuasion to share those new understandings. We see both aspects of development at work in the classical process of invention.

Consequently, when English teachers write "more development needed" on students' papers, we don't just mean "make your paper longer." More development means more thinking, more reading, more research, more building, more testing, more refining, more communicating. Think about what we mean by the phrases "professional development" or "personal development." Participating in professional development doesn't mean you just add "more teacher"; it means you grow and change. Writing and thinking need to grow and change, too, over the course of their development.

Development is also a matter of direction. Writing needs to go somewhere, and where it goes and how it gets there are up to the writer. In "The Shifting Relationships Between Speech and Writing," Peter Elbow describes good writing as *leading us on a journey through time* (2000, 162; italics in original). That is, effective writing moves readers through a series of moments. "Readers," Elbow explains, "are immersed in time as they read just as listeners are when they hear. We cannot take in a text all at once as we can a picture or diagram" (2000, 161). A skillful writer guides readers through a text by creating the same kind of directional energy we associate with works of fiction: a problem develops, anticipation and tension build, a resolution emerges, and perhaps the pattern begins again. This "itch and scratch" pattern, Elbow says, is what "holds the reader's experience together" (2000, 163). We sense this when we read stories.

But this is also what a good argument should do, too—move us emotionally and intellectually *and* move us through time, so that where we start is not where we end. The line in a line of reasoning is thus a kind of plotline. Well-developed and supported arguments follow a dramatic arc.

Of course, it's our job as teachers to help students develop this more sophisticated understanding. When applied to their own writing, a heightened sense of discovery and direction improves the quality of students' content and cohesion.

Thinking of development in terms of direction, for example, can help students create that itch-and-scratch experience for their readers. One of my students, Elinor, had drafted the following outline for her essay in response to *Farewell to Manzanar*, the 1973 memoir of life in a World War II internment camp by Jeanne Wakatsuki Houston and James D. Houston:

1. Introduction

2. Interviews with Japanese-Americans

3. Statistics on WWII internment camps

4. Children's experiences at Manzanar

5. Adults' experiences at Manzanar

6. Conclusion

At first glance, the outline seemed pretty static. So I pushed Elinor to see a logical progression of ideas in this order. "Why does the section on statistics come after the interviews?" I asked her. "What's the relationship between these two sections?" She wasn't sure. Instead of just treating "statistics" as the next item on her outline, I encouraged Elinor to think about how this section could take up and extend the work initiated by the previous section—perhaps by contextualizing the personal stories with big-picture data. The move from the specific (i.e., the interviews) to the general (i.e., the statistics) moves the argument forward.

In *A Short Course in Writing*, Kenneth A. Bruffee (2007) offers a set of questions that can further develop students' thinking. When students stall at the sentence or paragraph level of development, Bruffee tells them to anticipate the questions that might occur to their readers:

- What do you mean by that?
- Why?
- How come?
- Who says?
- So what? (2007, 112)

Taking on reader expectations as writing prompts can help advance a line of reasoning while creating greater cohesion.

Logic and Integrative Thinking

Developing a *line*, or a chain, of reasoning is a different sort of task from just providing reasons and evidence for a claim. When students are new to argumentation, they often take the "and another thing" approach, listing loads of reasons for a claim or claims that have nothing to do with one another. Paragraph A offers a reason, with evidence and examples. Paragraph B does the same. So does paragraph C. But it makes no difference whether paragraph A is swapped with B or C because the paragraphs aren't links in a chain of reasoning. The argument doesn't go anywhere because the sections are interchangeable. The organizational structure is a list, not a plot.

But if we want students to engage a whole system of thought, then we need to teach not only about reasons and evidence but also about the connections between claims, reasons, evidence, and ways of knowing. We need to teach integrative thinking.

Many students could use extra support connecting ideas in their writing. Karissa, for instance, was writing a paper about persuasion versus force in Orson Scott Card's novel *Ender's Game* (1985). About halfway through, she included a discussion of sibling rivalry. There was no clear connection between these two seemingly disparate topics, so I encouraged her to establish the link between ways of controlling people and family dynamics more directly. Here's what she came up with: "Because siblings are often in competition with each other, they frequently use both physical force and mental manipulation to get the upper hand."

Teaching logic as integrative thinking is the opposite of what students sometimes do with the idea of logos: just dropping in a handful of weighty statistics or some expert testimony to give a paper the veneer of authority. If these embellishments can be removed without harming the integrity of the essay, they're not really part of the essay's logic (i.e., how the text works). The logic of something governs how it's put together and functions. Logic lives in the deep structure.

That means that logical links between sections of a composition are functional links. Consider, for instance, the kinds of logical relationships that can exist between two paragraphs (see Figure 6.1):

FIRST PARAGRAPH →	SECOND PARAGRAPH
introduce a concept	provide an illustration
raise a question	broaden the scope of the question
describe a phenomenon	suggest an explanation
make a claim	provide supporting evidence
establish a general trend	describe an exception
describe something	make a comparison
summarize the general view	note an objection
present a common explanation	suggest an alternate explanation
describe an experience	offer an interpretation

FIGURE 6.1
Logical relationships

In each case, the second paragraph builds on, or develops, the thinking initiated by the first. That movement from one paragraph to the next is development. Describing paragraph structure as just a "sandwich" doesn't capture the dynamic and interconnected nature of paragraphs in a composition. (By the way, all of the logical relationships in Figure 6.1 can also exist between sentences.)

Logic Models

In research, logic models are guides that show links among ideas and resources. A logic model uses tools like flowcharts to describe how you get to the outcome and what each piece of the project contributes to the takeaway learning. It's an iterative process, open to modification. How does everything add up? That's the question a logic model asks. A logic model is a test of whether a project makes sense and flows from point to point.

Students can transfer this approach to their own writing by thinking of an argument as a logic model. For instance, *What are the available resources? How does each piece contribute to your purpose? What are the outcomes of your research/argument?* (By the way, I think we should call more of what we do when we engage in academic work "research").

ARGUMENT FLOWCHART

Creating a flowchart of their argument can help students see that we're reasoning *from* evidence *to* claims, not finding evidence to support claims. A flowchart represents logic as an internal system, not just something that makes you sound smart and mathy. See the student sample in Figure 6.2 from an argument about how the main character in Rodman Philbrick's *Freak the Mighty* (1998) changes over the course of the novel.

Directions to Students: Create a flow chart for your argument linking your evidence to your claims to your conclusions and the impact of your argument. Use the table below to chart this sequence or create your own visual representation of your argument's flow. Draw arrows connecting the elements of your argument.

Input (Evidence and Resources)	Processing (Claims)	Output (Conclusions and Impact)
"And now that I've written a book, I might even read a few. No big deal."	Max is more confident in himself.	This show that Max has overcame his fear of reading and the he now believes he can overcome other fears, all with a "No biggie" attitude.

FIGURE 6.2
Student sample of an argument flowchart for *Freak the Mighty*

Directions to Students: **Create a flowchart for your argument linking your evidence to your claims to your conclusions and the impact of your argument. Use the table in Figure 6.3 to chart this sequence or create your own visual representation of your argument's flow. Draw arrows connecting the elements of your argument.**

Input → (Evidence and Resources)	Processing → (Claims)	Output (Conclusions and Impact)

FIGURE 6.3
Argument flowchart

Creating a flowchart develops the directional awareness that aids in transfer of learning. It also helps students focus on the internal workings of a text (i.e., the logos). Writing that flows doesn't just sound nice; it moves from one idea to the next in a reasonable and cohesive manner.

> **Students get more out of instruction in argument and reasoning when what they learn helps them connect their thinking in other contexts. We hold onto our thinking by finding connections.**

I don't think these are skills that should be taught only to students in advanced courses. All students can draw on their natural ability as storytellers to develop lines of reasoning that go somewhere, and all students deserve to have their reasoning tested and strengthened through thoughtful feedback.

The Benefits of Literature

Literary texts are a particularly good way to develop students' critical reasoning skills. In "Writing Without Reading: The Decline of Literature in the Composition Class," rhetorician John C. Briggs calls for the integration of literature and composition as a means to improve the teaching of writing:

> It is time to rediscover literature's power to contribute to the teaching of composition, not only as a stimulus for ideas but also as a model and point of departure for the organization and presentation of those ideas. Literature should inform the study of invention, organization, syntax, and style—the matter and form of articulate thought. (2004, 19)

The study of literature not only offers students an excellent logical training ground but also helps students avoid some of the pitfalls they fall into when they read and write about controversial issues in the news. This does not mean that these kinds of nonfiction readings are not critically important for a well-rounded literacy education, but if we find students are struggling with evidence, warrants, and backing, they can practice these skills with literary texts that won't trigger their confirmation bias or inclination to make unfounded claims or faulty assumptions.

In addition, teaching argument through literary texts helps students see that there can be more than two sides to an issue. This is because, as Bruce Ballenger explains in *The Curious Writer*, literature can't easily be reduced to pro and con views:

> One of the things that literature—and all art—teaches us is the delightful and nagging complexity of things. By inclination and upbringing, Huck Finn is a racist, and there's plenty of evidence in *Huckleberry Finn* that his treatment of Jim confirms it. Yet there are moments in the novel when we see a transcendent humanity in Huck, and we can see that he can be a racist, *but . . .* It is this qualification—this modest word *but*—that trips us up in the steady march toward certainty. Rather than *either/or*, can it be *both/and*? Instead of two sides to every issue, might there be thirteen? (2008, 272)

In addition to resisting oversimplification, literature also makes clear the interconnections among ethos, pathos, and logos. Literary texts won't easily support a false dichotomy between logic and emotion.

Reading and writing arguments about literature helps students practice argument as open-minded inquiry. Because the imagined worlds we encounter are often so complex and destabilizing, literature forces us to take it on its own terms. It's hard to experience confirmation bias with a thematically ambiguous text. Students might come to class with a preexisting opinion on gun control, or abortion, but I'll bet anything most incoming eleventh graders don't have a preexisting opinion on the meaning of the green light at the end of Daisy's dock.

Analyzing Arguments in Literature

We can heighten students' awareness of how they develop and support their own arguments by having them analyze arguments in literature. An interesting one to use is the argument the Ghost makes in Shakespeare's *Hamlet* when he tries to persuade his son to avenge his death. Ask students to annotate and descriptively outline the speech, paying special attention to how the Ghost develops and supports his line of reasoning (see my sample annotations):

Ay, that incestuous, that adulterate beast,　　　[describes Claudius as an animal]

With witchcraft of his wit, with traitorous gifts,—　　　[characterizes foe as wicked and devilish]

O wicked wit and gifts, that have the power　　　[portrays C as Satanic tempter]

So to seduce!—won to his shameful lust	[explains Queen's seduction]
The will of my most seeming-virtuous queen:	
O Hamlet, what a falling-off was there!	[elevates ethos by comparison to C]
From me, whose love was of that dignity	[shows pain and grief caused by betrayal]
That it went hand in hand even with the vow	
I made to her in marriage, and to decline	
Upon a wretch whose natural gifts were poor	[laments Queen's preference for a "wretch"]
To those of mine!	
But virtue, as it never will be moved,	
Though lewdness court it in a shape of heaven,	[offers moral truth as an aphorism]
So lust, though to a radiant angel link'd,	[notes principles of vice and virtue]
Will sate itself in a celestial bed,	[establishes own virtuous ethos]
And prey on garbage.	[invokes images of angels and fiends]
But, soft! methinks I scent the morning air;	[heightens sense of urgency and constraint]
Brief let me be. Sleeping within my orchard,	[begins narrative testimony]
My custom always of the afternoon,	[supports murder charge through story]
Upon my secure hour thy uncle stole,	[acts as victim and eyewitness]
With juice of cursed hebenon in a vial,	[answers question of fact: what happened?]
And in the porches of my ears did pour	[describes his body as an edifice]
The leperous distilment; whose effect	
Holds such an enmity with blood of man	[intensifies horror through personification]
That swift as quicksilver it courses through	
The natural gates and alleys of the body,	[portrays body as a conquered city or castle]
And with a sudden vigour doth posset	[suggests invasion of the State of Denmark]
And curd, like eager droppings into milk,	[describes gruesome effects of poison]
The thin and wholesome blood: so did it mine;	[details corruption of pure substance]

And a most instant tetter bark'd about,	[intensifies emotional and physical pain]
Most lazar-like, with vile and loathsome crust,	
All my smooth body.	
Thus was I, sleeping, by a brother's hand	[draws a conclusion; identifies murderer]
Of life, of crown, of queen, at once dispatch'd:	[amplifies implications of the crime]
Cut off even in the blossoms of my sin,	[intensifies sense of untimeliness]
Unhousel'd, disappointed, unanel'd,	[appeals to emotion; expands on loss]
No reckoning made, but sent to my account	[adds crime of being denied reconciliation]
With all my imperfections on my head:	[suggests intense suffering in afterlife]
O, horrible! O, horrible! most horrible!	[demonstrates depth of pain]
If thou hast nature in thee, bear it not;	[appeals to Hamlet as son and heir]
Let not the royal bed of Denmark be	[issues direct command in graphic terms]
A couch for luxury and damned incest.	[describes ongoing sexual corruption]
But, howsoever thou pursuest this act,	
Taint not thy mind, nor let thy soul contrive	[adds a stipulation]
Against thy mother aught: leave her to heaven	[complicates mother's guilt]
And to those thorns that in her bosom lodge,	
To prick and sting her. Fare thee well at once!	[returns to sense of urgency]
The glow-worm shows the matin to be near,	
And 'gins to pale his uneffectual fire:	
Adieu, adieu! Hamlet, remember me.	[appeals to father-son relationship]

The Ghost's argument is both forensic (*Who done it?*) and deliberative (*What should we do now?*). After addressing a question of fact, he exhorts Hamlet to follow a course of policy: "Let not the royal bed of Denmark be / A couch for luxury and damned incest." But before making his case, the Ghost has already commanded Hamlet to "revenge his foul and most unnatural murder" and informed him of the identity of his murderer: the "serpent" who "now wears his crown." Then why is the subsequent argument necessary? This is the interesting question.

The Ghost's argument is a good example of why we typically can't just make a claim and be done with it. A claim needs to be fully developed and supported before it can move people to belief and action. The first rhetorical challenge the Ghost has to deal with is the shady reputation of ghosts in general. Horatio voices this concern when he tells Hamlet not to follow the Ghost lest it "tempt you toward the flood, . . . or to the dreadful summit of the cliff" (act 1, scene 5, lines 72–73). The Ghost will need to provide additional proof of his credibility.

Beyond this, there's the Ghost's purpose to consider. Hearing that his uncle killed his father puts Hamlet into a state of shock and confirms his worst fears. The Ghost needs to develop several other ideas and feelings in Hamlet in order to move him to revenge. So he moves Hamlet through shock to disgust to grief to outrage to pity to national pride to filial duty on the way to moving him to revenge. The emotional journey Hamlet experiences as a result of the Ghost's argument leaves him with a very different mind-set from what he had before.

You can have your students continue to analyze the way the Ghost develops and supports his argument by considering other components of this rhetorical situation:

- What does the Ghost's speech indicate about how well he knows his audience? What does he expect Prince Hamlet to do or feel? How do you know? What kind of relationship did they have?

- How do you evaluate the Ghost's ethos? Is he trustworthy? What do other characters say?

- How would you stage this moment? Is the Ghost spontaneous or conniving? Is this Iago-like trickery or in-the-moment reaction? Calculating or earnest?

- What questions does Hamlet have to consider in this persuasive situation? Which questions does the Ghost answer? Is Prince Hamlet satisfied with those answers?

- How do the structure and strategies of the Ghost's argument reflect his priorities?

- What's most important to the Ghost? Personal vengeance or political justice? Which claims are more fully developed and supported?

- Why do you think the Ghost says, "Taint not your mind against thy mother aught"? What are some possibilities? How does your interpretation of the Ghost's reasons for mentioning Gertrude impact your assessment of the Ghost's ethos?

- Why does Shakespeare have the Ghost suddenly snap out of his rant? What difference do you notice between what the Ghost is saying and what Shakespeare is saying?

- What's the tone of the scene? What feeling do you get? If this scene were in a movie, what kind of music would be playing (if any)?

- What's the narrative purpose of the scene? How does it help develop the plot? How does it build on your understanding of Hamlet's character?

I don't mean to suggest that students just sit down and write answers to these questions individually. The questions are there to model the kind of thinking we do when we engage texts rhetorically. Choose the questions that are right for your students and select a discussion strategy (like Think-Pair-Share or Socratic Seminar) that can help students engage these questions collaboratively.

After working through a full analysis, you could try this follow-up activity to extend students' thinking about the rhetorical possibilities and limitations in this scene from *Hamlet*.

GUIDELINES FOR GHOSTS

Directions to Students: **Create a list of guidelines for ghosts who need to give a family member a message from beyond the grave. What principles and constraints should a ghost keep in mind in order to make the most of their limited opportunities? Using the Ghost's speech in act 1, scene 5 of *Hamlet* as your source of information, generate a list of five key guidelines that can help ghosts deliver rhetorically effective messages.**

Reasoning from Evidence

Many students start their work as literary analysts with the idea that they can say anything they want about a text's meaning as long as they support their interpretation with evidence. Well, sort of. I think this is an inevitable departure point for students on the developmental trajectory of intellectual growth, and I don't want my students to feel that where they are starting is not a good place to be. But I don't want them staying there too long, either. As soon as they're ready, I introduce them to the idea that, while there may be many defensible interpretations of a text, there are also some indefensible ones.

A good lawyer knows when to tell a prospective client that she doesn't have a case. In the same way, a good reader needs to know when there isn't sufficient textual evidence to justify a particular reading of a text's theme. Which means, of course, that students need to know what counts as meaningful, cohesive evidence and how to analyze and interpret it. So, yes, you can say anything about a text as long as you support it, provided you define "support" as "substantiate through informed and responsible close reading and critical reasoning."

When Ginelle was writing her paper on Geoffrey Chaucer's *The Canterbury Tales*, she wanted to make an argument about how the Wife of Bath was an early feminist who rebelled against the gender conventions of her time. But she didn't have any historical evidence for these claims. We talked about what assertions she could reasonably make given the evidence she'd collected.

Ginelle: Back in the day, women had to just stay in the home and take care of their families, so the Wife of Bath is really different.

Me: OK, where do you see that in the text? Show me. Let's go through this together.

Ginelle: There's the husband's quote from the Bible. Here it says, "No man should let his wife go roam about." She's making a pilgrimage, so that shows she's more adventurous than other women.

Me: That's a helpful quotation. But why do you say *more* adventurous? What's your basis for making that comparison?

Ginelle: Well, you never hear about a woman from that time acting the way she acts.

Me: Are you making that claim based on evidence you've found? What *do* you hear about women in this time? How many texts from the period have you read?

Ginelle: So maybe I don't want to compare her. But it does seem like she's totally going against society. Like all those rules and warnings in her husband's book about bad women.

Me: Good! How do we view that book? Can we take it as a representation of society's view? Or do the words and actions of the other characters in *The Canterbury Tales* tell a different story?

Ginelle: I guess the book shows what she has to deal with. Maybe it doesn't represent everyone's view, but it does show the Bible's view and many famous men's views.

Me: Is there anything else significant about the book?

Ginelle: She says women would tell bad stories about men, too, if women wrote books.

Me: Why is that important?

Ginelle: She understands men and women don't have equal power. The women's side isn't being told.

Me: Does she do something about this?

Ginelle: Yes!

By the time we got to this point, Ginelle was on her way to a much more nuanced and defensible argument. Instead of making claims about what other women did during the time period (a subject she hadn't researched), Ginelle was able to reason from her evidence to make a claim about how the Wife of Bath rebelled against men's narratives by telling her own story.

We justify a particular interpretation of a literary work, Graff and Birkenstein note, through "the evidence provided by the work: its images, dialogue, plot, historical references, tone, stylistics details, and so forth" (2014, 194). This is what it means to develop and support a line of reasoning in literary analysis. What I especially love about teaching arguments through literature is the richness of the evidence pool; every word in a poem, play, short story, or novel is a potential data point.

Understanding Warrants

A warrant is a justification. How do you know if a writer has taken a claim too far? Search for the warrants. Warrants help tighten the links in a chain of reasoning by establishing meaningful connections between evidence and claims. Because warrants are typically implied in arguments rather than directly stated, students have to do some digging to uncover them.

Let's look at an example from Ginelle's essay on the Wife of Bath. In an early draft, Ginelle claimed that "the way [The Wife of Bath's Prologue] is written, one can automatically assume that it can be something from the twenty-first century." Her evidence for this claim included the Wife of Bath's frank comments about sexuality in her prologue:

> In wifehood I will use my instrument
> As freely as my Maker has it sent. [150]
> If I hold back, God bring me misery!
> My spouse shall have it day and night, when he
> Desires he may come forth and pay his debt.

I asked Ginelle to justify her use of that evidence as the basis for her claim by completing the "since" statement in Figure 6.4. I also added the word "therefore" to her claim to show her this was the conclusion she was drawing from her evidence:

EVIDENCE →	CLAIM
The Wife of Bath talks freely about sexual pleasure and desire.	Therefore, one can automatically assume The Wife of Bath's Prologue is from the 21st century.
Warrant	
Since …	

FIGURE 6.4
Connecting evidence and claims
Adapted from Rieke, Sillars, and Peterson (2005).

Ginelle tried a couple different responses using "since" as a sentence starter but quickly ran into trouble with the assumptions she was making.

1. The Wife of Bath talks freely about sexual pleasure and desire; therefore, one can automatically assume the Wife of Bath's prologue is from the twenty-first century since talking about sex is a defining characteristic of this period.

2. The Wife of Bath talks freely about sexual pleasure and desire; therefore, one can automatically assume the Wife of Bath's prologue is from the twenty-first century since people didn't talk freely about sex before the twenty-first century.

Neither statement stands up to historical scrutiny. In this case, the claim isn't warranted based on the available evidence. George Hillocks explains a warrant this way: "Such a statement is called a warrant because it explains why data are appropriate in support of a claim. That is, it warrants the data as support for the claim" (2005, 245). The warrant makes a claim reasonable. It's that implicit connection between evidence and claim that makes the audience think, *Yeah, OK, you can say that.*

Another way to get at the justification for a claim is to analyze the premises on which a writer's assertion is based (the idea of a *warrant* comes from Stephen Toulmin [(1958) 2003] while the closely related concept of a *premise* comes from Aristotle). Premises support conclusions. Try this exercise with your students.

Directions to Students: First, read "The Fabric Store" from *Brown Girl Dreaming* by Jacqueline Woodson. Then, choose the best answer for the item.

The Fabric Store

Some Fridays, we walk to downtown Greenville where
there are some clothing stores, some restaurants,
a motel and the five-and-dime store but
my grandmother won't take us
into any of those places anymore.
Even the five-and-dime, which isn't segregated now
but where a woman is paid, my grandmother says,
to follow colored people around in case they try to
steal something. We don't go into the restaurants
because they always seat us near the kitchen.
When we go downtown,
we go to the fabric store, where the white woman
knows my grandmother
from back in Anderson, asks,
How's Gunnar doing and your girls in New York?
She rolls fabric out for my grandmother
to rub between her fingers.
They discuss drape and nap and where to cinch
the waist on a skirt for a child.
At the fabric store, we are not Colored
or Negro. We are not thieves or shameful
or something to be hidden away.
At the fabric store, we're just people. (2014, 90–91)

1. Woodson's assertion that "at the fabric store, we're just people" relies on all of the following premises *except*:

   a. People are treated with respect and dignity.

   b. Being seen as "Colored or Negro" is different from being seen as "just people."

   c. Different contexts and relationships impact how we're viewed by others.

   d. People share a common human identity.

   e. Children see life differently from adults.

2. Which of the following statements best supports Woodson's assertion that "[at the fabric store] we are not thieves or shameful or something to be hidden away"?

   a. "We don't go into the restaurants because they always seat us near the kitchen."

   b. "They discuss drape and nap and where to cinch the waist on a skirt for a child."

   c. "my grandmother won't take us into any of those places anymore."

   d. "a woman is paid, my grandmother says, to follow colored people around in case they try to steal something."

3. Which of the following is *not* implied in the passage?

   a. The woman at the fabric store knows the grandmother's family members by name.

   b. The narrator and her grandmother feel welcome and respected at the fabric store.

   c. The end of segregation didn't automatically result in equal treatment for people of color.

   d. It takes a long time for the narrator and her grandmother to walk to Greenville.

   e. Being seated near the kitchen in a restaurant is a sign of disrespect.

Identifying the assumptions behind the words of other writers enhances students' power as critical readers. Identifying the assumptions behind claims in their own writing is one of the most challenging things we ask students to do. David Takacs, an environmental policy scholar and the author of *The Idea of Biodiversity*, explains why:

> Few things are more difficult than to see outside the bounds of your own perspective—to be able to identify assumptions that you take as universal truths but which, instead, have been crafted by your own unique identity and experiences in the world. (2003, 27)

Woodson's National Book Award–winning novel *Brown Girl Dreaming* makes this point eloquently.

Distinguishing Between Data and Claims

I want students to make the most of their opportunities. So if students open a section of an essay with a statement that doesn't do a lot of work for their argument, I'll often ask if they can connect that statement more directly to their line of reasoning. One of my students wrote the following topic sentence for his essay on Sandra Cisneros's *The House on Mango Street* (1989): "One character that stands out is Esperanza." Nothing wrong with that aside from a missed opportunity. I encouraged him to rewrite the sentence as an analytical claim and see which version of the sentence does the best job developing his argument. Here's the revision: "Esperanza stands out as a character who knows the importance of her identity."

DATUM OR CLAIM?

To help students see the choices they have for developing their arguments, I ask them to practice discerning between data and claims. Claim-forward topic sentences can help readers anticipate a writer's next move.

> *Directions to Students*: Identify each statement as either a datum (i.e., a piece of evidence) or a claim requiring support.
>
> (The sample exercise is based on the novel *Bless Me, Ultima*, by Rudolfo Anaya [1972].)
>
> 1.   Antonio is the protagonist of Rudolfo Anaya's novel.
>
> 2.   Antonio's complex sentence structure and mature vocabulary are primary means by which Anaya signals his protagonist's exceptionality.
>
> 3.   Diction is used throughout the passage.
>
> 4.   One technique Anaya uses to create a sense of frenzied chaos at Antonio's new school is collapsed, or enjambed, syntax; words in this passage rush headlong into other words without spaces to distinguish them.
>
> 5.   As the youngest child in his family, Antonio is the last to leave home for school.
>
> 6.   Imagery is another technique Anaya uses in this passage.
>
> 7.   Anaya's rapid, kaleidoscopic scan of the school playground provides a stark contrast to the quiet, meditative nature of his young protagonist.
>
> 8.   Although he does not understand English, Antonio feels relieved when "Red" offers to help him on his first day of school.
>
> 9.   From the myriad details and frenetic pace of Anaya's description, the reader can infer that the hyperperceptive Antonio undergoes sensory overload on his first day of school.
>
> 10.   Anaya also uses the cultural differences evident in the children's lunches to illustrate how disorienting and isolating the first day at a new school can be to a sensitive, nonnative speaker like Antonio.

Although I don't have any hard and fast rules for the kinds of topic sentences students should write, I do want students to be able to evaluate the effects of their rhetorical choices, especially the ways those moves advance their argument. A writer's moves should create movement.

Understanding Backing

What if someone in the audience challenges your ideas? Then we need to be able to back up our evidence with more substantial support. Toulmin calls this "backing" ([1958] 2003). Not all rhetorical situations call for this extra level of persuasion. As J. Vernon Jensen notes in *Argumentation: Reasoning in Communication*, "If the audience accepts the warrant, then there is no need to back it up" (1981, 55).

Backing responds to the question *How do you know?* Have you listened to an elementary school student with an iPhone question Siri lately? I have. It's fascinating. They can spin out an almost endless chain of questions.

My own two monkeys, ages nine and eleven at the time, had this scintillating exchange as I was driving them to school one day:

Dryden: How much wood would a woodchuck chuck if a woodchuck could chuck wood?

Ellerie: About two trees because that's all he'd need for food and shelter.

Dryden: How do you know?

Ellerie: I read it.

Dryden: Where's your proof?

Ellerie: I don't carry it with me.

Dryden: Why not?

Ellerie: No room.

And so on.

Whether my kids were genuinely interested in teasing out the logic behind this enduring question or just in teasing each other, I don't know, but I was impressed by their persistence and invention. This is the kind of dogged inquiry we want our students to practice when they apply their critical reasoning skills to a reading or writing task, especially when it's time for them to evaluate the logic behind their own arguments. *How do you know?* should be the insistent question of the voice in their heads.

We know what we know through our life experiences, both in school and outside of school. Surfacing our ways of knowing—and understanding how our unique journeys lead us to take particular positions on issues—is an important part of what we do when we examine the backing for a claim. Backing is a transformative concept for students to learn because it links knowledge to identity. I know what I know because I am a mother / a scientist / an immigrant / a teacher / a historian / a rabbi. Backing is generated and constrained by lived experiences.

Rieke, Sillars, and Peterson (2005) define backing as *"any support (specific instances, statistics, testimony, values, or credibility) that provides more specific data for the grounds or warrant"* (2005, 100; italics in original). Backing is the enriched support we bring in when the lightweight stuff isn't cutting it. Like infielders who call on their outfielders to back them up as they go for a ball, rhetors bring in backing as an extra line of defense. Bringing in additional disciplinary expertise and ways of knowing provides needed reinforcement.

The concept of backing thus has implications for how well we know what our sources know when we cite them in academic papers. Quoting from sources can sometimes be a little like the telephone game, especially if students are quoting a teacher's or writer's paraphrase of another source. If you haven't read what I've read, I tell students, you probably shouldn't quote my opinions on those texts.

Some questions to get students thinking about backing:

- What background does the reader need to understand this issue?
- What would you say to people who disagree with your position?
- Do you need additional historical or biographical evidence to make this claim?
- Why do you believe that? What makes you say so?
- Will your audience just accept this or will they challenge you, and if they do, how will you respond?
- How many writers would you need to read to make this claim?

BACKING BOOK TALKS

Backing book talks helps students see the importance of *depth* of knowledge—depth being the whole idea of backing and a necessary condition for transfer of learning. We don't back up our claims with superficial beginner's knowledge; we back up claims with mature expertise. Here's how you can show students what it looks like if they *don't* have the backing to lend extra support to their claims.

Directions to Teachers: Bring in a random selection of SparkNotes *or* CliffsNotes *guides on books your students have* not *read. (I know, I know—if there's a SparkNotes for it, it's almost a guarantee that your students haven't read the actual book.) You'll be distributing these notes guides to your students for the second part of the activity.*

Directions to Students:

Step 1: First, give a brief book talk to your peers on your favorite book of all time. It could be a novel, children's book, graphic novel, sports biography, or any other book you love. Give a brief description of the book and say why you think it's so great and everyone should read it.

Step 2: Now give a book talk on a book you've never read before using only the notes guide your teacher gives you or one you find yourself online. Describe the book's best qualities and explain why your peers should read it (you'll have to wing this based on what you read in the notes guide.) Good luck.

Step 3: Quick-write: What does it mean to really know something? How is a deep understanding of something different from a surface understanding?

Note: While your peers give their book talks, use a T-chart to compare the two talks, noting differences in ethos, pathos, and logos.

Another activity that lets students experience what a *lack* of backing feels like is a PowerPoint Swap. This could work as a fun, whole-class demonstration with a few volunteers or as a low-stakes pairs activity. It's best to keep the tone light and friendly so that students don't feel like they're being mocked for their ignorance.

> **Transfer of learning depends on deep conceptual and procedural knowledge. Backing is deep knowledge.**

POWERPOINT SWAP

Directions to Students: Give a PowerPoint presentation using a PowerPoint you did *not* create on a subject that's unfamiliar to you. This could be one of your teacher's PowerPoints or you could swap presentations with another student. As you try to present, pay attention to what it feels like to make statements based on only a partial or surface understanding of the subject. After presenting, debrief the activity, sharing what you noticed about having to make claims about a text when you can't back your assertions with deep knowledge.

(These activities also show students why we have to read the whole book.)

Testing Thesis Statements

A thesis statement is a writer's central claim. In my view, the time to check a thesis is after students have composed their drafts. One of my students reminded me of how important it can be to withhold initial judgments about students' introductions or thesis statements. In his reflective quick-write, George wrote, "I usually have no idea where to start. I can't remember the last time I didn't change how I'd started after writing the rest of the draft."

The following activity is based on thesis statements I pulled from students' interpretive argument essays on the novel *Bless Me, Ultima* (Anaya 1972) after they had completed their first draft.

BLESS ME, ULTIMA: VAGUE, NARROW, OR OK THESIS STATEMENTS

Adapted from an exercise in *Composition and Literature: A Rhetoric for Critical Writing* (Grassi and De Blois 1984, 132–134)

Directions to Students: Identify each of the following thesis statements as "vague," "narrow," or "OK." Remember, a vague thesis leaves key terms unspecified and is often so general it could refer to any work of literature. A narrow thesis is too simplistic and often focuses on an easily answered question about plot, setting, or character (e.g., "The play is about the main character's desire for revenge."). In other words, the narrow thesis is an obvious statement about the text that requires little argument or proof. The OK, or effective, thesis makes a defensible and focused claim in precise language about a complex textual issue.

1. Through the imagery, the author illustrates the theme. [vague]

2. Antonio's formal speech and sophisticated thought processes reveal him to be an unusually mature and intelligent boy. [OK]

3. By using a third-person omniscient narrator, Anaya allows the reader to experience the fear that overwhelms his sensitive protagonist on Antonio's first day of school. [OK]

4. Anaya's syntax demonstrates several ways that Antonio is different from the other students. [vague]

5. Antonio does not speak any English and has never been to school before. [narrow]

6. The chaotic imagery of the boisterous students and the rushed syntax of this passage perform the confusion and anxiety Antonio experiences on his first day of school and reveal him to be an exceptionally perceptive boy. [OK]

7. Anaya's vivid imagery, syntax, and diction paint a picture of Antonio's first day of school and reveal several of Antonio's unique characteristics. [vague]

Notice, for instance, how no. 5 is a narrow thesis because it reports a fact; you don't really need anything else to back up this statement. In contrast, no. 6 is a precise claim that cries out for support: in other words, a solid thesis. Furthermore, by bringing in stasis theory, we can see that the problem with the vague thesis statements is that the subject matter is not at issue. Without a point of disagreement, we have no reason to argue.

Making Choices About Arrangement

A rhetorical approach treats the structure of an essay, to use John T. Gage's words, as "something that is *generated* by the writer rather than as something *imposed* on the writer" (2000, xiii; italics in original). Don't try to follow someone else's formula, Gage tells students, reminding them that "form follows function." It's the writers' job to figure out the patterns and purposes of their compositions based on their own process of inquiry. Until we've sifted through the evidence, we don't know what our arguments are going to say or do yet.

Writers use a variety of strategies to develop their ideas in an essay: for example, analogy, cause and effect, compare and contrast, definition, illustration, description, narrative, and hypothesis. Writing rhetorically entails making thoughtful choices about such strategies. William Brandt explains, "The parts of an argument, and their effective ordering, is an important consideration in rhetoric" (1970, 16). The classical word for the process of determining the structure and order of an argument is *arrangement*.

In writing on the importance of structure and organization, Peter Elbow reminds us that effective writing gives readers "an *experience* of coherence and clarity" (2000, 163; italics in original); that is, it offers a felt sense of movement between anticipation and resolution. Elbow says we can give arguments a narrative feel by engaging readers in the story of our thinking (2000).

Students can make choices about the arrangement of their ideas and the experience they want to create for their readers by answering the questions Elbow poses:

- Where does this thinking start?
- Where is it going?
- What is the goal? (2000, 163)

These questions help students to think of their writing as a journey through time.

Foregrounding the importance of arrangement can move students away from treating an essay or a paragraph as a bag of stuff. Early drafts (including my own) often fit this description. I've seen essay drafts that were a bag of stuff about lying or a bag of stuff about women writers. (And I've written a bag of stuff about teaching literature rhetorically.) When a student shares a draft that hasn't yet been arranged in a strategic order, I can say, "OK, that bag of stuff is your evidence collection. You have a lot of data on women writers from different periods and countries who wrote in a lot of different genres on a lot of different subjects. So what are the connections and patterns? And what are the implications?" Writers need to do the organizational thinking for their readers.

Of course, the other big problem is when arrangement is treated as a matter of just following a predetermined formula. The five-paragraph essay isn't a rhetorical approach to a writing task because it skips the critical process of invention—that is, of finding the best available means of persuasion, including choices concerning arrangement.

Development Moves

In the best writing, a writer's moves give a text movement. These moves are directional as well as strategic. There are lots of ways to think about moves like concessions or counterarguments, but I especially like to think of these as development moves—ways to extend thinking rather than just add-on items to boost a writer's logic quotient.

There are moments when texts say, "See where this is going?" (sometimes in these exact words). If our students don't see where the text is going, we need to help them anticipate and recognize writers' development moves and make effective choices in their own compositions.

Concessions

Practicing the art of conceding helps students get on the ambiguity roller coaster. If they've started out on one trajectory in their interpretation, see whether you can get them to do an about-face. In a skillful demonstration of how to make a rhetorical concession, Gerald Graff and Cathy Birkenstein say of the warrant, for instance, "Although such concepts can be useful, we believe most of us learn the ins and outs of argumentative writing not by studying logical principles in the abstract, but by plunging into actual discussions and debates" (2014, xxv).

One common move in academic argumentation is to start with a concession. This opening gambit says, "OK, OK, I know I'm crazy / stubborn / old-fashioned / in left field / whatever, but hear me out." Watch how Deborah Appleman effects this move in *Critical Encounters in High School English*, her book about teaching literary theory to high school students: "In the face of today's turbulence and the seemingly urgent need for pragmatic education, it seems almost ludicrous to suggest that the study of literary theory could have any relevance to the education of young people" (2000, 1). Appleman's concession of her subject's seeming absurdity disarms readers of potential objections to her claims before she has even made them.

Wait for It . . .

The opening concession, as experienced readers know, is typically followed by a strategic shift that introduces the writer's thesis. After candidly admitting significant obstacles to persuasion, the writer goes ahead and makes his or her argument anyway. I tell students if you see the words "seems" or "appears" in the opening paragraphs of a text, watch out. The writer may be setting you up for a fall.

As readers, we experience movement through time directly when we anticipate an impending turn or counterpoint. When Thomas Newkirk, for instance, writes in *Minds Made for Stories* that Louise Rosenblatt "attempted to deal with [the] question" of the differences, if any, between reading informational and aesthetic texts, my reader radar is instantly alerted to the fact that he has used the word "attempted," and I immediately sense where we're going next—that Newkirk will say Rosenblatt's attempt was not a total success. I'm not surprised, therefore, when a few lines down the page, Newkirk makes his turn, asking, "But is that the way reading works?" (2014, 12). I've already moved ahead with him in time, imagining his next move as a writer.

You can encourage your students to try opening one of their own essays with a concession. Applying insights gained through reader experiences to their own writing is the kind of transfer that empowers students as communicators.

Starting with a Refutation

Here's an old and easy one although it can be an ethos trap: starting with a refutation. This was one of my favorite devices in my undergraduate days, as the following excerpt from one of my old essay introductions shows:

> Thomas Marc Parrott, a professor of English at Princeton University,
> wrote in his preface to William Shakespeare's comedy, *As You Like It*,

that this play "presents few problems of interest to the critical student"
and that "it is a play to be enjoyed rather than analyzed" (Parrott 515).
This preface, first drafted in 1938, would likely be refuted by most
contemporary Shakespearean scholars, and it seems probable that the
playwright himself would have had difficulty supporting Professor Parrott's
conclusions. Although *As You Like It* is a delightful text that is admittedly
less problematic than such works as *The Merchant of Venice* or *Measure for
Measure*, it serves as such a rich exploration of the transitory nature of
perception that it can hardly be deemed unworthy of rigorous study.

The problem with starting with a refutation is that you need to have enough juice in your
ethos to pull it off, something I didn't understand myself as a new college student. I imagine
my professors winced more than a few times whenever I tried to refute the claims of scholars
I didn't actually know anything about.

Counterarguments

Can I really take this person on? Do I have enough status or credibility myself to disagree
with one of the big names in the field? If I'm a newcomer or a student, how can I present my
ethos in a way that seems reasonable and self-aware? How can I make myself heard? Can I
make my unknown status an asset in my argument? Can I use a David and Goliath approach?

We can encourage students to have courage and speak their truth while also anticipating
the impact of their words and the way their ethos might help or hinder them in achieving
their purpose. These questions help students think through their strategy for developing
and supporting an argument through counterarguments:

- What do your other sources say?
- What role do you play in this rhetorical situation?
- What role does the source you're challenging play?
- How much evidence do you have for your counterargument?

By the way, addressing a counterargument may not always be an appropriate move. Interpretive arguments about literature are frequently developed through other means than
counterarguments.

The "We're Not Done Yet" Move

This move works for expository writing and for literary writing that calls for social action:
it's the "we're not done yet" move. After acknowledging and celebrating shared achievements,
this development move takes a turn toward a future course of action, calling for audience

members to build on the momentum of past successes. I encountered this move in an e-mail from my faculty union:

> We are proud of the contract that we just won, but we realize that the salary improvements were only a small step towards correcting many years of frozen salaries and growing salary inequities. To help fix these issues, we will be reopening negotiations on salary in May. In order to most effectively represent you at these negotiations, CFA is collecting data on the effects of salary stagnation on faculty lives through a survey. It is very important that we collect as much information and as many individual stories as possible. E-mail to CFA members from Steven Levinson, chapter president, California Facility Association, Monterey Bay Chapter, on February 24, 2015.

We also see characters make this move in literary texts—like when the Ghost returns to remind Hamlet of his unfinished business.

A Narrative

Stories contain their own internal movement but also function to shape expository arguments in important ways (as was the case with the Ghost's retelling of his murder in the garden). A narrative creates a *kairotic* experience—a special moment in a text that heightens the reader's sense of being fully present in the writer's world and journeying with the writer toward a new understanding. Adding a narrative can be a powerful way to move an argument forward.

The List with a Twist

The "list with a twist" is a subspecies of the rhetorical twist I describe in Chapter 2, "Reading Closely and Critically" (remember the Haunted Mansion portraits?). This is that head fake writers pull through an abrupt change in direction. The ability to anticipate, recognize, and deploy this move enhances students' transfer opportunities between reading and writing, as well as between literary and informational texts.

See what you notice about how Thanhha Lai deploys this move in *Inside Out and Back Again* (2011), a novel in verse about a young girl's journey from Saigon to Alabama at the end of the Vietnam War. The excerpt that follows describes the moment when the narrator, ten-year-old Hà, prepares to flee the fallen city with her family:

Choice

Into each pack:
one pair of pants,
the pair of shorts,

three pairs of underwear,
two shirts,
sandals,
toothbrush and paste,
soap,
ten palms of rice grains,
three clumps of cooked rice,
one choice.

I choose my doll,
once lent to a neighbor
who left it outside,
where mice bit
her left cheek
and right thumb.

I love her more
for her scars.

I dress her
in a red and white dress
with matching hat and booties
that Mother knitted.

April 27

In this example, the movement is from the practical to the deeply poignant. The two-word line "one choice" is the pivot point in this chapter, the moment that makes clear the enormity of the narrator's loss in leaving her home and country. The choice of a doll, too, as the one precious and nonessential item Hà carries with her emphasizes the pain and vulnerability of children in times of war. As with the Stretching Portrait Poems activity I share in Chapter 2, reading and writing this kind of rhetorical twist helps students understand that texts often end up in very different places from where they start—and that the most significant meanings often follow the shift.

Seeing the setup and knowing what will follow is part of being a fluent reader. One of my students shared his excitement that he'd independently noticed a shift in a writer's choices: in this case, a series of long, complex sentences in a paragraph, capped off by a surprisingly short sentence. "I finally caught it," he said with a look of satisfaction. When students try something like the "list with a twist" in their own writing, I find they're far more likely to recognize that move in others' writing.

Qualifiers

Protective older brother Laertes tells Ophelia, the "best safety lies in fear" (*Hamlet*). This may not have been welcome advice to Ophelia, but it is a good tip for writers. Knowing our argument's vulnerable spots and qualifying our assertions accordingly can be an important development move. Assertions are more defensible when they're qualified. Sometimes a qualification deserves a significant chunk of an argument's real estate. If students have made a sweeping generalization that could get them into trouble with their audience, I'll ask, "Do you want to qualify this claim?" My student who claimed that every parent in the world should read *Romeo and Juliet* to understand today's teenagers better was in danger of basing her argument on several fallacies, including sweeping generalization, false analogy, and hasty conclusion. She needed to add a whole section on the play's context to deal with this issue. Lesson learned: We can argue for a text's enduring relevance without overstating its connections to our own time or ignoring its historical differences.

Note: Words like *often, sometimes, may, might, can, could, some,* and *many* can help walk an argument back when it wanders too far out on a limb.

Creating Cohesion and Coherence

Do you find yourself writing the following kind of feedback on your students' papers?

"How is this paragraph related to your thesis?"

"How does this example support your claim?"

"Transition needed."

"What's the logical relationship here?"

"How did you get to this idea?"

Writers create cohesion and coherence by practicing integrative thinking. When writing lacks cohesion, it's usually because "everything is cooked separate," as Huck Finn would say. Logic is a matter of relationships.

To continue the cooking metaphor (the same metaphor, by the way, that Peter Elbow uses to describe the composition process in *Writing Without Teachers* [2000]), I'd like to use an example from one of my favorite Food Network shows: *Chopped.* The premise behind the show is as simple as it is entertaining. Contestants are given a basket of mystery ingredients and have to assemble something fabulous from their available resources in a limited amount of time. How rhetorical. Writers face the same basic setup. We get our metaphorical basket of cheese curls, apple cider, and peppermints and have to find a way to turn it into a cohesive and enjoyable experience for our judges.

The secret to composing a successful dish or text is finding the connections between the ingredients. In writing, those connections largely happen through transitions. Transitions serve not just to hold together the text but also to hold together the reader's experience—that movement through time that Peter Elbow (2000) and Thomas Newkirk (2014) describe.

Transitions help readers and writers navigate texts. They're a response to the following kinds of writerly questions:

- How do I get from one paragraph to the next?
- How do I connect these ideas?
- How do I keep my reader with me?

At their most effective, transitions tighten the logic in a chain of reasoning. Transitions such as the student favorite "with this in mind" don't tell me much about the logical relationship between ideas. There's some connection there—that's why we're thinking about both ideas—but the nature of the connection is left unspecified. I try to help students think strategically about the work their transitions do to advance the logic of their arguments.

Building Cohesion Through Signal Words and Key Terms
WORD TILES FOR "TO BUILD A FIRE"

Word Tiles is a sorting strategy that encourages students to work out the logical connections among terms or ideas. For this activity, students physically manipulate the individual tiles into groups or piles of their choosing. (I find it saves time to cut out the word tiles for students in advance.) See the example on Jack London's short story "To Build a Fire (1908)."

> *Directions to Students:* On the following page, there are several words that appear in Jack London's short story "To Build a Fire." First, cut out each word to create individual tiles if this hasn't already been done for you. Then, sort the word tiles into your own categories. Next, record your groupings and your reasons for grouping them on a separate sheet of paper. Try grouping the words in three different ways, and record your thinking each time.

cold	judgment	then
gray	menacing	on the other hand
dim	fire	if
pall	warmth	safe
gloom	frost	fault
ice	Sixty Mile	mistake
snow	camp	next
Dawson	danger	quickly
Bering Sea	but	this
frailty	yet	however
immortality	also	battle
instinct	when	panic

MAKING SIGNAL WORDS VISIBLE

In addition, students can study how other writers create logical coherence through a close reading of a text's structure.

Directions to Students: Sometimes signal words are implied rather than directly stated. In the passage from "To Build a Fire," signal words have been added in brackets to clarify the causal relationship London establishes in this pivotal scene. Read the passage and then discuss the questions that follow with a partner.

But before he could cut the strings, it happened. It was his own fault or, rather, his mistake. He should not have built the fire under the spruce tree. He should have built it in the open. But it had been easier to pull the twigs from the brush and drop them directly on the fire. Now the tree under which he had done this carried a weight of snow on its boughs. No wind had blown for weeks, and [hence] each bough was fully freighted. Each time he had pulled a twig he [consequently] had communicated a slight agitation to the tree—an imperceptible agitation, so far as he was concerned, but an agitation sufficient to bring about the disaster. [Thus] High up in the tree one bough capsized its load of snow. This [in turn] fell on the boughs beneath, capsizing them. This process [then] continued, spreading out and involving the whole tree. It grew like an avalanche, and it descended without warning upon the man and the fire, and the fire was [thereby] blotted out! [As a result] Where it had burned was a mantle of fresh and disordered snow.

Note the different logical implications of the signal words.

- Which words suggest a conclusive cause-and-effect relationship?

- Which words indicate a probable cause-and-effect relationship?

- Which words suggest innate or essential causality (i.e., cause-and-effect relationships that are determined by general principle and not merely sequence or circumstances)?

- Which words suggest conditional causality (i.e., cause-and-effect relationships that vary according to sequence or circumstances)?

- What other key words indicate the extent of the man's responsibility?

Now turn and talk to an elbow partner about these questions and what you noticed when you read the passage.

LOGIC HAIKUS

I created this activity to help students see how transition words function in a text. The compact form of the haiku offers a thumbnail of how the logical moves work together.

Directions to Students: Create a haiku for each of the sets of logical transitions that follow. As you write your poem, pay attention to how the transitions, or "signal words," structure your thinking.

Example: *First, we plant the seed*
                     Then, we water, watch, and wait.
                     Finally, we eat.

Yes
And
So

Granted
Admittedly
But

If
Or
Then

First
Then
Now

Consider
So too
Thus

The following examples come from a sixth-grade class:

Granted, you may thrive.
Admittedly, you may fail.
But you were warned first.

First you go to school.
Then you do very well in school.
Now you can have a job.

The poems help students to notice moves that do different work in a text how and also how they work together.

Conclusion

A significant aspect of learning to write rhetorically is the ability to determine how the structure, content, and development of a composition meet the demands of a particular rhetorical situation. In determining the length and organization of their compositions, students must evaluate the effectiveness of their choices for their given audience and purpose. In this manner, students practice key competencies of the Common Core State Standards, such as the ability to "develop claims(s) and counterclaims fairly and thoroughly" (CCSS. ELA-Literacy.W.11-12.1b), "create cohesion" (CCSS.ELA-Literacy.W.11-12.1c), "develop the topic thoroughly" (CCSS.ELA-Literacy.W.11-12.2b), and "produce clear and coherent writing in which the development, organization, and style are appropriate to task, purpose, and audience" (CCSS.ELA-Literacy.W.11-12.4). In deciding what constitutes *thorough* development, a *unified* whole, and *coherent* writing *appropriate* to task, purpose, and audience, students exercise the critical judgment necessary to write in a variety of genres and disciplines at the postsecondary level. The mental agility required for these decisions is the basis for transferable learning.

CHAPTER SEVEN

Communicating with Self and Others in Mind

When we ask students to think for themselves and to understand themselves as thinkers—rather than telling them what to think and have them recite it back—we help foster habits of introspection, analysis, and open, joyous communication.

—DAVID TAKACS

It was bedtime at our house, and my thirteen-year-old son didn't want to put down his book and turn off the light. The book was Edward Bloor's novel *Tangerine* (1997), and Dryden was almost to the end.

"This book is getting *good*," he said, then added with a sly look, "but it's a school book."

"So?" I asked.

"If it's a school book, it's the worst book in the world."

I gave him a teacher look. "Because?"

"It's homework," Dryden said. Nothing more to explain.

I. A. Richards calls rhetoric the "study of misunderstanding and its remedies" ([1936] 1965, 3). What we have here is a misunderstanding. Novels like *Tangerine* don't say, "Finish me by Friday, or you'll get a zero." They say, "Listen to me. I am telling you a story." But students don't always hear this message because they're not thinking about books as voices in an ongoing conversation or about their own roles in this interchange of ideas. A school book is just an assignment.

This same assignment-centric thinking also dominates when it's time for students to write in school. Until something or someone helps them flip the switch from the writer's to the reader's perspective, many students complete academic tasks as if they're going to be machine-scored. They don't yet see texts as acts of communication between real human beings. This chapter is about flipping that switch, about turning the spotlight on identity, audience, and the reader-writer relationship, so that students communicate with self and others in mind. Ethical and effective communication is the master practice that makes all other forms of collaborative problem solving possible.

In his work on rhetoric and literature, James Phelan says that a rhetorical approach's "only major initial commitment is to the idea that authors design texts as purposive communicative actions" (2010, 227). Teaching literature rhetorically means teaching literature as communication. When we focus on the communicative purposes and practices of writers, readers, texts, and literary characters, we help students understand that they're not just completing assignments; they're developing communication skills they'll use throughout their academic, professional, and personal lives.

Transfer of Learning

It's become a commonplace to say that good communication skills are necessary for success in life. But every day we see abundant evidence that tells us good communication doesn't just happen. That's because ethical and effective communication depends on a sophisticated awareness of how various identities and value systems function in rhetorical situations. These include the speaker's or writer's identity, the complex individual and collective identities of audience members, and the needs and values of all participants in a conversation. The idea of *the rhetor*, in particular—the speaker or writer—is a key concept for transfer of learning. *Audience* is also an essential transfer term (Yancey, Robertson, and Taczak 2014).

When communication goes wrong, it's usually because these interdependent factors have been overlooked—a lesson United Airlines CEO Oscar Muñoz learned the hard way. Muñoz's inept response to the forcible removal of a passenger from an overbooked UA flight in April 2017 was widely panned on social media for its insensitivity to UA's customers. The airline's initial insistence that it was justified in ejecting the passenger because he refused to leave the plane didn't satisfy people who saw video of the limp and bloody man being dragged down the aisle. On the ensuing public relations disaster, communications specialist Sam Singer had this to say: "Denying someone else's emotional response to a situation only makes customers, the public and the media even angrier and more outraged" (Diaz 2017). Muñoz's apology, when it finally came, was a day late and a dollar short.

Achieving a deep understanding of the complex roles people play in acts of communication represents a major threshold crossing for learners (take note, CEOs). This understanding also helps students apply their learning in diverse contexts. Two of the key principles in *Understanding Writing Transfer*, one of the books to come out of Elon University's research seminar on critical transitions and the question of transfer, stress the importance of audience and identity (Moore and Bass 2017):

- Successful writing transfer requires transforming or repurposing prior knowledge (even if only slightly) for a new context *to adequately meet the expectations of new audiences* and fulfill new purposes for writing.

- Students' dispositions (e.g., habits of mind) and *identities* inform the success of their unique writing transfer experience. (2017, 4–7; emphasis added)

Although these principles specify writing transfer, I've found they apply equally to students' reading experiences and skills. Thinking about themselves as the audience for texts, for instance, deepens students' understanding of audience knowledge, expectations, and needs. Likewise, the ability to recognize and analyze different identity components—both their own and others'—helps students as writers and readers.

Identity Impacts Understanding

If you've ever been in a fight with someone, you probably have a good sense of the way identity impacts understanding. Why are our versions of events so different? What influences our interpretation of a situation? Our understanding of a conflict is directly related to the role we play in that situation. The possible scenarios are endless: advocate, ally, or target; older sibling or younger sibling; novice or expert; parent or child; buyer or seller; teacher or student; friend, acquaintance, or partner; accuser or accused. How we see ourselves in a particular context profoundly shapes our perception of the exchange.

Especially with people we care about, we might be willing to just agree to disagree because we don't want to damage our relationship. Jessica, one of my students, wrote about her frustration with family disagreements: "I always tone down my own opinion and almost pretend that I'm on their side, so we can just stop talking about it." When we can't communicate across our differences, we disengage. This is why a narrow focus on argumentation as claims supported by logical reasoning and evidence doesn't move us far enough toward the dialogic and deliberative decision-making practices needed to solve twenty-first-century problems. We can pile up reason on top of reason, but if something in our character or personal history blocks us from understanding each other, then the exercise of our logic is futile.

Communication scholars Josina Makau and Debian Marty caution against the harmful effects of embedding argument instruction in poor communication habits "that actually diminish [students'] understanding of themselves and their world": for instance, teaching students "to view those who disagree as opponents" or "to reject reflecting on or reconsidering their own assumptions, ideas, and beliefs" (2013, 13). We need to consider more than just how a series of "true" statements might lead to a rational conclusion; we need to consider the complex psychosocial factors that contribute to ethical and effective communication.

These factors are also crucial in literary analysis. Compare, for example, Tybalt's feelings of resentment and bitterness in *Romeo and Juliet* to Iago's in *Othello*. Each character has his own particular needs and motives, and our insights into what makes one character tick only get us a small way toward understanding the other character. Tybalt's resentment arises from his pride and partisanship as a Capulet; Iago's resentment arises from his sense of neglect as Othello's captain and whatever other mysterious malevolence motivates the man who says "I am not what I am." The role Tybalt plays in his family is different from the role Iago plays in the military. Each villain's unique identity and brand of resentment requires a customized character analysis.

One of the threshold concepts in Linda Adler-Kassner and Elizabeth Wardle's *Naming What We Know* speaks directly to this idea—that "writing enacts and creates identities and ideologies" (2015, 48). Writing and reading express and shape our various social roles and beliefs. We can help students better understand themselves and others as thinkers and communicators by asking them to do some identity work.

Doing Identity Work

In my classes, doing identity work starts with telling students that their identities matter. The following are some of the opening gambits I use to send this message; all work nicely as icebreakers and community builders. I've found that the more time I spend getting to know my students, the more I can help them.

NAME STORIES

I've noticed how much easier it is for me to remember new students' names after hearing the story of how they were given or acquired their name. I've also noticed that more students speak up in class earlier in the semester when I start the term with this activity. By telling the story of their name, students seem to claim a space for themselves in the classroom. They belong because they are known.

> **Directions to Students:** In a five-minute quick-write, tell the story of how you got your name. You may choose to write about the name on your birth certificate or your nickname. Be prepared to share your name story with the class.

PHONE PICTURES

Phone picture stories are another way I invite students to explore their personal identities (thank you, Vanessa Lopez-Littleton, for teaching me this strategy). The first time I tried this strategy I was surprised and touched by how much I learned about my students from just one picture.

Directions to Students: Choose a picture on your phone that represents a significant memory. Share your picture with the class, telling us why that picture is important to you.

WALK-UP MUSIC

The entrance music used by Major League Baseball players when they step up to the batter's box or pitching mound tells fans a lot about the image a player wants to project. Walk-up music is part of a baseball player's ethos—that mindfully constructed public self that rhetoricians Edward P. J. Corbett and Robert J. Connors describe in *The Elements of Reasoning* (2000). You might start this activity by sharing examples of walk-up music used by current MLB players. Then ask students to choose their own walk-up music and describe in a quick-write how their choice represents values and personal qualities that are important to them (see Figure 7.1).

Directions to Students: What would your walk-up music be if you were a Major League Baseball player? In a ten-minute quick-write, describe what song you would choose to be your personal entrance music and how this song represents your identity or "ethos." After writing your quick-write, if possible, play a clip of the music you've chosen for the class and explain why that song is an appropriate choice for you.

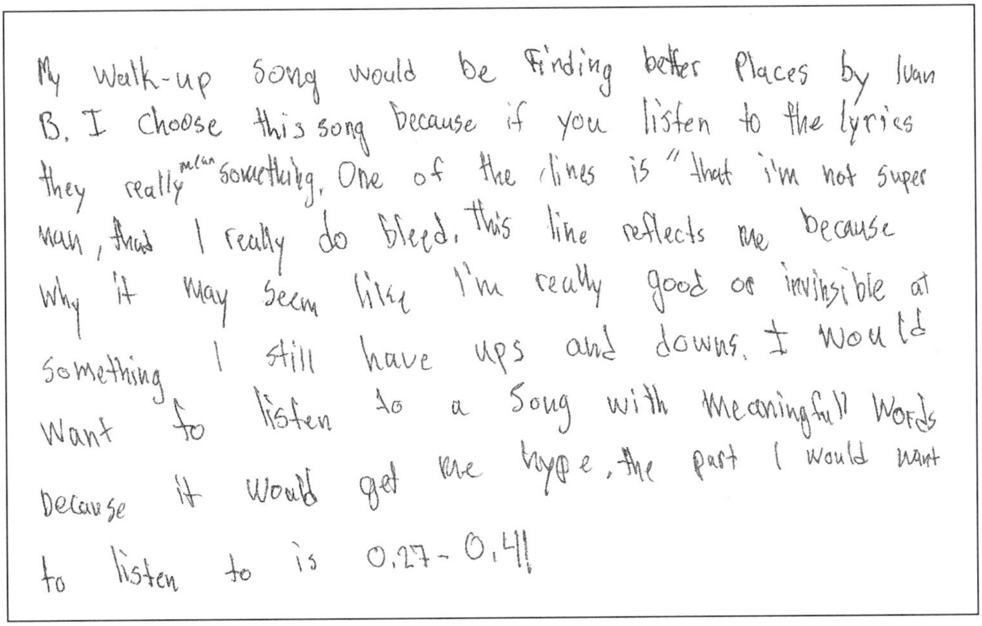

My Walk-up song would be Finding better places by Ivan B. I choose this song because if you listen to the lyrics they really mean something. One of the lines is "that i'm not super man, that I really do bleed, this line reflects me because why it may seem like I'm really good or invisible at something I still have ups and downs. I would want to listen to a Song with Meaningful Words because it would get me hype, the part I would want to listen to is 0.27 - 0.41

FIGURE 7.1
Student Walk-Up Music

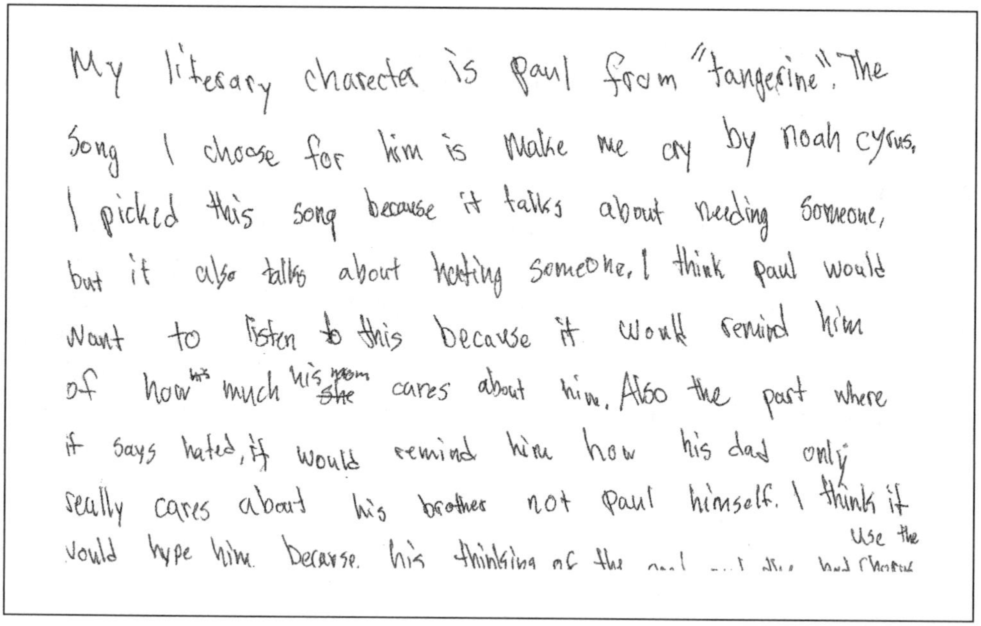

My literary charecter is Paul from "tangerine". The
Song I choose for him is Make me cry by noah cyrus.
I picked this song because it talks about needing someone,
but it also talks about hurting someone, I think paul would
want to listen to this because it would remind him
of how much his mom cares about him. Also the part where
it says hated, it would remind him how his dad only
really cares about his brother not Paul himself. I think it
would hype him because his thinking of the ....

FIGURE 7.2
Walk-Up Music for a Fictional Character

If you have a class that buys into this idea, you can even have students play their walk-up music throughout the semester or year whenever they come up to the front of the room to give presentations. Alternatively, you could ask students to choose walk-up music for a fictional character from a literary text and explain why this music is an appropriate representation of the character. (See Figure 7.2.)

"I" STATEMENTS

Another community-builder I use is Katie Egan Cunningham's "I" statements (2015) from her book *Story: Still the Heart of Literacy Learning*. I like to have everyone write their responses to the four sentence starters below and just have folks share out as the spirit moves them. This is a good activity to do when the class is sitting in a circle.

I am happy . . .

I love it . . .

I remember . . .

I am frustrated . . .

Sharing my own responses gives me a chance to open up, too:

- I am happy when my kids giggle together in the backseat when I'm driving.

- I love it when my husband brings me coffee on vacation.

- I remember when my dad told us about my mom's skiing accident.

- I am frustrated by my inability to do more than one thing well at a time.

Even though we're just sharing little blurbs about ourselves through these activities, we're getting to know each other better and helping everyone to feel more comfortable in our classroom. These activities also affirm the personal knowledge and experiences we all bring to our learning community. Community and communication go hand in hand. As one of my colleagues likes to say, "The quality of the communication affects the quality of the community."

READING LIST INTRODUCTIONS

In Mary Shelley's *Frankenstein* ([1818] 1983), Victor Frankenstein's creation gives us the key to understanding his character through a reading list: Plutarch's *Lives*, Milton's *Paradise Lost*, and Goethe's *Sorrows of Werther*. To understand the creature, one must understand Milton's fallen angel—a being similarly outcast and despised yet also possessing great eloquence and persuasive power. Reading what the creature reads increases our capacity to empathize with his profound sense of isolation, envy, and thwarted potential.

Drawing on the idea of reading as an empathy builder, this next activity makes the point that the words of other writers give us a language for understanding ourselves and our world. Here's the idea: Students list the titles of five texts that would help someone else get to know them better. Because many of my students don't have a ready catalog of favorite books to list, I encourage them to include song and poem lyrics, magazines, and texts they've written themselves.

Directions to Students: Create a reading list for someone who would like to get to know you better. What readings could help that person better understand and empathize with your background, experiences, values, and interests? Use the prompt below.

To understand me better, read these five texts:

1.

2.

3.

4.

5.

My students' reading lists offer important windows into their worlds:
Abel's List:

1. *Sports Illustrated* magazine

2. Professional Bull Riding (PBR)

3. Santana—"Black Magic Woman"

4. *Under the Same Moon*

5. Martin Luther King, Jr.'s and Cesar Chavez's speeches

Jasmine's List:

1. *The Fault in Our Stars*

2. *In the Time of the Butterflies*

3. "It Is What It Is" by Drake

4. *To Kill a Mockingbird*

5. Project on "My Journey"

COMMUNICATION PERSONAL INVENTORY

The personal inventory is a way to continue developing students' identity awareness through a consideration of their assets, needs, and learning contexts. This activity takes a little more time and reflection and may not be suitable to whole-class sharing.

> *Directions to Students*: Answer each of the following questions after taking some time to consider your response. Keep these responses in mind as you read and write for different purposes and audiences.

1. Have anyone's words impacted me especially strongly?

2. What do I like best about myself as a communicator?

3. Whom do I trust? How did these people earn my trust?

4. Who are my communication role models?

5. What are my strengths and weaknesses as a speaker?

6. What are my strengths and weaknesses as a listener?

7. How easy is it for me to open up to others?

8. How is the class I'm in now different from any other class I've taken?

9. Who am I in this classroom community?

10. What is my style of communication?

An alternative to the full inventory is to ask students to choose three of these questions to answer in a reflective quick-write.

Inclusive Learning Community Norms

Establishing learning community norms is something else we do early in a new semester. Ethical communication is principled communication, which means we have principles we follow—such as the belief that everyone has the right to be heard or that we need to understand before we argue. *We need each other to solve problems* is another principle that guides my classroom approach; that's why everyone's presence and participation are so important. Our learning community norms are informed by our principles.

I've never forgotten Marilyn Tabor saying, in one of her excellent workshops on leading professional conversations, that every time she's neglected to norm a group before discussion, she's regretted it. Ditto for me. It seems funny that just asking a class (or a group of teachers) to agree not to multitask during our time together is enough to eliminate texting or social media distractions, but often it is. The same is true of attendance reminders and plagiarism warnings. The times I've had problems with learners disengaging from our group are usually the times when I've forgotten to set and monitor our learning community norms.

The following are my go-to norms for most learning situations. In proposing these, I always distinguish between norms and rules and make the point that the norms only work if they actually describe how we all want to do business together. I also invite learners to propose their own norms for our community. Here's my list (see if you can infer the principles behind the norms):

> **Checking in:** Ask students whether they feel like active and valued participants in their learning community. Encourage them to share their responses through talk or writing.

- Listen with the purpose of understanding
- Use technology in support of the group's learning
- Minimize multitasking and side conversations
- Promote equity of voice and participation
- Assume the best about others
- Be fully present and prepared in all class meetings

You'll notice, too, that I'm using the phrase "inclusive learning community norms" instead of just "learning community norms." I want all my students to know that they're needed and valued members of our community. My campus defines "inclusive excellence" as enabling all members of our community to do the following:

- Feel a sense of belonging
- Fully engage in campus life

- Achieve their academic or professional goals

  (https://csumb.edu/diversity?_search=inclusive+excellence)

That about captures everything I'm trying to do as an educator.

Identity Is Complex

Becoming a self-aware communicator requires extensive analysis and reflection. Our identities are complex. Different aspects of who we are inform our response to rhetorical situations in different ways. For example, a female software engineer who is asking her employer for a raise might feel empowered by her outstanding record of performance but disadvantaged by the gender pay gap in her field. Her reputation as an engineer and status as a woman are interrelated, but distinct, components of her identity. In another situation—say, for instance, a presentation to a local school board on ways to increase the number of girls in advanced science courses—this same woman could enjoy the privileged status of an expert consultant. The reason for this, explain Maurianne Adams, Lee Anne Bell, and Pat Griffin, the editors of *Teaching for Diversity and Social Justice*, is because "individuals hold multiple complex and cross-cutting social group memberships that confer relative privilege or disadvantage differently in different contexts" (2007, 3).

Socially responsible communication acknowledges these situational differences in identity and social status. To help students understand this idea, I ask them to map their own identity components through an Intersectionality Map. The term *intersectionality* refers to the way different identity factors—such as gender, ethnicity, and sexuality—intersect with one another and to the way identities intersect with different social groups, institutions, belief systems, and forms of power. Attending to the diversity of students' intersecting identities promotes integrative thinking and reflection (see Figure 7.3).

INTERSECTIONALITY MAP

Directions to Students: Create a diagram or visual representing the different identity components that contribute to your sense of self. Draw circles for different social groups you feel you belong to. Link circles you see as overlapping or closely related to each other.

An Intersectionality Map makes the same point that Keith Grant-Davie makes about rhetors in rhetorical situations: "Rhetors need to consider who they are in a particular situation and be aware that their identity may vary from situation to situation" (1997, 269). After completing their Intersectionality Maps, students then reflect on persuasive situations that were particularly impacted by one or more of their identity components.

Directions to Students: Write a three- to five-minute narrative about a persuasive situation you encountered that had a particularly strong impact on one or more aspects of your personal identity. Were you trying to persuade someone or was someone trying to persuade you? What was it about this situation that made you especially aware of who you are? What was at stake? Be prepared to read your narrative aloud.

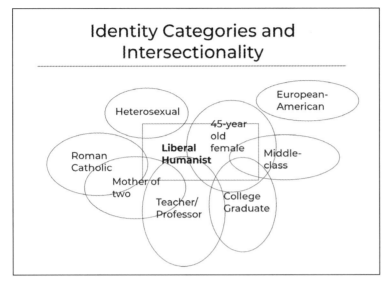

FIGURE 7.3

Intersectionality Map

When we communicate with texts as readers (the audience), we need to be mindful of all that we're bringing to this experience: our needs, interests, and expectations that contribute to our construction of reading. This is an important idea in reader response approaches to literature. In *Literature as Exploration*, Louise Rosenblatt makes the point that "the reading of a particular work at a particular moment by a particular reader will be a highly complex process. Personal factors will inevitably affect the equation represented by book plus reader" ([1938] 1995, 75). The following prompt helps students to think about these ideas.

> *Directions to Students*: Think about how all your different identity components invoke different power dynamics in your reading experiences. What kinds of texts make you feel invited or included? What kinds of texts make you feel excluded? Explore your responses to these questions in a five-minute quick-write.

We also talk about the way different aspects of our identity serve as filters, influencing what we see in texts because of who we are in place and time. In "The Myth of the Rhetorical Situation," Richard E. Vatz writes, "No situation can have a nature independent of the perception of its interpreter or independent of the rhetoric with which he chooses to characterize it" (1999, 226). So. We have to not only try to figure out what is going on with other people but also be keenly aware of how our own beliefs and emotions, and even our language choices, filter what we're experiencing.

This idea can be a heavy cognitive lift for younger students. Law professor David Takacs boils all this down to an accessible question: "How does who you are shape what you know about the world?" (2003, 27). Our stance or position, Takacs argues, biases our way of knowing. Drawing on this idea, we can imagine each of those identity circles in our intersectionality profile as a lens with a different tint or prescription. Change lenses, and we change the view. My selection of lenses, moreover, is different from yours.

No wonder, then, that effective and ethical communication isn't something we tend to just pick up on the fly.

ANALYZING THE INTERSECTIONALITY OF CHARACTERS

The concept of intersectionality can also be applied to literary characters. This can be an especially enlightening act of transfer. Using the idea of intersectionality, we can consider how different characters we've been reading about experience their various group memberships and levels of social status. The following sample scenarios explore the intersectionality of the title character from Junot Díaz's novel *The Brief Wondrous Life of Oscar Wao* (2007) and of the young Firoozeh Dumas in her memoir, *Funny in Farsi* (2003). Try creating intersectionality profiles of characters in the works of literature your students are reading.

> **Directions to Students**: For each sample scenario, consider the different group memberships and social privileges and/or disadvantages the person described might experience. Then answer the questions that follow in a quick-write or pairs conversation.
>
> **Sample Scenario 1**: A young male "ghetto nerd," growing up in a Dominican family in New Jersey; likes fantasy fiction and comic books; speaks in formal, academic English; not good at sports or romance; overweight; doesn't like to fight; single mom has cancer; older sister is a "punk chick"; idealistic
>
> **Sample Scenario 2**: Seven-year-old Iranian girl; moved to Whittier, California; loves Barbies; father is an engineer and a Fulbright scholar; two big brothers; English language learner; new kid in second grade; mother is stay-at-home mom; funny

What are the character's needs, values, and beliefs? What kinds of power relations might this person experience in his or her daily life? In his or her reading experiences?

Try adapting these questions to suit the needs of your own students and offer additional support through small-group and whole-class discussion. Students will need help understanding how identity intersects with power and what forms power can take (e.g., political, social, economic, psychological, physical).

For example, one of my students wrote a paper calling for more public support for the arts. She described her own love of museums and concert halls and argued that "disadvantaged" and "underprivileged" youth in her community should have the same opportunities to enjoy exhibits and performances that she had. Her paper was full of references to "the less fortunate."

I asked her how those word choices might impact how others would see her. I also gently asked whether she would call people "the less fortunate" if she were talking to them face to face. (And, yes, I'm thinking of my own assumptions, values, and privileges as I'm writing this now and of the power I have to uplift or embarrass students.) Communicating with awareness of self and others involves awareness of the assumptions we make about ourselves and others. This work isn't easy, but it offers payoffs far beyond the classroom.

Doing this kind of identity work can help us reorient ourselves when we react defensively to people who don't share our views. Instead of angrily thinking, "How can anyone not know this?" we can take a step back and examine our assumptions. My experience is not your experience.

Identity and Identification

Identity plays a key role in persuasion—one of the reasons why students need to learn to communicate with self and others in mind. In *A Rhetoric of Motives*, Kenneth Burke says that, in order for persuasion to take place, the audience must identify with the speaker or writer; that is, the listeners or readers must see themselves as being like the rhetor in some important way. According to Burke, this process of "identification" involves sharing common interests and concerns but not necessarily the same motives (1969, 19). While still unique individuals, rhetor and audience become "one body" through the act of persuasion (Burke uses the word "consubstantial"). They are both "joined and separate" (1969, 21).

For an example of how this works, consider the following NPR story on political protests. In "Researchers Examine the Psychology of Protest Movements," social science correspondent Shankar Vedantam (2017) talks with two Stanford University researchers who found that more extreme and violent protest tactics, such as breaking windows, cause bystanders to distance themselves from the protesters' interests, resulting in an adverse effect on their movement. Their discussion illustrates Burke's theory of identification:

> VEDANTAM: Willer [one of the researchers] thinks this is because when people see a protest, they ask themselves whether they can see themselves identifying with the protesters. He explains what happens inside the minds of the audience.
>
> WILLER: I might have agreed with their cause, but the way they're doing it is not the way I would have done it. And so I think that's the risk with extreme protest tactics, is they lead people—observers, bystanders—to answer that question—am I like those people? Should I go join them?—in the negative where they might have said, yeah, I am like them. I'm going to join that movement.

GREENE [host of *Hidden Brain*]: So, Shankar, it really is a matter of empathy. I mean, can I feel like I'm there with this group of people I'm watching, or is this not something I would ever do?

As the Stanford study suggests, persuasion is ultimately a matter of empathy. And empathy is a matter of identifying with and more deeply appreciating the humanity of other people.

Broadening Our Perspectives

What is so special about imaginative literature is that it creates the experience of empathy; we don't see an issue just through our own eyes but also through the eyes of the author and characters. Powerful works of literature compel us to read them on their own terms. This heightened awareness of others' perspectives is what lifts us out of the limits of our own experience.

The following activity is modeled on educational resources developed by the Peace Corps (2016) to help students view a situation from more than one point of view and "explain how various people may interpret the same reality in different ways." I created the following examples below using literary texts. This activity also asks students to appreciate similarities and differences, an essential ability for transfer of learning.

Directions to Students: **Imagine how the behaviors that follow might be interpreted by people from different cultural or personal perspectives. For each scenario, write two different interpretations of the behavior representing these different points of view, keeping in mind that there are many complex responses different individuals can have to these scenarios.**

1. (from *The Scarlet Letter*) A woman is publicly punished for committing adultery by being forced to wear a scarlet letter "A" on her chest. How might this act be interpreted by a seventeenth-century Puritan? By a twenty-first-century feminist?

   Response 1:

   Response 2:

2. (from *Romeo and Juliet*) Two teenagers fall in love and secretly get married without their parents' permission. How might this act be viewed by a sixteenth-century father? By a twenty-first-century high school student?

   Response 1:

   Response 2:

3. (from *Julius Caesar* or *The Absolutely True Diary of a Part-Time Indian*) A friend betrays a friend for a greater good. How might this act be viewed by the person who is betrayed? By the person who betrays the friend for a good reason?

   Response 1:

   Response 2:

> The stance we take on an issue is intimately connected to our role in the rhetorical situation.

4. (from *Beloved*) A mother who is a runaway slave kills her child in order to save her from slavery. How might this act be viewed by a person who has never been enslaved? By a person who has been enslaved?

    Response 1:

    Response 2:

Try debriefing this learning experience by asking students to respond to the following question: How does our perspective impact our perception? Taking advantage of literary study to examine different perspectives gives students more opportunities to experience and develop empathy.

Ethos

We can build on students' understanding of character development by applying the rhetorical concept of *ethos* to their analysis of literary texts. While perspective and persona, image and identity, are not the same things, these concepts are contained in the idea of ethos, or "the markers of character" (Farrell 1999, 83). Ethos is a high-utility concept. All academic disciplines ask students to consider the image they create for themselves in their writing. Notice, for instance, how this syllabus from a business writing course at my university pays special attention to the construction of a writer's ethos:

All written correspondence leaves a lasting impression. Remember to:

- be respectful, not demanding;

- be modest, not arrogant;

- be polite, not sarcastic;

- be positive and tactful, not negative and condescending;

- avoid being overly direct or overly indirect;

- avoid being too informal or formal;

- be concise, not blunt;

- be accurate by paying attention to details! Don't be careless—appearance of your message counts! (Business Writing and Critical Thinking II [BUS 304], California State University, Monterey Bay)

Constructing a compelling ethos depends on our ability to understand who we are and the roles we play in different rhetorical situations. This identity work is critical to effective communication. Thomas Newkirk says, "The character of the speaker/writer is absolutely crucial—unless this person is trusted, no logical appeal will have much force" (2014, 108).

After doing intersectionality work with my students, I also encourage them to be aware of how power and privilege operate in rhetorical situations. The following questions can trigger this thinking:

- Who am I in this rhetorical situation?
- What privileges do I have?
- What power dynamics do I need to be mindful of in this situation?

Ethos and Academic Writing

What about ethos and the use of the first person in academic writing? The best way I've found to answer this question is to point students to the works of scholarship published in a given field. Can we find articles in journals of literary criticism or language studies, for instance, in which the author says, "I think" or "In my view"? We sure can. Answering this question rhetorically means understanding what works for a target audience, starting with the editor or the instructor.

When students reference their own identity in their writing, they need to be mindful of the effects of this choice. In one of those behind-the-scenes musings I often encounter in student writing, one of my students started her essay on Orson Scott Card's novel *Ender's Game* (1985) with, "I'm not completely sure what kind of literary technique I want to focus on for this assignment." So I wrote on her paper, "Think about how you are situating yourself in the ongoing academic conversation on this text. What kind of ethos have you constructed for yourself? Why have you made these choices?"

I try not to ask questions on my students' papers that I already have an answer to. If I write, "Do you want to use academic English here?" by a student's use of a casual phrase in a research paper, I want that student to believe that I really am asking for her opinion about her language options and that I'm not implying that I think she *should* be using academic English. The final choice and responsibility are the writer's.

I always cringe when I hear baseball coaches ask young players questions they can't answer with dignity: "Why are you swinging at that outside pitch?! What were you thinking?!" I remember, too, hearing sociolinguist Deborah Tannen talk about her mother seeing her on a television show, and, clearly unhappy about her daughter's choice of hairstyle, calling Tannen the next day to ask, "Do you *like* your hair like that?"

> **Question: When is the first-person point of view a rhetorically effective choice? Answer: When the writer has created a compelling ethos.**

These are not the kinds of questions I want to pose to my students. Instead, I want to pose questions that trigger writer's brain, questions that genuinely help students think about their choices as writers and about the effects of those choices, particularly in terms of the kind of relationship they create with their audience. (My feedback should also model the clean communication practices I want my students to use—so no sarcasm or ridicule.)

I want students thinking, *If I make this move, will I help or hinder my chances of winning my reader over? And if my opening moves make it a little harder for my reader to identify with me or see where I'm going—but I have a good reason for beginning this way—then what will I need to do later on to get my reader to see things the way I do?*

Establishing Who You Are and Why You Care

The following sentence frames can help students establish who they are in a particular rhetorical context and why they care about the question at issue (note the academic use of first person):

As a _____, I do this because . . .

As a _____, I understand this . . .

My intention is . . .

Based on my experience with . . .

Drawing on my personal knowledge of . . .

I contribute to _____ by _____. (What contribution do you make to the field? How do you do this? What research methods do you use?)

Here at [name of organization], we understand that . . .

Developing an Identity as a Rhetor

Rhetor is a word I'm using more often with my students now. The rhetor identity carries with it the capacity and expectation to engage in civic discourse. Rhetors take rhetorical action to effect change. It's an academic identity that comes with a built-in sense of agency. By calling students *rhetors*, we tell them, "You have something important to say, and you're going to say it. And people are going to listen." This can be a transformative identity for students.

Keith Grant-Davie describes rhetors as "those people, real or imagined, responsible for discourse and its authorial voice" (1997, 269). Rhetors, Grant-Davie says, need to be "aware that their identity may vary from situation to situation" (269). He adds that rhetors can also play several roles at once, including the roles the audience brings to its perception of the rhetor. When I volunteer to supervise my children's school field trips, for instance, I take on the role of a chaperone: someone who has the authority to give directions. I bring my educator identity, too, and am not afraid to use my teacher voice if I have to. But the students also see another (perhaps more accessible) role: I'm Dryden and Ellerie's mom. Each role elicits a different response.

We give students opportunities to rethink their identities as communicators when we ask them to reflect on the following kinds of questions:

- Who am I as a rhetor? What can I do? How can I develop my skills further?
- How do my rhetorical skills and knowledge help me in life?
- How do my rhetorical actions impact my relationships with people?
- How do the roles I play vary across different situations?

Applying Knowledge of Ethos to Character Analysis

In fictional works, students can use their knowledge of ethos and rhetors to analyze a narrator's image or credibility (as I demonstrate in Chapter 5, "Negotiating Voices and Meaning") or to analyze other characters in the text.

If you teach British literature, *Beowulf* offers terrific material for this kind of analysis, especially if you're using Seamus Heaney's brilliant translation. My favorite moment for this kind of close reading comes early in the poem in the scene in which Unferth—a name that suggests discontent—challenges Beowulf's heroic reputation. Unferth says, "Are you the Beowulf who took on Breca in a swimming match on the open sea, risking the water just to prove that you could win? It was sheer vanity made you venture out on the main deep" (Heaney 2000, 35). Unferth then tells his version of the story, claiming that Breca outswam Beowulf and "came ashore the stronger contender" (35). You were defeated by Breca, the jealous Unferth tells Beowulf, and you'll be defeated by Grendel, too,

Here's where it gets good. As Sheldon said on *The Big Bang Theory*, "Trash talk is a traditional component in all sporting events." Beowulf is as adept at verbal sparring as he is at hand-to-hand combat. My students love Beowulf's retort:

> *Well, friend Unferth, you have had your say*
> *About Breca and me. But it was mostly Beer*
> *that was doing the talking. The truth is this:*
> *when the going was heavy in those high waves,*
> *I was the strongest swimmer of all.* (37)

After recounting one astounding, superhuman deed after another—swimming in full armor, killing nine sea monsters—Beowulf concludes by saying, "Now I cannot recall any fight you entered, Unferth, that bears comparison" (39–41), adding that if Unferth were truly as courageous as he claims to be, Grendel wouldn't still be a problem. Oh snap.

This scene is a great departure point for analyzing Beowulf's ethos. We can consider how he sees himself, how he's viewed by a unworthy rival, how he's viewed by other characters, and how he appears to us. We can analyze the strategies the Beowulf poet uses to diminish Unferth's credibility while enhancing Beowulf's.

We can also consider Beowulf as a *rhetor*, someone who takes rhetorical action. While Beowulf's rhetorical choices are clearly of the old school agonistic tradition (and not the dialogic communication skills I'm trying to teach my students), he effactually prevents Hrothgar's thanes from questioning his heroic status. Analyzing the consequences of Beowulf's rhetorical actions enriches our understanding of his character. (See Figure 7.4.)

My next step for analyzing Beowulf's ethos and rhetorical skill is to have students compare his pre- and postbattle speeches. What does Beowulf say before he fights Grendel? What does he say afterward? Does he make good on his boasts? From there, I invite students to make some cross-context connections by comparing Beowulf to twenty-first-century professional athletes.

BEOWULF'S POSTGAME INTERVIEW

Directions to Students:

Step 1: Rewrite Beowulf's postbattle speech as a twenty-first-century postgame interview. If this is a new genre for you, watch some videos of postgame interviews of professional basketball players or football players on ESPN to get the idea. Choose the approach Beowulf will take to the reporter's questions: Will he be humble, defensive, arrogant, understated, or funny? Give credit to his teammates? Or claim all the glory for himself? Be sure Beowulf's tone and language choices match the communication style you've selected for him.

Step 2: Explore the following questions in a quick-write. How are Beowulf's pre- and postbattle speeches similar to twenty-first-century athletes pre- and postgame interviews? How are they different?

FIGURE 7.4
Analyzing Beowulf's ethos

The Step 2 quick-write is critically important for training students to avoid logical fallacies such as sweeping generalizations and false analogies. Effective transfer depends on a keen understanding of similarities and differences between contexts. I think one of the reasons reader response criticism (an approach I find really valuable for engaging students) sometimes comes under fire is because of a tendency for students to overstate similarities between different historical, cultural, and ideological contexts when making connections between a text and their own lives. Students who say how they can totally relate to Juliet's conflict with her parents because their own parents are just as strict and controlling are missing some of the nuances of sixteenth-century gender roles and family dynamics. Transfer of learning scholars talk about this as negative transfer—an inappropriate application of prior learning or experience to a new text, a task, or a context. The challenge is finding relevant connections between different situations.

Analyzing Communication Styles

Depth of understanding is important for transfer of learning. Pattern recognition is also important (Perkins and Salomon 2012). To deepen students' understanding of the complexities of communication, I have them analyze the communication styles of different literary characters using a feature analysis matrix. The matrix asks students to note characters' patterns of behavior in the following areas: persuasive strategies, collaborative problem solving, listening to understand, making connections, obstacles to understanding, and relationship building. I point out that not all these areas are aspects of effective and ethical communication; in most cases, creating obstacles to understanding is *not* an ethical move, but you could get into a philosophical discussion with your students about whether the end justifies the means. Similarly, persuasive strategies, as Plato notes, can be used for honorable or dishonorable purposes. It will be up to the students to evaluate the consequences of the characters' communication choices.

I had a lot of fun creating the following example using J. K. Rowling's *Harry Potter and the Order of the Phoenix* (2003); see Figures 7.5 and 7.6.

You can imagine how this activity works with novels like *Ender's Game*, *Lord of the Flies*, or *Wuthering Heights*. Analyzing characters' communication practices offers new insights into characters' needs, motives, strengths, and weaknesses. Considering Lady Capulet and Heathcliff as *rhetors* opens up an entirely different angle of approach to these characters, one that offers additional explanations for why their relationships with others are the way they are. Focusing on communication practices helps students get more out of their literary reading.

Communication Feature Analysis Matrix

Title and Author of Literary Text: Harry Potter and the Order of the Phoenix by J. K. Rowling

Directions to Students: Create a list of 4-6 characters from a work of literature you are studying. Write the names of these characters in the far left column. Then, for each character, place a check mark in the box for each communication behavior that is typical of that character. Mark all that apply.

Literary Characters	Persuasive Strategies							Collaborative Problem Solving							Listening to Understand					Making Connections						Obstacles to Understanding							Relationship Building				
	supports claims with evidence	shares personal stories	uses humor	uses deductive reasoning (if...then...)	appeals to own authority or power	appeals to fear or anger	appeals to self-interest	negotiates agreements	explores multiple perspectives	contributes own insights	tests different solutions	works to build consensus	compromises	seeks additional information	paraphrases others' words (mirrors)	summarizes others' views	checks for understanding	postpones judgment	asks clarifying questions	reflects on past experiences	draws on prior knowledge	sees similarities and differences	relates to others' experiences	synthesizes information	sees the big picture	interrupts others	deceives self or others	dominates conversations	threatens to harm others	withdraws	insults others or calls names	uses sarcasm or ridicule	encourages others	validates others	promotes equity of participation	expresses empathy	sets ground rules or norms
Harry	X	X	X	X	X			X	X	X	X	X	X	X	X	X	X	X	X	X	X	X	X	X	X			X	X		X	X	X	X	X	X	X
Hermione	X	X	X	X	X			X	X	X	X	X	X	X	X	X	X	X	X	X	X	X	X	X	X					X				X	X	X	X	X
Malfoy			X		X	X	X		X					X							X	X				X	X	X			X	X	X	X	X			X
Professor Snape	X			X	X	X			X	X				X						X	X	X	X		X	X					X		X	X				X
Dolores Umbrage			X	X	X	X							X														X	X	X	X				X				X
Dumbledore	X		X	X	X			X	X	X	X	X		X		X			X	X	X	X	X	X	X						X		X	X	X	X	X

FIGURE 7.5

Communication Feature Analysis Matrix for *Harry Potter and the Order of the Phoenix*

Communication Feature Analysis Matrix

Title and Author of Literary Text: _____.

Directions to Students: Create a list of 4-6 characters from a work of literature you are studying. Write the names of these characters in the far left column. Then, for each character, place a check mark in the box for each communication behavior that is typical of that character. Mark all that apply.

Literary Characters	Persuasive Strategies							Collaborative Problem Solving							Listening to Understand					Making Connections						Obstacles to Understanding							Relationship Building				
	supports claims with evidence	shares personal stories	uses humor	uses deductive reasoning (if...then...)	appeals to own authority or power	appeals to fear or anger	appeals to self-interest	negotiates agreements	explores multiple perspectives	contributes own insights	tests different solutions	works to build consensus	compromises	seeks additional information	paraphrases others' words (mirrors)	summarizes others' views	checks for understanding	postpones judgment	asks clarifying questions	reflects on past experiences	draws on prior knowledge	sees similarities and differences	relates to others' experiences	synthesizes information	sees the big picture	interrupts others	deceives self or others	dominates conversations	threatens to harm others	withdraws	insults others or calls names	uses sarcasm or ridicule	encourages others	validates others	promotes equity of participation	expresses empathy	sets ground rules or norms

FIGURE 7.6

Communication Feature Analysis Matrix (see Appendix 22)

Facilitating Collaboration

Employers want graduates who can collaborate, but collaborative learning is often students' least favorite learning modality. I think part of the reason for this is because the kind of communication students experience in collaborative groups often causes people to shut down instead of engage. We downshift—that is, become less invested and motivated—when we feel we're not being heard. We get interrupted, someone else is off task, we're told we're wrong, and we start to pull back from the group. Instead of working together and working to understand, our focus shifts to self-protection. Group work becomes one of those I-just-need-to-get-this-over-with experiences—a sure sign that students aren't thinking about leveraging their learning in the future. Rather, what they often carry with them is a fixed sense that they don't like group work and a fixed desire to avoid group work as much as possible.

> Students can also use the **Communication Feature Analysis Matrix** as a reflective tool to analyze their own communication practices.

Setting students up for successful collaboration is work we need to do as teachers. In addition to our regular learning community norms, when my students do group projects or whole-class discussion, I offer these guidelines:

- Communicate with self and others in mind
- Allow people to finish speaking before you respond
- Increase the "wait time" between questions and comments to encourage someone who hasn't spoken yet to jump into the conversation
- Practice listening silently
- Paraphrase what others have said to check for understanding
- Engage in dialogue, not debate

As teachers, we can also direct traffic and practice our own situational awareness, especially if we need to be alert to the kinds of messages students hear from their peers and the world outside our classrooms. In writing about identity and agency, I don't mean to suggest that the responsibility for success lies entirely with students. Much of what causes students to feel they don't belong in academic conversations is external to the student—and often related to systems of injustice like racial oppression or gender discrimination. Some college programs also intentionally try to weed students out because they simply can't handle the number of students who want to enroll in their majors. There are many reasons the students we serve in our classes can fall out of the educational pipeline. This makes it all the more important for us to help our students make their voices heard and to send them the message that, as a society, we need the unique contributions that only they can make.

A side note: If we've taught counterarguments as "counterpunches," here's where that combative approach to argument can come back to bite us (as, of course, a combative approach *would*). Students who only know how to throw punches aren't much help during group deliberation and decision making.

The Reader-Writer Relationship

Reading and writing are also a type of collaboration. Thinking about audience and author in terms of reader-writer interaction can be a new idea for many students. This kind of rhetorical thinking exemplifies Peter Elbow's and Thomas Newkirk's points about writing operating in time, so that the reader goes on a journey with the writer. Good writers, Newkirk (2014) says, create "dynamic" experiences for their readers, raising their expectations and moving them toward the writer's stance in that pattern Elbow describes as "itch and scratch" (2000, 163). After talking over this idea with one of my classes, a student shared that he'd actually looked up what happens when we physically scratch an itch on our body; he learned that the more we scratch, the more the nerves in our skin intensify the sensation of the itch. Good writing does this, too; the more we read a compelling text, the more we want to read. Our anticipation results from our interaction with the writing.

I want to share an example from Tim Gillespie's excellent book *Doing Literary Criticism*. Gillespie's introduction shows his keen awareness of both his own identity as a teacher-writer and of his audience's interests and level of expertise. Here's what he says:

> I'm not a specialist. Like most high school teachers, I'm a generalist who is mediating between the demands of my academic discipline, the expectations of my school and community, and the needs of my students. . . . Though I have a couple of degrees in English, I am less an expert than a curious learner, an idiosyncratic reader, and a translator looking for what works with students. As such, I need your collaboration as a fellow teacher, seeker, and reader. If you see any prejudices in my explanations or ways of organizing this vast body of thinking, bring them up for discussion with your students; I'm counting on you and your students to balance my biases and fill the holes in my knowledge. (2010, 18)

Gillespie's request for help establishes a sympathetic connection between writer and reader. His message is "we're all in this together," not "I know more than you"—a wise move from a writer who clearly knows the high caliber of teacher likely to be reading a professional development book.

For an example from a literary text, see how Emily Dickinson negotiates this relationship, creating for herself what might almost be called an anti-ethos:

I'm Nobody! Who are you? by Emily Dickinson

I'm Nobody! Who are you?
Are you – Nobody – too?
Then there's a pair of us!
Don't tell! they'd advertise – you know!

How dreary – to be – Somebody!
How public – like a Frog –
To tell one's name – the livelong June –
To an admiring Bog!

As Dickinson's poem shows, taking a stance—in this case, on the issue of fame and self-promotion—constructs a particular kind of identity and reader-writer relationship.

Dickinson draws her reader in to the private world of the "nobodies" who eschew the garish displays of the "somebodies" with their cult of celebrity.

Understanding Audience Needs, Interests, and Expectations

Communicating with others in mind is a key aspect of a rhetorical approach. We write in the presence of others, imagining how they'll react to our words as we compose our texts. When we talk about audience expectations, we're really making predictions about audience reactions.

The Audience Group Résumé is an activity that helps students research the shared background, experiences, and values of specific audiences. This activity works best with genres that have fairly narrow audiences, such as children's literature, YA novels, blogs, and magazine articles (today's magazines are more specialized than ever). It also works when students personally know their audience, as is the case when they write to their peers, teachers, family members, or school administrators. The Audience Group Résumé probably isn't suited to texts like the Harry Potter series with massive worldwide readerships.

Audience Analysis: Group Résumé (adapted from Ellen Levy)

Directions to Students: **Describe the general characteristics of the audience for a text (e.g., your own or a published writer's) using the following criteria. Think of this as a collective summary of the audience's attributes, experiences, and qualities: in other words, a group résumé. Although there will probably be many audience members who are exceptions to this profile, your task is to understand the typical needs, interests, knowledge, expectations, and feelings of the target audience as the writer understands them.**

Title and author of the text: _____

Year of publication: _____

Typical education level of the audience (e.g., high school diploma, bachelor's degree):

_____

Audience's level of knowledge about the topic (e.g., novice, expert): _____

_____

The issues and topics that are important to this audience: _____

_____

The audience's attitude toward the topic: _____

_____

_____

The languages the audience speaks: _____

_____

_____

The experiences, talents, and interests that influence the audience's perspective: _____

_____

_____

_____

The occupations or social roles that influence the audience's perspective (e.g., careers, family roles, peer groups): _____

_____

The greatest challenge this audience faces: _____

_____

_____

The top priorities for this audience:_____

_____

_____

References: (Note: Character references testify to the truth of the attributes listed on someone's résumé. In this case, your references will literally be the reference works—biographies, histories, surveys, interviews, and so forth—that support your claims about the audience. Include a citation for each of your listed references.)

_____

_____

_____

_____

_____

It's also a good idea to assign this activity as a group research project, so that students share the responsibility of finding the historical, biographical, or critical reference works they need to complete the audience résumé. The following texts are especially good choices for this kind of collective audience analysis: *To Kill a Mockingbird*, *The Adventures of Huckleberry Finn*, *The Crucible*, "The Yellow Wallpaper," and *1984*.

LET'S PLAY *HOW WELL DO YOU KNOW YOUR READER?*

Do you remember the *Newlywed Game?* This is the same idea, only the couple testing its knowledge of each other is a writer and the reader. Focusing on the reader-writer relationship makes clear that writing is a relational art; writing succeeds as an act of communication when it builds the right sort of relationship with its audience. This doesn't mean that as readers we always have to like a writer or narrator (or agree with their ideas) to be moved by them. But we do need to understand each other. If writers and their readers don't understand each other, then communication fails.

For the following activity, you can choose to have students either take on the roles of famous authors and their contemporary readers (be as specific as possible; for example, John Steinbeck and literary readers and critics of the 1930s) or just be themselves and think about the real audiences they try to reach as students (e.g., their peers, teachers, parents).

Once students have had a chance to answer their questions individually, I like to stage the full game show by having three or four "couples" take a seat together at the front of the room and answer their questions in front of a live audience. If you want to be really corny, you can play the old *Newlywed Game* theme song as students take their seats on the "stage." Choose a student volunteer to act as the host and read the questions or take on this role yourself. Writers will give their answers first (decide in advance if you want them to show their answers on cards or just read them off their paper). Then readers share their responses. Keep track of how many points each couple earns for correct answers and announce the winning pair at the end. Feel free to be lenient in judging "matching" answers. Have fun!

> *Directions to Students:* For this activity, you will be working in pairs to determine how well a writer knows his or her reader. Each "couple" will consist of one writer and one reader. You'll both be answering a set of questions individually (no peeking or talking!) before revealing your answers during the game show.
>
> Step 1: Read one of the writer's compositions together and talk over what it means. This could be a student essay (if you're playing as yourselves) or a published poem, article, or short story (if you're playing as a famous author and his or her reader).
>
> Step 2: Answer your individual questions. For the writer, these will be based on how well you know your reader. For the reader, these will be based on how well you know yourself. Do not compare answers at this point!
>
> Step 3: You're ready to play *How Well Do You Know Your Reader?*—the game that tests the quality of a reader-writer relationship. The game show host will now ask for your responses to your previously answered questions. Your couple earns one point each time your answer matches your partner's response to the same question. The pair with the most matches wins.

Questions for the Writer:

1. "Here's the concern I have about what you've written." How would your reader finish this thought?

2. What is your reader's biggest pet peeve as a reader?

3. When is your reader most likely to lose interest in what you've written—at the beginning, the middle, or the end?

4. What would cause your reader to stop reading what you've written?

5. What does your reader like best about what you've written?

6. What does your reader like least about what you've written?

7. What adjective best describes your reader?

8. What was your reader's first impression of you as a writer?

9. What other writers does your reader like?

10. Why is your reader reading what you've written?

    a. They were forced to.

    b. They want to learn something new.

    c. They're reading for pleasure (could include aesthetic or intellectual pleasure).

Questions for the Reader:

1. "Here's the concern I have about what you've written." How would you finish this thought?

2. What is your biggest pet peeve as a reader?

3. When are you most likely to lose interest in what the writer's written—at the beginning, the middle, or the end?

4. What would cause you to stop reading what the writer's written?

5. What do you like best about what the writer's written?

6. What do you like least about what the writer's written?

7. What adjective best describes you as a reader?

8. What was your first impression of the writer?

9. What other writers do you as a reader like?

10. Why are you reading what the writer's written?

    a. I was forced to.

    b. I want to learn something new.

    c. I'm reading for pleasure (could include aesthetic or intellectual pleasure).

When you debrief this activity with your students, be sure to discuss the diversity of perspectives encompassed by real audiences. One audience member's view of a text will differ from another's. Nevertheless, writers can increase the likelihood of reaching their target audience by researching audience cares and concerns and anticipating typical audience reactions.

Understanding Value Hierarchies

How can students evaluate whether an act of communication is ethical? One way to do this is to create a value hierarchy. Ethical judgments of behavior are based on the values of the judge. What is a top priority for one judge may not be as important to another judge. By creating value hierarchies, students can explore the way different people (including literary characters) have different needs and priorities.

CHARACTER VALUE HIERARCHY

Directions to Students:

Step 1: Create a value hierarchy for a character in a work of literature you are studying. Begin by listing ten of the character's top priorities in life. These can be one-word needs or values, like *love, power, honor, dignity, loyalty, survival, friendship*. Then rank the character's values from 1 to 10, with number one being the value that is most important to this character.

Step 2: After creating your value hierarchy, explore the following questions in a quick-write: How do you see your character using their value hierarchy to make critical decisions? What textual evidence do you have that supports your ranking of the character's values? Are any of the character's values in conflict or tension with one another?

Step 3: Finally, evaluate the character's communication choices in a conversation with a partner or a small group. Discuss the following questions: How do the character's values compare to your own? Do you think the character's choices are ethical? Feel free to bring in other criteria for making your judgments, such as the consequences of the character's choices.

When it's time for students to write their own compositions, they can revisit this idea. Ask your students how their value hierarchies might be different from the value hierarchies of members of their audience. Comparing and contrasting value hierarchies further develops students' situational awareness.

Reaching Real Audiences

Most of our students, when they write in their future lives, will not be writing for publication. That means that they'll likely be writing for smaller groups of readers that they may know personally (e.g., employers, colleagues, professors, family members). And while these individuals will still probably be part of a larger discourse community with its own expectations for communication (e.g., the insurance industry, the hospitality industry, agribusiness, the tech world, academia), our students need practice drilling down to audience specifics.

One business writing guide I found describes its audience as people "who communicate business and technical ideas in English and who need practical answers to questions about writing in the world of work" (Shipley Associates 1985, vii). Not surprisingly, this real-world resource has a strong rhetorical orientation. In contrast to style guides that only present the rules of grammar, spelling, and mechanics, this guide answers questions about audience, purpose, and rhetorical strategy, including the following:

- How do you present ideas that your readers will not like or will not accept?
- How do you write for managers? For peers?
- When should you use visual aids?
- How should you use key words? (Shipley Associates 1985, vii)

Notice how these questions take a rhetorical interest in a writer's choices and the effects of those choices in specific scenarios. In explaining how language conventions change over time, the guide likewise offers an eminently rhetorical message:

[Conventions] evolve as the language adapts to printing presses, computers, space shuttles, television, new industries, changing social concerns and political issues, new perspectives on history, new economic theories—in short, to everything in a constantly changing world. (vii)

Note, as well, how the reference to space shuttles and the omission of the Internet and social media mark this text as pre-twenty-first century, a fitting example of the scale of change our language has to cope with.

Shifting from a Writer's Perspective to a Reader's Perspective

As a writer, I know exactly those things that cause me the most stress, and I bet most of our students do, too. Any unfinished writing task can weigh heavily on our minds. We become preoccupied with the grunt work of just cranking out a draft. But in focusing on our own needs as writers ("I just need to find an opening" or "I just need to write the conclusion"), we forget that our readers' needs are even more important to accomplishing our purpose. In much real-world writing, unmet reader needs equal an unread text.

The table in Figure 7.7 compares differences in writer needs and reader needs in source-based academic writing. Ask students to talk about what happens if readers' needs aren't met.

WRITERS' NEEDS	READERS' NEEDS
Complete the task	Be informed, entertained, or inspired
Get started	Get engaged
Get from one paragraph to the next	Stay engaged
Introduce sources	Understand who is saying what
Provide reasons and evidence	Be convinced
Write a conclusion	Experience a meaningful conclusion
Make the deadline	Make sense

FIGURE 7.7
Comparing writers' needs to readers' needs

Writers' needs are important—something Peter Elbow has written about at length—but writers who focus *only* on their own needs are a bit like employees who do a job just for the paycheck. Giving more attention to readers' needs (including their own) prepares students to be more responsive and responsible communicators.

Success in Life and Work

Any instructional approach that aims to promote students' post-secondary success needs to consider the importance of communication. "Being heard, known, and understood," write Makau and Marty, "are widely recognized as key elements in the fulfillment of

> **A writer's needs are not the reader's problem; however, the reader's needs *are* the writer's problem.**

human potential" (2013, 1). I've been saying all along that literature helps us respond to the cares and concerns of others. I believe this with all my heart. Imaginative literature also helps us better understand our own place in the world.

In the category of "Reflection and Self-Assessment" on AAC&U's Integrative Learning VALUE Rubric (2009), growth is measured by the way a student "demonstrates a developing sense of self as a learner, building on prior experiences to respond to new and challenging contexts." Uncoupled from a rhetorical awareness of our own and other people's needs, identities, values, and relationships, academic work can become an exercise in proving that we're right and someone else is wrong. I think of the activity I saw posted on Pinterest that offered to teach argumentation skills through a "Socratic Smackdown." Crushing an opponent is not my idea of productive problem solving. Nor does it jibe with the National Research Council's description of success: "Success in work and life in the 21st century is associated with cognitive, intrapersonal, and interpersonal competencies that allow individuals to adapt effectively to changing situations rather than to rely solely on well-worn procedures" (2012, 70). Chief among those intrapersonal and interpersonal competencies is the ability to communicate ethically and effectively.

Conclusion

Students cross the threshold from school-based literacy practices to communication-based literacy practices when understanding and responding to others become more important than completing an assignment or earning a grade. Communicating with self and others in mind is ultimately about communicating with caring.

While I was writing this book, I daily encountered messages that gave me hope or caused me great dismay. Words have real consequences. I'm grateful to the many educational leaders—principals, superintendents, teachers, university presidents—who made sure their words were heard during times when we were deeply concerned for the safety and well-being of our students. Their public commitments to diversity of thought and the protection of all members of our school communities provided much-needed guidance and reassurance. These good people did what the fourth-century philosopher, Augustine of Hippo, reminds us we can all do when we communicate with caring:

> When we are weighed down by poverty, and grief makes us sad; when bodily pain makes us restless, and exile despondent; or when any other grievance afflicts us, if there be good people at hand who understand the art of rejoicing with the joyful and weeping with the sorrowful, who know how to speak a cheerful word and uplift us, then bitterness is mitigated, worries are alleviated, and our troubles are overcome. (Rotelle 1986, Letter 130, 2)

CHAPTER EIGHT

Reading and Writing with Passion

What you fall in love with, what seizes your imagination, will affect everything. It will decide what will get you out of bed in the morning, what you do with your evenings, how you spend your weekends, what you read, whom you know, what breaks your heart, and what amazes you with joy and gratitude. Fall in love, stay in love, and it will decide everything.

—ATTRIBUTED TO FR. PEDRO ARRUPE, S.J.

What I want most for my students is that they'll flourish in life. Above all, this is the future I'm trying to prepare them for. A flourishing life is a joyful and meaningful life. And so I want their educational journey to be full of opportunities for them to find their passions and fulfill their promise, especially when it comes to reading and writing. The best literacy experiences are those that "begin in the gut," as Barry Lane says (2016, 158), that inspire and move us, reminding us that words, *our* words, have the power to change the world.

This final chapter is thus about changing the measure for postsecondary success from academic proficiency to intellectual passion, from workforce preparation to liberal learning, and from diploma or degree completion to a life well lived. You'll find strategies for further developing students' understanding of exigence, purpose, and *kairos*—key rhetorical concepts for transfer and engagement. You'll also find a defense of the value of literature in secondary school curricula. Frankly, I don't know how we'd nurture our students' passion for reading and writing if literature were not part of our approach. Implicit in all of this is the importance of student agency and choice.

Emotion and Transfer of Learning

My choice of the word *passion* in the title of this chapter is strategic. These days, emotion seems to have something of a bad name in education. We're encouraged by some professional development programs to teach our students to avoid emotional appeals in their writing and to beware of emotional manipulation in the writing of others. Patrick Clauss and John Duffy, directors of writing programs at the University of Notre Dame, raised this issue in their post to the NCTE Teaching and Learning Forum on the false dichotomy between argument and persuasion: "What is so problematic about these binaries, aside from their reductive qualities, is how they suggest to teachers and students that not only is argument divorced from the complications of character and emotion, from *ethos* and *pathos*, but that invoking these in an argument represents an ethical lapse" (Duffy and Clauss 2016). The scholarship on emotion, engagement, and transfer of learning tells a different story—a point that Clauss and Duffy make in their essay. Emotion is a powerful resource and ally in the pursuit for deeper learning, not a weakness to be overcome.

What we've learned from transfer research is that the things we carry are the things we care about. Emotionally engaging students in literary texts helps them not only communicate more effectively by heightening their awareness of pathos and audience but also hold onto their thinking longer and make more meaningful connections. In his work on transfer, David N. Perkins talks about "lifeready learning" as involving "understanding-as-caring" (2014, 115). Emotion helps students retain and internalize learning. In *Student Engagement Techniques: A Handbook for College Faculty*, Elizabeth F. Barkley claims that "emotional associations can have a particularly potent influence on transfer, as emotions usually have a higher priority than cognitive processing for commanding our attention" (2010, 21). Barkley's conclusion is based on the work of leading educational psychologists, including Brophy (2009), Svinicki (2004), Wlodkowski (2008), and Sousa (2006; 2009).

Not surprisingly, Louise Rosenblatt anticipated this connection between emotional engagement and transfer a half-century earlier. In *Literature as Exploration*, she sees the "response to literature and the process of reflection as a prelude to action in life itself" ([1938] 1995, 216). We act on our learning when our learning has been personally meaningful.

Passion Is the Antidote to Apathy

One of the community-building activities I use when I facilitate workshops is to ask teachers to identify the single greatest challenge they face in the classroom. Workshop after workshop, the answer is the same: apathy. (I don't always ask whether they mean their apathy or their students'.) On one memorable occasion, a table of teachers said its greatest challenge was the way varying degrees and kinds of social privilege caused some students to *appear* apathetic in school while others appeared engaged.

A little knowledge of Greek goes a long way in helping us understand the connection between pathos and apathy.[1] One meaning of apathy is that it is "without pathos." In the *Secret History of Emotion: From Aristotle's Rhetoric to Modern Brain Science*, Daniel M. Gross explains that "the English word *apathy* is related to the Greek *apatheia*, which means, literally, without passion-as-suffering" (2007, 52; italics in original). Gross is quick to point out that the classical meaning of suffering has more to do with what one experiences or undergoes than the sensation of pain (2007). Thus, in the classical sense, we can suffer pleasure. *Apatheia* is the absence of emotional experiences.

It's hard to see the teaching of pathos as a problem in education if teachers see the absence of passion as one of their biggest classroom challenges. This is where narrow implementations of the Common Core go most awry. Passion is not the enemy of logic; passion drives logic. We engage in sustained reading, sustained writing, sustained intellectual inquiry out of a sense of passion, not detachment. Talk to any scientist, mathematician, or philosopher about their scholarship for a few minutes and watch their eyes light up and gestures grow animated. Research is *exciting*. Our human hearts and minds have a profound need to wonder. Why do we talk of sending humans to Mars when the same data can be obtained by robots? Because it's not just the data we want. It's the story—the awe-inspiring experience that can only be captured through human senses and human words.

Reading with Passion

This is why it makes no sense to talk about literature without discussing emotional impact. As readers of literature, we have to be prepared for devastating moments of beauty and disabling moments of insight. Some books lay us low before they lift our spirits. Some books tell us what we *need* (but don't want) to hear, a fact that doesn't take the pain out of the sucker punch they deliver. In these moments, we are feeling, as James Phelan puts it, the full force of the narrative's "designs on its audience" (2010, 219). Arundhati Roy's novel *The God of Small Things* (1998) is one of those texts I reread with fear and trembling although I know I'll find a little mercy at the end. At the same time, writing like Roy's celebrates the remarkable potentialities of human hearts and minds. We are not machines. We cannot be reduced, as a report on academic literacy says in describing the desired competencies of entering college students, to a "mere list of skills" (Intersegmental Committee of the Academic Senates of the California Community Colleges, the California State University, and the University of California 2002, 12). If we and our students don't feel a little shaky after reading Shakespeare's *MacBeth* or *Othello* or Toni Morrison's *Beloved*, we're doing something wrong.

----

1. *Of course, another term related to pathos is* empathy, *which the* Oxford English Dictionary *defines as "the ability to understand and appreciate another person's feelings, experience, etc."*

When I teach Kazuo Ishiguro's *The Remains of the Day* ([1989] 1993), for example, the questions my students explore during analysis are all about emotion and what happens when we repress emotions:

- Is there such a thing as irreparable loss?
- What is our capacity for resilience, renewal, and redefinition in the face of devastating loss and regret?
- Can we make a mistake that ruins our lives? Is it ever too late for change?
- What kind of pain does Stevens suffer? What kind of loss does he experience?
- How does his suffering compare with other kinds of heartache?

Lovers of literature experience a kind of comfort and wholeness that transcends the pain we feel from imaginatively entering into the suffering of our fellow creatures. Sometimes just the form of a poem can be reassuring, the elegant stanzas a reminder that at least some of us have used our powers doing more than getting and spending.

Why do I personally need literature in my life? Because great art makes my soul feel its worth. Rosenblatt says, "A great work of art may provide us the opportunity to feel more profoundly and generously, to perceive more fully the implications of experience, than the constricted and fragmentary conditions of life permit" ([1938] 1995, 37). The most profound teaching experiences I've had in my twenty plus years in education have been around the shared study of literature. Nothing quite touches the power of literature for creating transformative classroom moments. The days students cry or shed their facade or finally break their silence are always the days when we read literature. For me, it's imaginative literature that makes things get real. Time and again, I've seen literature spark life-changing learning.

What Students Say . . .

For my students, reading with passion also means reading with purpose and pleasure. This is what they wrote in their journals on the topic:

Ulises: Topics that make me feel more passionate about writing or help with reading comprehension are LGBTQ+ topics, injustice topics. I like talking or bringing up LGBTQ+ topics as much as possible to educate or bring light to it because no one else will.

Priscilla: I read with passion when I'm thoroughly interested in a book. The readings have to either do with documentaries, the government, or an issue that would impact myself.

Kevin: One way to get myself to read with passion is to have something to read that has many things that have happened in my life. Like if I read a book about my hometown, I want to read more.

Jubbylyn: I read with passion when the book speaks to me. I like mystery, romance, horror, fiction, war, history, the human body, and animals.

Antonio: I read with passion when an article, or book, starts to excite me. This is usually a reading that is "heroic."

My students' responses reminded me of the importance of a point Maryanne Wolf makes in her powerful book *Proust and the Squid: The Story and Science of the Reading Brain*: "As every teacher knows, emotional engagement is often the tipping point between leaping into the reading life or remaining in a childhood bog where reading is endured only as a means to other ends" (2008, 132).

You can invite your students to share their own passions through the following writing prompts:

QUICK-WRITE

> *Directions to Students*: What inspires you to do your best work? When do you read and write with passion?

QUICK-WRITE

> *Directions to Students*: Describe a time when you got lost in a good book. What was the book? What did it feel like to live in the world the writer had created? How did you feel when the book was over?

The Right Words at the Right Time

Kairos is the Greek term for "the right words at the right moment." In *Naked Reading: Uncovering What Tweens Need to Become Lifelong Readers*, Teri S. Lesesne describes the transformative power of the right book: "When we find the books that meet the needs and interests of our students, we are placing them squarely on the road to a lifetime of reading. We never know how one right book at the right time in the right hands might impact a tween" (2006, 88).

Finding the right book can be like this: You've been driving in traffic for hours, fatigued and stressed by the demands of work-a-day life, and all of a sudden you find you've turned off the main highway and are now the only car on a country road, driving through a tunnel of oaks as the mist softly rises from an autumn field. It's an astounding experience of full consciousness. Literary reading is arresting; it suspends time, lifting us out of the everyday.

How many times have I found the right book at the right moment? What would my heart-torn teenaged self have done without Emily Brontë's fierce genius? And how sorely my middle-aged self needed books like Sena Jeter Naslund's *Ahab's Wife* (2005), with its mature understanding of the way time takes the edge off even the sharpest horror and loss. One of my students wrote in her journal about the way Sandra Cisneros's *The House on Mango Street* marked a turning point in her life: "This book helped me because before I was insecure and after reading it, I wasn't so insecure."

For many of our students, the right book is also the first book, as in the first book they've finished in a long time . . . or ever. If we don't help more of our students find the right books for them, we have to face the fact that our students aren't just not reading with passion; they're probably not reading at all.

Kylene Beers encourages teachers to ask reluctant readers an important question: "If you absolutely had to read a book, what would it need to be like for you to enjoy it?" (2003, 285). Her students came up with a list of features they find appealing in works of fiction:

- Thin books and short chapters
- White space
- Some illustrations, especially of characters
- Well-defined characters
- Plots with a lot of action that begins right away
- Mysteries
- Funny books
- Characters their age or only slightly older
- Characters who face tough choices
- Realistic language
- An easily defined conflict (2003, 285–288)

Teaching *kairotically* means making the most of our opportunities to reach our students, wherever they are in their educational journey. If they don't (yet) enjoy reading literary texts, we need to increase their access to books that meet their needs and interests. As Leila Christenbury says, "If we want our students to respond to literature, then it is crucial that we choose literature—or let them participate in the choosing of literature—to which they can have a response" (2000, 147).

PEER READING QUIZZES

I've been thoroughly persuaded by Penny Kittle (2003) and Kelly Gallagher (2004) that reading choice and volume matter. How much our students read is one of our most important concerns as English teachers. If the only books our students have access to are required core novels, we have to assume that many of our students are just fake reading, i.e., reading a notes guide or an online summary instead of the actual text. From a communications standpoint, fake reading and writing are even worse than no reading and writing because students are practicing ways to obstruct and obscure authentic communication.

Allowing more instructional space for students to choose the right books at the right time for themselves can help. The following peer reading quiz offers support for free reading choices. I like using these kinds of conversations as assessments because they feel like the opposite of busywork. Talking over a scene's significance is what we do at book club. When possible, I use this same approach when I meet with students for individual reading conferences, too.

Directions to Students: You and your partner will be assessing each other on your understanding of your individual books. Your teacher will also be checking in on your conversations. Take turns following these steps.

Step 1: Open your partner's book to a random page and read it aloud (two to three paragraphs are usually good).

Step 2: Then ask the following questions: What's happening here? What's the context? Why is this passage important to the book as a whole?

I find that students are unwilling to bluff their way through a face-to-face conversation. If they haven't actually read the book, they usually fess up. And if they *have* read the book, then they have a fun intellectual discussion that doesn't involve any busywork.

Reading for a Writer's Exigence

In *Appeals in Modern Rhetoric*, M. Jimmie Killingsworth explains that exigence "is what moves a person to write and what defines a topic" (2005, 27). He further elaborates:

> Exigence has to do with what prompts the author to write in the first place,
> a sense of urgency, a problem that requires attention right now, a need that
> must be met, a concept that must be understood before the audience can
> move to a next step. (27)

The writer is moved to take a position, says Killingsworth, and in turn tries to move the audience toward that same position. We appeal to others—that is, reach out—through our emotions and identity, as well as our reasoning. An appeal is a request for empathy.

Reading with passion often involves feeling empathy for the writer's exigence. We learn to care about the problem or need that the writer cares about, even if we ultimately don't end up sharing the writer's position. Reading for the writer's source of inspiration can help us be more inspired readers ourselves.

We can shift students' exigence for reading from completing an assignment to understanding an act of communication. Students who I know would listen empathetically and even reverentially to a real Anne Frank talking in person about her years hiding from the Nazis nevertheless complain that reading her book is "boring." The book becomes just an assignment to get through—something an English teacher is making them do that has no connection to the experiences of real human beings. The context is all school, as if the book—and the suffering and heroism it describes—only exists in school book rooms, waiting to be checked out to the students who will be forced to read it. When students view books exclusively as "schoolwork," there's little chance of them feeling connected to the wider community of readers who have chosen to read the work for its own sake.

Understanding Pseudo-boredom

To counteract this kind of disengagement from challenging texts, I teach my students about the difference between academic boredom and real boredom. Academic boredom is a special kind of boredom. Unlike the boredom we associate with repetitive or simplistic tasks—think assembly line work here—academic boredom results from cognitive overload rather than from lack of stimulation. The brain has too much to deal with, rather than too little, and so it shuts down, says "Thank you, but I've already had my fill today," and defends the student against further stress by allowing him or her to tune out for the class. Academic boredom, or what composition scholar Charles Bazerman calls *pseudo-boredom*, is thus a type of guard dog against feelings of confusion and insecurity.

I've seen this happen in my own classes more times than I like to admit. I distribute a reading to a class that I consider absolutely fascinating—oh, say, Ralph Waldo Emerson's "Self-Reliance" or some passages from Henry David Thoreau's *Walden*—and the students make a good faith effort to dutifully read what I've assigned for about five minutes. Then it starts: the shifting, the sighs, the slumping, the cell phones. *I* know that what I've distributed is life-changing, electrifying material that should rivet my students' attention to the page. *They* look like they've been in line at the Department of Motor Vehicles for days—exhausted, resigned . . . broken. This is not the face of engagement.

Yet I also know that this is boredom with a difference. Reading *Walden* is not the same as standing in line at the DMV, reading Emerson nothing like capping bottles in a factory (although students may at first experience similar reactions). As Bazerman explains, "Genuine boredom occurs when you are reading material you already know only too well. . . . Pseudo-boredom comes when you feel you just cannot be bothered to figure out what all the new information and ideas mean" (1995, 22–23). Scholars from the Boredom Research Group (real name) offer a more technical distinction: Whereas the academic boredom associated with over-challenging situations can produce complex feelings of anger, anxiety, hopelessness, and shame in some students, the boredom induced by under-challenging tasks simply results in low levels of enjoyment (Acee et al. 2010). Students can thus mean many different things when they say, "This is boring" (Acee et al. 2010).

My job as a teacher is to alert my students to these situational differences in meaning. One of the ways I've tried to help my students distinguish between real boredom and "fake" (i.e., academic) boredom is through a metacognitive approach to academic reading that asks students to notice when they're feeling tired, disengaged, confused, frustrated, and disinterested, and then to apply a fix-up strategy to deal with the source of boredom. In other words, I try to train students to develop their radar for situations that might trigger defensive boredom. The goal of this approach is improved self-awareness, persistence, and personal responsibility.[2]

We begin by completing an anticipation guide, or survey, that asks students to agree or disagree with various statements related to academic reading and boredom (see Appendix 24). For example, "It's not fun to do something until you're good at it" or "The best way to handle confusion is to just keep reading." I usually follow this with a whole-class discussion and quick-write on the most divisive statements. Statements on how to handle distractions tend to draw the biggest reactions ("Ignore them!" "Be disciplined!" "Take a break!"). Because I'm asking my students to consider an attitude change, I want to be sure they have sufficient time and support to explore their feelings. Next, we discuss the special features of academic reading that can induce pseudo-boredom, such as assumed background knowledge, dense information, and academic English (Schleppegrell 2004)—and compare academic texts to materials they might use for pleasure reading. The important point for students to understand is that academic boredom is a response to tasks that feel too hard, not too easy.

I then share with them the following "Top Ten List of What Students Might Really Mean When They Say 'This Is Boring'":

1. I don't want to work this hard.

2. I'm confused.

3. I don't have a purpose for reading.

4. I've never done this before.

5. I don't have any questions I want answered.

6. I'm tired or hungry.

----

2. *I don't mean to suggest that engagement is primarily a student responsibility. "Self-Reliance" and* Walden *warrant additional teacher support and scaffolding. My point is rather that pseudo-boredom is a defensive response that interferes with students' ability to listen to a text.*

7.   I'm preoccupied with something else.

8.   I don't feel like I'm very good at this.

9.   I don't see the connections between this activity and future learning or work.

10.   I have another agenda.

While this list is mostly a conversation starter based on what I think students mean by "boring," the general idea of multiple meanings of boredom is research based (Pekrun et al. 2010; Acee et al. 2010). To introduce the idea that students have some control over their responses to texts, I ask them to talk with a partner about one counterstrategy they could use for one of these causes of boredom. For example, pairs might brainstorm ways to generate questions or make predictions for no. 6 or might discuss sources of support and clarification for no. 2. After participating in this activity, one student wrote, "It's almost as if my mind wants to distract me." Some of her "boredom busters" included stretching for ten minutes, drinking a full glass of water, or even swimming laps when stressed or preoccupied.

We then discuss strategies for making difficult reading assignments active and engaging. In particular, we focus on self-monitoring and fix-up strategies to improve students' comprehension while also reflecting on how, where, and when they read can affect what they understand. See Chapter 2, "Reading Closely and Critically," for examples of these strategies.

When Henry David Thoreau describes reading as "a noble intellectual exercise" that requires us to "stand on tip-toe" and "devote our most alert and wakeful hours to" ([1854] 1937, 94), I want my students to know exactly what he means. These activities help students see that meaning-making is not shouldered by writers alone; readers, too, have to work hard to create tiptoe-standing literacy experiences, especially with academic texts. As Bazerman writes, "The cure for real boredom is to find a more advanced book on the subject; the only cure for pseudo-boredom is to become fully and personally involved in the book already in front of you" (1995, 23).

Writing with Passion

While we don't always write with a lump in our throat or a chip on our shoulder, I think some of the most powerful writing happens this way. We've all been in situations when we were just going through the motions as writers, and there's certainly a great deal of perfunctory writing we encounter in school and out. But just going through the motions doesn't serve us or our audience well. I avoid reading perfunctory writing. I shouldn't write it or teach it.

Rhetorical knowledge changes how students write when it matters most. For students who feel uncomfortable describing their achievements in statements of purpose or scholarship applications, for example, an understanding of exigence can be liberating. Discussing *why* it's important that they've done good work and will continue to do good work—what drives them and what's at stake—transforms a college essay from a hoop jump to an authentic vision statement.

The following three activities invite students to write from the heart.

GRADUATION SPEECHES

Directions to Students: Write your own three- to five-minute graduation speech. What has your educational journey meant to you? What were your most significant turning points or challenges? How did your reading and writing experiences contribute to the person you've become? How will you use this learning in your future life? Begin your graduation speech with a quotation from one of your favorite works of literature.

If you choose to have students read these aloud during class time, be sure to have a box of tissues handy.

WRITING ROGUE

What do we do when we care so much about an issue that the "rules" don't matter anymore? We go rogue. I admit, I totally cheered for the National Park Service when it started tweeting out data on climate change in anticipation of a federal communications shutdown in January 2017. The rogue Twitter account of Badlands National Park in South Dakota broadcast numerous facts about climate science before being silenced, but by that time, several alternative NPS accounts had joined the Twitter rebellion. Rogue NASA and Environmental Protection Agency accounts soon followed (Capatides 2017).

Going rogue can be a powerful way to create or disrupt *kairos*, as California governor Jerry Brown did when he violated the formal decorum of gubernatorial addresses by telling a group of scientists at a conference in San Francisco that "California will launch its own damn satellites" if the White House stops NASA from studying climate change. In its coverage of the governor's speech to the American Geophysical Union, *NBC News* noted that "Brown abandoned all niceties" (Johnson 2016)—a fitting move since one of Brown's points was that shock is sometimes necessary to spur change. Brown's *kairos*-savvy rhetorical choices emphasized the urgency and exceptionality of the situation.

WRITING ROGUE

This assignment is an invitation to students to ditch the directions and follow their hearts.

Writing rogue gives students practice finding a workaround when the usual way of doing things doesn't work. In contrast to the uncertainty students often experience as newcomers to academic writing ("I don't know what to say/do." "I don't how to start." "What do you want this to be about?"), when students go rogue, they usually know exactly what they want to say.

FIGURES 8.1 A AND B

Students writing rogue on the topic of college and career readiness

Directions to Students:

Step 1: Read the following writing prompt: In a well-organized, multiparagraph essay, identify and describe the key academic skills, knowledge, and dispositions (or "habits of mind") that contribute to college and career readiness. Explain why these competencies and attitudes are essential for postsecondary success and what students can do to develop them.

Step 2: Now go rogue! Instead of responding to the prompt in Step 1, identify a different but related issue that you'd rather respond to. Your challenge is to successfully depart from the assigned topic while still acknowledging the original rhetorical situation. How can you turn this conversation in a more interesting and timely direction?

Possible responses (only if you're stuck, remember: the point of this exercise is to write about something that *you* genuinely care about instead of limiting yourself to an assigned subject):

- Experiences of underrepresented students
- Alternatives to college education
- Obstacles to college success
- Problem of finding the right college
- Student debt
- The stress of preparing for college
- Benefits of taking a year off
- College readiness versus career readiness
- Value of work experience

Writing rogue can be the appropriate rhetorical response in situations in which there's a deep disconnect between writing tasks and students' lived experiences—for instance, students who have never been outside their hometowns who are asked to write about the benefits of study abroad on a college placement test. While it's a risky move, a skillful rhetor could take the here's-my-reality approach and change the conversation. (See Figures 8.1a and 8.1b on the previous page.)

I've seen students write successfully against the grain of a prompt during high-stakes standardized tests. An ironic response to a question of policy, for instance ("We don't need to take this action in the future because the future world will no longer care about this issue."). Or a satiric response to the test genre itself ("I know you expect this type of essay, so here it is."). When done with wit, intelligence, and skill, these rogue essays score just as well as more conventional ones, I've found.

Note: What about the student who wants to write on the assigned "boring" topic? Since the purpose of the activity is for students to experience a sense of agency as writers, I can't force a student to obey my advice to go rogue. Resisting deviation from the assignment may be the form of independence they choose. This assignment brings up the unusual possibility that students could refuse to disobey me.

GOFUNDME REQUEST

A GoFundMe Request is another authentic task that invites students to write with passion.

> *Directions to Students*: Write an appeal to donors for an online fund-raising campaign to support a need you learned about through reading a work of literature. Be sure to explain what makes this problem urgent and important right now and what you hope to accomplish through your donors' gifts.

For a reputable example of a GoFundMe campaign, see the following video featuring Alton Pitre, a senior at Morehouse College, whose college tuition was partially supported by a GoFundMe campaign. The video was posted by the Institute for Higher Education Policy (IHEP) as part of its #CollegeNotPrison campaign (www.facebook.com/instituteforhighereducationpolicy/videos/10158360900275111/).

> WPA, NCTE, and NWP's *Framework for Success in Postsecondary Writing* warns that "standardized writing curricula or assessment instruments that emphasize formulaic writing for non-authentic audiences will not reinforce the habits of mind and the experiences necessary for success as students encounter the writing demands of postsecondary education" (2011, 3).

Writing for a "Yes" or a "No"

When I was the English Department chair at Buena Park High School, part of my job was to figure out how many times administration would say "no" to our department's requests before we'd finally get what we wanted. I assumed we'd nearly always encounter initial resistance, and we did. If we had given up the first or second time our ideas were shot down, we'd have accomplished considerably less (although we never did get that backyard trampoline Silva asked for).

One of the most important life lessons I've learned is that sometimes you have to take several noes before you get a yes. Negotiating rejection is a key aspect of problem solving. There are several different kinds of noes that can ultimately comprise our path to success:

- The investment no (the no you pay for the price of learning what you need to know to get that yes down the road)
- The redirection no (the no that steers you away from an unproductive channel to more fruitful endeavors)
- The "I wasn't really listening" no (the default response from an audience predisposed to answer in the negative)
- The paying-your-dues no (you'll get your yes eventually)
- The numbers-game no (multiple attempts matter!)

The variety and implications of these different forms of rejection influence how we accomplish our goals. Some projects need built-in refusal time. If you know that a no or two (or several) are a predictable part of the process for a particular communication context and purpose, you allow yourself some extra response time.

If only our students could build a time machine and get a firsthand look at the real writing purposes that will be a part of their future lives. Their first taste of writing for an authentic purpose often comes through a scholarship essay or job application. It's that yes/no factor that distinguishes real-world purposes from many school purposes.

Writing for a "Yes" or a "No," Not a Letter Grade

I happen to think high-stakes, on-demand writing is some of the most authentic writing high school students encounter. The SAT, AP, or college placement tests have that "yes" or "no" quality that characterizes real-world writing. In many real-world contexts, the effectiveness of an act of communication is measured by a yes-or-no response, not a letter grade or a rubric score. Either the response to the writing is a yes (e.g., "Yes, we'll hire you." "Yes, we'll pass the legislation." "Yes, we'll publish your article." "Yes, we'll fund your project."), or it's a no. Many high-stakes tests have a similar nature (e.g., "Yes, you earn college credit." "Yes, you can take freshman English."). These are not writing situations in which aimless meandering around a topic is going to pass muster. Instead, students need to be ready to identify their purpose in writing straight out of the gate because—unlike classroom-based, process essays—on-demand writing tasks give students only one opportunity to influence the decision of their audience.

WRITING ASSIGNMENT: STARTING WITH A NO

This is one of those tasks that can often produce the right amount of mad.

> *Directions to Students*: Imagine that you've already been told no: "No, you can't have the money for this school event." "No, you can't take this special elective." "No, you can't wear that to the school dance." "No, you can't bring that person as your date." "No, you can't play that song at commencement." Write a rebuttal to the person who has told you no, explaining why you deserve a yes to your request. Carefully consider your purpose, audience, context, and timing. Keep in mind that you already have a history with this audience now.

Our students also need to develop an awareness of how multiple requests and refusals shape reader-writer relationships. Often, preserving goodwill and a creditable ethos can be the key to ultimate success. Other times, it's a case of the squeaky wheel finally getting the oil. We can move people to action by irritating them, but we have to evaluate whether what we sacrifice in goodwill will have unwanted repercussions. Attention to *kairos* and audience helps us make informed decisions about how we persist in the face of rejection.

Prompts for Quick-Writes

- How does a no change how we write?

- How do you know when not to take no for an answer?

- How does a prior no change the rhetorical situation? What rhetorical strategies are needed in this situation?

When Purpose Meets Passion
THANK-YOU NOTES TWO WAYS

Directions to Teachers: You might want to start this activity by sharing YouTube videos of people opening gifts with varying reactions. Show some clips of superexcited kids getting the present of their dreams. Then show some clips of people who are obviously disappointed with what they've received (perhaps an ugly sweater?).

Directions to Students: Imagine you've received two different presents—a gift you love and a gift you hate—and you have to write thank-you notes for each one. No opting out! Try to make each note as sincere and respectful as you can. You may *not* use sarcasm in the note to the gift giver who got it wrong. Follow the steps below.

Step 1:

A. Write a thank-you note for the gift you absolutely love, the gift you've always wanted, the gift you never thought you would actually get but have just received. And it's even better than you thought it'd be! Express your over-the-top joy and gratitude to the giver in a heartfelt thank-you note. (5 minutes)

B. Now write a thank-you note for the gift that you weren't so pleased to receive, the gift that is so *not* you, that has nothing to do with your tastes, values, interests, and likes. You will never use or enjoy this gift. But you have to write a thank-you note anyway to acknowledge the generosity of the giver. Write your note as politely as you can. (5 minutes)

Step 2: Compare your two thank-you notes. How would you describe the tone of each? What is the voice or ethos of the writer of each note? (Yes, the writer is the same person, but do we see the same side of this person in each note? Or does the image or impression we get of this person change from one letter to the next?) What are the primary and secondary purposes of each note? What goal or objective is the writer trying to accomplish with each note? What drives or motivates each note?

Step 3: Reflective Quick-Write: How does having a heartfelt purpose for writing change how we express ourselves? Why do we write differently when we feel passionate about our subject?

Literature and Life Readiness

As I've shared before, David N. Perkins offers a standard by which to judge the value of curricula that I find really useful: lifeworthiness. Perkins defines "lifeworthy" learning as "likely to matter in the lives learners are likely to live" (2014, 8).

I tried Perkins's suggestion to identify what I learned during my first twelve years of education that still matters in my life today, not counting basic literacy and numeracy skills. At the top of my list were those works of classic literature my father read to my sister and me as children. From novels such as *The Secret Garden, Oliver Twist, Little Women, Watership Down,* and *The Hobbit,* I learned that I was not alone, that writing heals, that the world was more than what I could see of it, that humans have a vast capacity for joy and kindness, as well as for suffering and cruelty. I learned to trust in the resourcefulness of the human mind and the resilience of the human spirit. What do I remember from my first twelve years in school? I remember the stories.

Literature of all kinds, narrative and otherwise, has the power to transform lives. In a time when liberal education in general and the humanities in particular are frequently under attack, I don't want to be on the side questioning the value of teaching literary analysis to our students. The genres and purposes of academic and artistic texts are relevant and important, not only to workplace communication but to democratic participation, as well. People who read, write, and critique imaginative literature tend to be more engaged in some sectors of the "real world" than those who don't. The 2004 National Endowment for the Arts Report *Reading at Risk* notes that those who read literature have higher participation levels in a variety of civic activities:

> Literary readers are much more likely to be involved in cultural, sports and volunteer activities than are non-readers. For example, literary readers are nearly three times as likely to attend a performing arts event, almost four times as likely to visit an art museum, more than two-and-a-half times as likely to do volunteer or charity work, and over one-and-a-half times as likely to attend or participate in sports activities. (National Endowment for the Arts 2004, 5)

Literary readers also vote at considerably higher rates (National Endowment for the Arts 2009, 3).

I don't want to teach my students to take a predominantly instrumentalist approach to literature either, reading every text with an eye to its use value. "What's in this for me?" is not the first question I want students to ask about a poem or a novel. But I do think one of the benefits of closely studying enduring works of literature is that we inevitably end up making connections to our own lives. When we find those gems in the literary tradition that explain where an idea comes from or why a word means what it means, we're energized with insider knowledge.

Ultimately, reading literature must be more than the means to an end. As Maryanne Wolf puts it in *Proust and the Squid,* we want students to make the leap into "the reading life" (2008, 132). Literary reading is rich with intrinsic rewards; it is worth doing for its own sake. *And it* offers students abundant opportunities to "extend their integrative abilities into the challenges of personal, professional, and civic life," as AAC&U (2009) recommends in its Integrative and Applied Learning VALUE Rubric.

A lifelong passion for reading and writing will support students' best work in any setting.

> Teaching for transfer doesn't mean students read literature only with an eye to its real-world applications. Students are still reading for discovery and pleasure and starting with an open mind, not demanding that a text prove its worth and relevance before giving it a fair chance.

Teaching with Passion

We know when our heart isn't in our work. There have been days in my teaching life when I was just going through the motions, trying to keep my head above water while checking off items on someone else's to-do list. On those days, I wasn't teaching for transfer.

How else do we know when we're not teaching for transfer? We're not teaching for transfer if we've done so much scaffolding for our students and their work is so assignment specific that students are unlikely to see a purpose beyond a mark in the grade book. We're not teaching for transfer if we find ourselves saying things like, "You need to do this because it's on the test." Or if students ask, "Why are we doing this?" and we say, "because it's in the Common Core" (without addressing *why* that standard is in the Common Core in the first place). We're not teaching for transfer if we share our academic expectations but not our intellectual passions. Perfunctory instruction doesn't produce lifeworthy learning.

Here's my top ten list of things teachers say when we're not teaching for transfer (I've said most of these myself at one time or another):

10. "Don't worry about the logic behind this—just trust me."
9. "We've always done it this way."
8. "This will be the last time you'll ever have to do this."
7. "We've been told we have to do this, so we're doing it."
6. "I suffered through this, and you have to, too."
5. "I'm glad that's behind us!"
4. "I don't enjoy this any more than you do."
3. "Let's get this over with."
2. "That's just the way it is."
1. "You need to know this because it's on the test/in the standards."

In contrast to the messages these statements send, when we teach literature for transfer, we invite students to respond to the exigence of making meaningful connections between literary studies and their own past, present, and future lives. For many of us, this is what makes learning exciting. Following our passions means connecting one series of dots after another, like illuminated points of light on a runway leading us home. It's integrative thinking that builds the personal, academic, and professional networks that support our best work, bringing together the diverse ways of knowing and being that shape who we are.

Teaching for transfer ultimately means teaching with passion.

Conclusion: The Things We Carry

We take with us what is precious. The learning that students carry into their future lives should be lifeworthy learning, learning that helps them live joyful and meaningful lives. Caring deeply about reading and writing enriches our lives immeasurably—today and tomorrow.

I carry with me the vision of my students' remarkable potential. Year after year, I'm humbled by the quality of human being that walks into my classroom: Kevin, who has lost both his parents but has learned that grief does not have to be disabling; Jasmine, who balances studying with caring for her sick mother; Erick, who has discovered he is most motivated and engaged when helping others; Jubby, who draws her dreams; Ulises, who advocates for LGTBQ+ students; and Moises, whose quiet statements command the attention of the whole room.

Each new year gives me a chance to practice a lesson I learned from my grandmother, a brown-eyed farm girl from Oklahoma: Seeing the best in people brings out the best in people. It's not hard to see all the excellent qualities my students bring to our learning communities. Sometimes I feel like my job is just to feed these bright souls on their journey and stay out of the way of the wonder at work. I'm honored by what my students have been willing to share of their lives and hopes with me.

Our students are kind, creative, and resilient. They're carrying a wealth of personal and cultural assets with them into their future lives. Nothing gave me more encouragement than seeing the way our students responded to the sweeping political tensions and challenges during the past few years. If we take the thousands of pictures of signs held by young people during the civil rights marches of 2017 and 2018 as representing the voice of this generation, their message is "diversity and inclusion," not "isolation and division." Those posters that read "If you build a wall, my generation will tear it down" gave me tremendous hope for our future. These kids have got our back. (See Figure 8.2.)

I have no doubt they will make the world a better place. And I think of my own amazing two middle schoolers, our son, Dryden, and our daughter, Ellerie. The generation of students we now serve in our classrooms is one of the most caring and connected groups of people the world has known; they're far more likely to build bridges than walls. This is what some of my students say they want for themselves:

> **Priscilla:** I want to be happy in my life. . . . I want to have a career that I enjoy and to be able to help people. Ultimately, I want to make my family proud of who I've become.

FIGURES 8.2 A AND B

These good people give me great hope.

Jasmine: [To] know that I am where I want to be.

Viviana: The thing I want the most would be traveling around the globe with my family and friends. I want to give back something to them in rewards of their sacrifices that they made for me.

Kevin: In the future, I hope that I would have found a job that I love and learn to make more connections with more people.

With our help, our students will continue to build bridges of understanding, integrating and applying their learning, reading critically, reasoning thoughtfully, negotiating differences, solving problems, communicating ethically and effectively, and living joyfully. The future is in good hands.

Appendix Contents

Appendix I

Student Sample of Assignment Comparison

Assignment (compare & contrast)

Argument Essays
- thesis is limited to the text in the prompt
- Supporting your argument w/ evidence presented to you
- Analyze more in depth to back you up in your position
- your own view
- Short in length
- dialogic
- different audience

(center overlap)
- bad words
- sentence fragments
- transitions
- Quotations
- pre-read
- outline
- connect reading to writing

Research Paper
- what everyone thinks about it not your opinion
- build writers knowledge on topic of our choice
- research & expand more on information found
- it is more longer than essay
- compare information found
- audience different
- more evidence
- more writing, commentary
- more than one perspective
- need scholar sources
- pick our own topic

Appendix 2

AAC&U Integrative Learning VALUE Rubric

INTEGRATIVE LEARNING VALUE RUBRIC

for more information, please contact value@aacu.org

Association of American Colleges and Universities

The VALUE rubrics were developed by teams of faculty experts representing colleges and universities across the United States through a process that examined many existing campus rubrics and related documents for each learning outcome and incorporated additional feedback from faculty. The rubrics articulate fundamental criteria for each learning outcome, with performance descriptors demonstrating progressively more sophisticated levels of attainment. The rubrics are intended for institutional-level use in evaluating and discussing student learning, not for grading. The core expectations articulated in all 15 of the VALUE rubrics can and should be translated into the language of individual campuses, disciplines, and even courses. The utility of the VALUE rubrics is to position learning at all undergraduate levels within a basic framework of expectations such that evidence of learning can by shared nationally through a common dialog and understanding of student success.

Definition

Integrative learning is an understanding and a disposition that a student builds across the curriculum and co-curriculum, from making simple connections among ideas and experiences to synthesizing and transferring learning to new, complex situations within and beyond the campus.

Framing Language

Fostering students' abilities to integrate learning—across courses, over time, and between campus and community life—is one of the most important goals and challenges for higher education. Initially, students connect previous learning to new classroom learning. Later, significant knowledge within individual disciplines serves as the foundation, but integrative learning goes beyond academic boundaries. Indeed, integrative experiences often occur as learners address real-world problems, unscripted and sufficiently broad, to require multiple areas of knowledge and multiple modes of inquiry, offering multiple solutions and benefiting from multiple perspectives. Integrative learning also involves internal changes in the learner. These internal changes, which indicate growth as a confident, lifelong learner, include the ability to adapt one's intellectual skills, to contribute in a wide variety of situations, and to understand and develop individual purpose, values and ethics. Developing students' capacities for integrative learning is central to personal success, social responsibility, and civic engagement in today's global society. Students face a rapidly changing and increasingly connected world where integrative learning becomes not just a benefit but a necessity.

Because integrative learning is about making connections, this learning may not be as evident in traditional academic artifacts such as research papers and academic projects unless the student, for example, is prompted to draw implications for practice. These connections often surface, however, in reflective work, self assessment, or creative endeavors of all kinds. Integrative assignments foster learning between courses or by connecting courses to experientially-based work. Work samples or collections of work that include such artifacts give evidence of integrative learning. Faculty are encouraged to look for evidence that the student connects the learning gained in classroom study to learning gained in real life situations that are related to other learning circumstances, extra-curricular activities, or work. Through integrative learning, students pull together their entire experience inside and outside of the formal classroom; thus, artificial barriers between formal study and informal or tacit learning become permeable. Integrative learning, whatever the context or source, builds upon connecting both theory and practice toward a deepened understanding.

Assignments to foster such connections and understanding could include, for example, composition papers that focus on topics from biology, economics, or history; mathematics assignments that apply mathematical tools to important issues and require written analysis to explain the implications and limitations of the mathematical treatment, or art history presentations that demonstrate aesthetic connections between selected paintings and novels. In this regard, some majors (e.g., interdisciplinary majors or problem-based field studies) seem to inherently evoke characteristics of integrative learning and result in work samples or collections of work that significantly demonstrate this outcome. However, fields of study that require accumulation of extensive and high-consensus content knowledge (such as accounting, engineering, or chemistry) also involve the kinds of complex and integrative constructions (e.g., ethical dilemmas and social consciousness) that seem to be highlighted so extensively in self reflection in arts and humanities, but they may be embedded in individual performances and less evident. The key in the development of such work samples or collections of work will be in designing structures that include artifacts and reflective writing or feedback that support students' examination of their learning and give evidence that, as graduates, they will extend their integrative abilities into the challenges of personal, professional, and civic life.

Glossary

The definitions that follow were developed to clarify terms and concepts used in this rubric only.

- **Academic knowledge:** Disciplinary learning; learning from academic study, texts, etc.
- **Content:** The information conveyed in the work samples or collections of work.
- **Contexts:** Actual or simulated situations in which a student demonstrates learning outcomes. New and challenging contexts encourage students to stretch beyond their current frames of reference.
- **Co-curriculum:** A parallel component of the academic curriculum that is in addition to formal classroom learning (student government, community service, residence hall activities, student organizations, etc.).
- **Experience:** Learning that takes place in a setting outside of the formal classroom, such as workplace, service learning site, internship site or another.
- **Form:** The external frameworks in which information and evidence are presented, ranging from choices for particular work sample or collection of works (such as a research paper, PowerPoint, video recording, etc.) to choices in make-up of the portfolio.
- **Performance:** A dynamic and sustained act that brings together knowing and doing (creating a painting, solving an experimental design problem, developing a public relations strategy for a business, etc.); performance makes learning observable.
- **Reflection:** A meta-cognitive act of examining a performance in order to explore its significance and consequences.
- **Self Assessment:** Describing, interpreting, and judging a performance based on stated or implied expectations followed by planning for further learning.

Appendix 2 — cont.

AAC&U Integrative Learning VALUE Rubric

A|A C&U Association of American Colleges and Universities

INTEGRATIVE LEARNING VALUE RUBRIC

for more information, please contact value@aacu.org

Definition

Integrative learning is an understanding and a disposition that a student builds across the curriculum and cocurriculum, from making simple connections among ideas and experiences to synthesizing and transferring learning to new, complex situations within and beyond the campus.

Evaluators are encouraged to assign a zero to any work sample or collection of work that does not meet benchmark (cell one) level performance.

	Capstone 4	Milestones 3	Milestones 2	Benchmark 1
Connections to Experience *Connects relevant experience and academic knowledge*	Meaningfully **synthesizes connections** among experiences outside of the formal classroom (including life experiences and academic experiences such as internships and travel abroad) to **deepen understanding** of fields of study and to broaden own points of view.	Effectively **selects and develops** examples of life experiences, drawn from a variety of contexts (e.g., family life, artistic participation, civic involvement, work experience), to **illuminate** concepts/theories/frameworks of fields of study.	**Compares** life experiences and academic knowledge to infer differences, as well as similarities, and **acknowledge perspectives** other than own.	**Identifies** connections between life experiences and those academic texts and ideas perceived **as similar and related** to own interests.
Connections to Discipline *Sees (makes) connections across disciplines, perspectives*	Independently creates wholes out of multiple parts (synthesizes) or draws conclusions by combining examples, facts, or theories from more than one field of study or perspective.	Independently connects examples, facts, or theories from more than one field of study or perspective.	When prompted, connects examples, facts, or theories from more than one field of study or perspective.	When prompted, presents examples, facts, or theories from more than one field of study or perspective.
Transfer *Adapts and applies skills, abilities, theories, or methodologies gained in one situation to new situations*	Adapts and applies, independently, skills, abilities, theories, or methodologies gained in one situation to new situations to solve **difficult problems or explore complex issues in original ways.**	Adapts and applies skills, abilities, theories, or methodologies gained in one situation to **new situations to solve problems or explore issues.**	Uses skills, abilities, theories, or methodologies gained in one situation in a new situation **to contribute to understanding of problems or issues.**	Uses, in a basic way, skills, abilities, theories, or methodologies gained in one situation **in a new situation.**
Integrated Communication	Fulfills the assignment(s) by choosing a format, language, or graph (or other visual representation) **in ways that enhance meaning,** making clear the interdependence of language and meaning, thought, and expression.	Fulfills the assignment(s) by choosing a format, language, or graph (or other visual representation) to **explicitly connect content and form,** demonstrating awareness of purpose and audience.	Fulfills the assignment(s) by choosing a format, language, or graph (or other visual representation) that **connects in a basic way** what is being communicated (content) with how it is said (form).	Fulfills the assignment(s) (i.e. to produce an essay, a poster, a video, a PowerPoint presentation, etc.) **in an appropriate form.**
Reflection and Self-Assessment *Demonstrates a developing sense of self as a learner, building on prior experiences to respond to new and challenging contexts (may be evident in self-assessment, reflective, or creative work)*	Envisions a future self (and possibly makes plans that build on past experiences) that have occurred across multiple and diverse contexts.	Evaluates changes in own learning over time, recognizing complex contextual factors (e.g. works with ambiguity and risk, deals with frustration, considers ethical frameworks).	Articulates strengths and challenges (within specific performances or events) to increase effectiveness in different contexts (through increased self-awareness).	Describes own performances with general descriptors of success and failure.

Reprinted with permission from *Assessing Outcomes and Improving Achievement: Tips and Tools for Using Rubrics,* edited by Terrel L. Rhodes. Copyright 2009 by the Association of American Colleges and Universities.

Appendix 3 — Sonnet 15 Annotation Cue Cards

Annotation Cue Cards for Group Analysis of a Text: Sonnet 15 by William Shakespeare

Comment: The phrase "everything that grows" focuses our attention on all plant and animal life on earth, including human beings.

Question: What does "holds" mean in this line? Is this like possession or ownership? Or more like a plane's holding pattern, a temporary position?

Comment: The first two lines are about how all living things are at their best for just a short time.

Question: What does Shakespeare mean by "this huge stage"? Is this a metaphor?

Comment: The words "but" (meaning "only") and "little" in line 2 stress the ephemeral nature of physical beauty; beauty is fleeting.

Comment: "Nought" means "nothing."

Comment: We perform our little lives under the watch of the cosmos.

Comment: The pronoun "this" points to the arena of action where our human dramas take place.

Question: Do "cheered" and "checked" mean the same thing in this line? Are both words about nurturing life? Or does "checked" refer to constraints on growth?

Comment: This second subordinate clause ("When I perceive . . .") introduces another observation that prompts thoughts about mortality.

Question: What does "vaunt" mean? What are the connotations of this word?

Comment: The rhyming words "increase" and "decrease" suggest that growth and decay are two sides of the same coin.

Comment: This phrase suggests that humans, like plants, begin to rot or fade after reaching their prime.

Comment: This word in the final couplet takes us back to the plant metaphor, making the poet seem like a gardener with the power of extension or renewal.

Question: Does "grafting" always refer to something you do to a plant or living thing (e.g., skin graft)?

Appendix 3 — cont.

Comment: Write your own annotation on this card and say it aloud whenever it naturally fits into the group analysis of the text.

Question: What does "Time debateth with Decay" mean? Are they arguing with each other? It sounds like they're trying to do the same thing in the sonnet.

Question: Why are "Time" and "Decay" capitalized? Is this a type of figurative language?

Comment: Maybe the debate is more of a contest or a competition. Time and Decay are both striving to make the young old.

Comment: Write your own annotation on this card and say it aloud whenever it naturally fits into the group analysis of the text.

Question: What does "sullied" mean? What are the connotations of this word?

Comment: Write your own annotation on this card and say it aloud whenever it naturally fits into the group analysis of the text.

Question: Who's at war with Time? It can't be Decay because Decay doesn't love the person the speaker's addressing.

Comment: The speaker reassures his beloved that the poem itself will give back the youth and beauty Time takes away.

Question: Write your own question on this card and ask it whenever it naturally fits into the group analysis of the text.

Question: Write your own question on this card and ask it whenever it naturally fits into the group analysis of the text.

Question: Write your own question on this card and ask it whenever it naturally fits into the group analysis of the text.

Appendix 4

Descriptive Plot Outlining

Descriptive Plot Chart

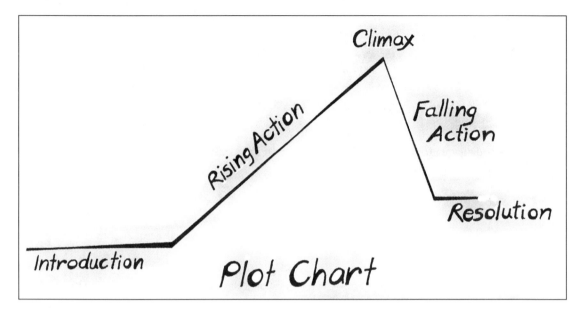

Directions: Draw a plot diagram (see above) representing the events in your selected narrative. You may choose to diagram the narrative as a whole OR to diagram the dramatic arc for a particular moment or scene. On the outside of your diagram, list what happens at each point. Then, inside the diagram, describe what each event does rhetorically. Your descriptive statements should reveal how the events function in the text. In other words, what impact does the event have on the reader, character(s), or theme? What is the effect or purpose of that event? See the list of verbs below for ideas on how to write your "does" statements.

Verbs for "Does" Statements for Literary Analysis:

closes	intensifies	counters	undermines
amplifies	pauses	balances	suggests
introduces a complication	invites	heightens	challenges
builds to a crescendo	introduces	increases	surprises
expands	questions	qualifies	frustrates
contracts	softens	reverses	confuses

Appendix 5

Student Sample of Say, Mean, Matter, Do for *The Absolutely True Diary of a Part-Time Indian*

Say (Quotation and page number)	Mean (Paraphrase and/or close reading of quotation)	Matter (Connection to the theme; significance to the work as a whole)	Do (Effect on the reader and/or text; rhetorical function or move)
"But I had to stand eventually, and when I did, I knew that my best friend had become my worst enemy" (Alexie 53).	Junior is telling the readers that Rowdy has just become his worst enemy, though he is his best friend. R. does not support J.'s decision to go to an all – white school, even if it is going to benefit Junior.	This quotation connects to theme of friendship present in the novel. To have friends is a huge deal, especially for adolescents. A common concern that students at a new school often have is whether or not they will make new friends. J. already gets bullied and pushed around and R. has been there to stand up for him. But now R. has broken a friendship with J. and he is lonelier than ever.	When I read this quote, personally I felt extremely bad for Junior. He is not getting the true support from a true friend, so it made me question as a reader, "Is Rowdy truly Junior's best friend as Junior says he is?" This quote, readers will later see, will have a huge impact on Junior's and Rowdy's relationship till the end of the novel and it will also serve as juxtaposition to Junior's new friends that he will make.
"'Son,'" Mr. P. said. 'You're going to find more and more hope the farther and farther you walk away from this sad, sad, sad reservation'" (Alexie 43).	Junior's teacher advises Junior to leave the reservation in order to obtain a better education and overall a better lifestyle. The repetition of words in this quote places an emphasis on how important this decision is for Junior and also how important it is to Mr. P. that Junior leaves his home.	This is the start of the turning point of the novel, where Junior may or may not leave the reservation, which is a huge deal for the Indians, because it is not common for an Indian on a reservation to leave to better themselves. As a result, if Junior leaves, havoc can occur.	As a reader, it questions us to whether or not Junior will leave. It placed this effect on me as well as illustrating that a teacher, a grown adult, is telling Junior this. No one from before ever brought up to Junior on how he could find more hope for himself. Therefore, it showed me that this teacher is portraying as a true role model towards Junior.

Teaching Literature Rhetorically: Transferable Literacy Skills for 21st Century Students by Jennifer Fletcher. Copyright © 2018. Stenhouse Publishers.

Appendix 6

Student Sample of Descriptive Plot Outline for *Ender's Game*

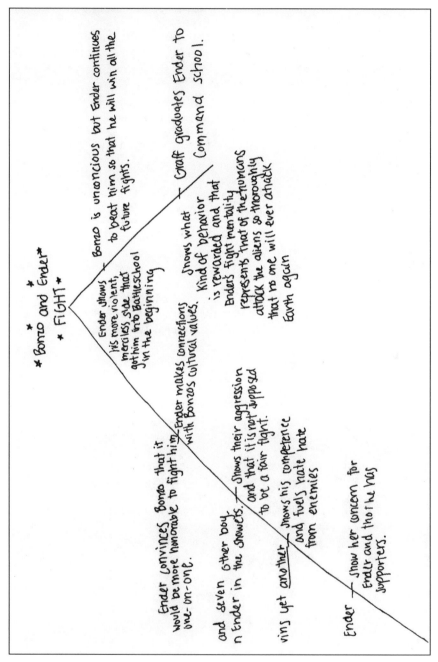

Appendix 7

Descriptive Plot Outline for "The Most Dangerous Game"

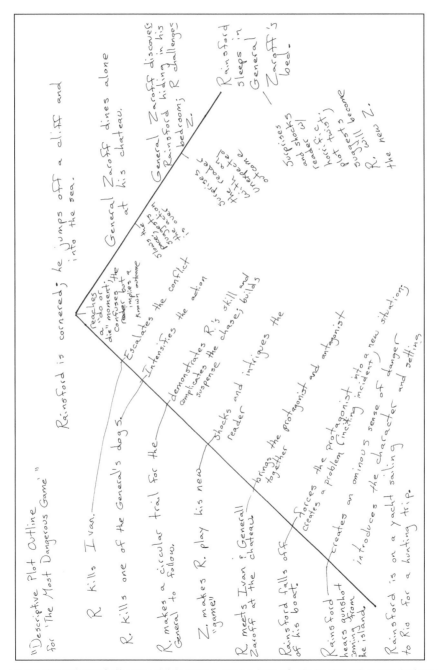

"Descriptive Plot Outline for 'The Most Dangerous Game'"

Rainsford is on a yacht sailing to Rio for a hunting trip. — introduces the character and setting

Rainsford hears gunshot coming from the island. — creates an ominous sense of danger

Rainsford falls off of his boat. — forces the protagonist into a new situation; creates a problem (inciting incident)

R. meets Ivan & General Zaroff at the chateau. — brings the protagonist and antagonist together

Z. makes R. play his new "game." — shocks the reader and intrigues the

R. makes a circular trail for the General to follow. — demonstrates R.'s skill and complicates the chase; builds suspense

R. kills one of the General's dogs.

R. Kills Ivan.

Rainsford is cornered; he jumps off a cliff and into the sea. — reaches a "do or die" moment; confuses the reader but implies a known outcome

General Zaroff dines alone at his chateau. — Escalates the conflict

General Zaroff discovers Rainsford hiding in his bedroom; R challenges Z. — Intensifies the action — surprises the reader with an unexpected outcome

Rainsford sleeps in General Zaroff's bed. — surprises and shocks w/ reader (i.e., a horrific twist); plot twists suggest R will become the new Z.

Appendix 8

"The Storyteller" by H. H. Munro (Saki) (1870-1916)

Narrator One: It was a hot afternoon, and the railway carriage was correspondingly sultry, and the next stop was at Templecombe, nearly an hour ahead. The occupants of the carriage were a small girl, and a smaller girl, and a small boy. An aunt belonging to the children occupied one corner seat, and the further corner seat on the opposite side was occupied by a bachelor who was a stranger to their party, but the small girls and the small boy emphatically occupied the compartment.

Narrator Two: Both the aunt and the children were conversational in a limited, persistent way, reminding one of the attentions of a housefly that refuses to be discouraged. Most of the aunt's remarks seemed to begin with

Aunt: "Don't,"

Narrator Three: and nearly all of the children's remarks began with

Cyril, Girl One, and Girl Two: "Why?"

Narrator One: The bachelor said nothing out loud.

Aunt: "Don't, Cyril, don't,"

Narrator Two: exclaimed the aunt, as the small boy began smacking the cushions of the seat, producing a cloud of dust at each blow.

Aunt: "Come and look out of the window,"

Narrator Three: she added. The child moved reluctantly to the window.

Cyril: "Why are those sheep being driven out of that field?"

Narrator One: he asked.

Aunt: "I expect they are being driven to another field where there is more grass,"

Narrator Two: said the aunt weakly.

Cyril: "But there is lots of grass in that field,"

Narrator Three: protested the boy;

Cyril: "there's nothing else but grass there. Aunt, there's lots of grass in that field."

Aunt: "Perhaps the grass in the other field is better,"

Narrator One: suggested the aunt fatuously.

Cyril: "Why is it better?"

Narrator Two: came the swift, inevitable question.

Aunt: "Oh, look at those cows!"

Appendix 8 — cont.

Narrator Three: exclaimed the aunt. Nearly every field along the line had contained cows or bullocks, but she spoke as though she were drawing attention to a rarity.

Cyril: "Why is the grass in the other field better?"

Narrator One: persisted Cyril.

Narrator Two: The frown on the bachelor's face was deepening to a scowl. He was a hard, unsympathetic man, the aunt decided in her mind. She was utterly unable to come to any satisfactory decision about the grass in the other field.

Narrator Three: The smaller girl created a diversion by beginning to recite "On the Road to Mandalay." She only knew the first line, but she put her limited knowledge to the fullest possible use. She repeated the line over and over again in a dreamy but resolute and very audible voice; it seemed to the bachelor as though some one had had a bet with her that she could not repeat the line aloud two thousand times without stopping. Whoever it was who had made the wager was likely to lose his bet.

Aunt: "Come over here and listen to a story,"

Narrator One: said the aunt, when the bachelor had looked twice at her and once at the communication cord.

The children moved listlessly towards the aunt's end of the carriage. Evidently her reputation as a story-teller did not rank high in their estimation.

Narrator Two: In a low, confidential voice, interrupted at frequent intervals by loud, petulant questionings from her listeners, she began an unenterprising and deplorably uninteresting story about a little girl who was good, and made friends with every one on account of her goodness, and was finally saved from a mad bull by a number of rescuers who admired her moral character.

Girl One: "Wouldn't they have saved her if she hadn't been good?"

Narrator Three: demanded the bigger of the small girls. It was exactly the question that the bachelor had wanted to ask.

Aunt: "Well, yes,"

Narrator Two: admitted the aunt lamely,

Aunt: "but I don't think they would have run quite so fast to her help if they had not liked her so much."

Girl One: "It's the stupidest story I've ever heard,"

Narrator Three: said the bigger of the small girls, with immense conviction.

Cyril: "I didn't listen after the first bit, it was so stupid,"

Narrator One: said Cyril.

Teaching Literature Rhetorically: Transferable Literacy Skills for 21st Century Students by Jennifer Fletcher. Copyright © 2018. Stenhouse Publishers.

Appendix 8 — cont.

Narrator Two: The smaller girl made no actual comment on the story, but she had long ago recommenced a murmured repetition of her favourite line.

Bachelor: "You don't seem to be a success as a story-teller,"

Narrator Three: said the bachelor suddenly from his corner.

Narrator One: The aunt bristled in instant defence at this unexpected attack.

Aunt: "It's a very difficult thing to tell stories that children can both understand and appreciate,"

Narrator Two: she said stiffly.

Bachelor: "I don't agree with you,"

Narrator Three: said the bachelor.

Aunt: "Perhaps you would like to tell them a story,"

Narrator One: was the aunt's retort.

Girl One: "Tell us a story,"

Narrator Two: demanded the bigger of the small girls.

Bachelor: "Once upon a time,"

Narrator Three: began the bachelor,

Bachelor: "there was a little girl called Bertha, who was extra-ordinarily good."

Narrator One: The children's momentarily-aroused interest began at once to flicker; all stories seemed dreadfully alike, no matter who told them.

Bachelor: "She did all that she was told, she was always truthful, she kept her clothes clean, ate milk puddings as though they were jam tarts, learned her lessons perfectly, and was polite in her manners."

Girl One: "Was she pretty?"

Narrator Two: asked the bigger of the small girls.

Bachelor: "Not as pretty as any of you,"

Narrator Three: said the bachelor,

Bachelor: "but she was horribly good."

Narrator One: There was a wave of reaction in favour of the story; the word *horrible* in connection with goodness was a novelty that commended itself. It seemed to introduce a ring of truth that was absent from the aunt's tales of infant life.

Bachelor: "She was so good,"

Narrator Two: continued the bachelor,

Appendix 8 — cont.

Bachelor: "that she won several medals for goodness, which she always wore, pinned on to her dress. There was a medal for obedience, another medal for punctuality, and a third for good behaviour. They were large metal medals and they clicked against one another as she walked. No other child in the town where she lived had as many as three medals, so everybody knew that she must be an extra good child."

Cyril: "Horribly good,"

Narrator Three: quoted Cyril.

Bachelor: "Everybody talked about her goodness, and the Prince of the country got to hear about it, and he said that as she was so very good she might be allowed once a week to walk in his park, which was just outside the town. It was a beautiful park, and no children were ever allowed in it, so it was a great honour for Bertha to be allowed to go there."

Cyril: "Were there any sheep in the park?"

Narrator One: demanded Cyril.

Bachelor: "No;"

Narrator Two: said the bachelor,

Bachelor: "there were no sheep."

Cyril: "Why weren't there any sheep?"

Narrator Three: came the inevitable question arising out of that answer.

Narrator One: The aunt permitted herself a smile, which might almost have been described as a grin.

Bachelor: "There were no sheep in the park,"

Narrator Two: said the bachelor,

Bachelor: "because the Prince's mother had once had a dream that her son would either be killed by a sheep or else by a clock falling on him. For that reason the Prince never kept a sheep in his park or a clock in his palace."

Narrator Three: The aunt suppressed a gasp of admiration.

Cyril: "Was the Prince killed by a sheep or by a clock?"

Narrator One: asked Cyril.

Bachelor: "He is still alive, so we can't tell whether the dream will come true,"

Narrator Two: said the bachelor unconcernedly;

Bachelor: "anyway, there were no sheep in the park, but there were lots of little pigs running all over the place."

Cyril: "What colour were they?"

Appendix 8 — cont.

Bachelor: "Black with white faces, white with black spots, black all over, grey with white patches, and some were white all over."

Narrator Three: The storyteller paused to let a full idea of the park's treasures sink into the children's imaginations; then he resumed:

Bachelor: "Bertha was rather sorry to find that there were no flowers in the park. She had promised her aunts, with tears in her eyes, that she would not pick any of the kind Prince's flowers, and she had meant to keep her promise, so of course it made her feel silly to find that there were no flowers to pick."

Girl One: "Why weren't there any flowers?"

Bachelor: "Because the pigs had eaten them all,"

Narrator One: said the bachelor promptly.

Bachelor: "The gardeners had told the Prince that you couldn't have pigs and flowers, so he decided to have pigs and no flowers."

Narrator Two: There was a murmur of approval at the excellence of the Prince's decision; so many people would have decided the other way.

Bachelor: "There were lots of other delightful things in the park. There were ponds with gold and blue and green fish in them, and trees with beautiful parrots that said clever things at a moment's notice, and humming birds that hummed all the popular tunes of the day. Bertha walked up and down and enjoyed herself immensely, and thought to herself: 'If I were not so extraordinarily good I should not have been allowed to come into this beautiful park and enjoy all that there is to be seen in it,' and her three medals clinked against one another as she walked and helped to remind her how very good she really was. Just then an enormous wolf came prowling into the park to see if it could catch a fat little pig for its supper."

Cyril, Girl One, and Girl Two: "What colour was it?"

Narrator Three: asked the children, amid an immediate quickening of interest.

Bachelor: "Mud-colour all over, with a black tongue and pale grey eyes that gleamed with unspeakable ferocity. The first thing that it saw in the park was Bertha; her pinafore was so spotlessly white and clean that it could be seen from a great distance. Bertha saw the wolf and saw that it was stealing towards her, and she began to wish that she had never been allowed to come into the park. She ran as hard as she could, and the wolf came after her with huge leaps and bounds. She managed to reach a shrubbery of myrtle bushes and she hid herself in one of the thickest of the bushes. The wolf came sniffing among the branches, its black tongue lolling out of its mouth and its pale grey eyes glaring with rage. Bertha was terribly frightened, and thought to herself: 'If I had not been so extraordinarily good I should have been safe in the town at this moment.' However, the scent of the myrtle was so strong that the wolf could not sniff out where Bertha was hiding, and the bushes were so thick that he might have hunted about in them for a long time without catching sight of her, so he thought he might as well go off and

Teaching Literature Rhetorically: Transferable Literacy Skills for 21st Century Students by Jennifer Fletcher. Copyright © 2018. Stenhouse Publishers.

Appendix 8 — cont.

catch a little pig instead. Bertha was trembling very much at having the wolf prowling and sniffing so near her, and as she trembled the medal for obedience clinked against the medals for good conduct and punctuality. The wolf was just moving away when he heard the sound of the medals clinking and stopped to listen; they clinked again in a bush quite near him. He dashed into the bush, his pale grey eyes gleaming with ferocity and triumph, and dragged Bertha out and devoured her to the last morsel. All that was left of her were her shoes, bits of clothing, and the three medals for goodness."

Girl Two: "Were any of the little pigs killed?"

Bachelor: "No, they all escaped."

Girl Two: "The story began badly,"

Narrator One: said the smaller of the small girls,

Girl Two: "but it had a beautiful ending."

Girl One: "It is the most beautiful story that I ever heard,"

Narrator Two: said the bigger of the small girls, with immense decision.

Cyril: "It is the only beautiful story I have ever heard,"

Narrator Three: said Cyril.

Narrator One: A dissentient opinion came from the aunt.

Aunt: "A most improper story to tell to young children! You have undermined the effect of years of careful teaching."

Bachelor: "At any rate,"

Narrator Two: said the bachelor, collecting his belongings preparatory to leaving the carriage,

Bachelor: "I kept them quiet for ten minutes, which was more than you were able to do."

Bachelor: "Unhappy woman!"

Narrator Three: he observed to himself as he walked down the platform of Templecombe station;

Bachelor: "for the next six months or so those children will assail her in public with demands for an improper story!"

Appendix 9

"The Storyteller" Annotation Cue Cards

Directions to the Teacher: Distribute the following comments and questions on individual slips of paper or index cards. It's best if the cards aren't in order. You may not have enough cue cards for each student to have one, but you should have enough "plants" around the room so that you have lots of responses when you ask your students to help you annotate Saki's story. A few students will receive "wild cards" on which they can write their own comments or questions—you can add more "wild cards" as students become more proficient in annotation.

As part of a second reading of the text, read sections of the story aloud, calling for those students with cue cards to add their comments or questions at the relevant moments. Encourage students to put their cue cards in their own words. Add your own critical "Think-Aloud" comments as appropriate. Be sure to pause frequently to ask if anyone has anything to contribute and remind students to annotate their own copies of the story during this process. Let students know it's OK if they don't see a spot to share their cue card; they can make up their own comments or questions instead.

Comment: The opening description suggests a dreary atmosphere.

Comment: Sounds like a dull and boring situation.

Question: Why don't we get the bachelor's name?

Question: What is the narrator's tone when he says the children remind one of a housefly?

Comment: The children want storytellers to know the reason for everything.

Comment: The word "emphatically" suggests the children took over the space.

Question: Does the narrator see the bachelor the same way the aunt does?

Question: How are the aunt's thoughts different from the bachelor's thoughts?

Comment: A "frown" suggests unhappiness and a "scowl" suggests dislike or disapproval.

Question: Can we believe this? Is the aunt credible?

Comment: This shows the narrator finds the aunt boring, too.

Question: What's this poem about? Is it important?

Question: Is this from the children's or narrator's point of view? Or both?

Appendix 9 — cont.

Comment: Suggests Aunt's view of good behavior is oppressive and boring.

Comment: The word "lamely" suggests the aunt doesn't really know what she's doing.

Question: Is the aunt trying to teach the children a moral lesson or keep them busy on the train? Or both?

Question: Is the bachelor using the children as inspiration?

Comment: The oxymoron "horribly good" catches the children's interest.

Question: Is Bertha supposed to remind us of the aunt?

Comment: This shows the aunt thinks the bachelor will have the same problems with the children's questions that she had.

Question: Children's values and interests are different from the aunt's.

Comment: Write your own annotation on this card and say it aloud whenever it naturally fits into the group analysis of the text.

Comment: Write your own annotation on this card and say it aloud whenever it naturally fits into the group analysis of the text.

Comment: Write your own annotation on this card and say it aloud whenever it naturally fits into the group analysis of the text.

Question: Write your own question on this card and ask it whenever it naturally fits into the group analysis of the text.

Question: Write your own question on this card and ask it whenever it naturally fits into the group analysis of the text.

Question: Write your own question on this card and ask it whenever it naturally fits into the group analysis of the text.

Appendix 10

Say, Mean, Matter, Do for "The Storyteller"

Directions: **Choose several quotations from the text to record in the following chart. Then practice paraphrasing each quotation and analyzing its significance to the work as a whole, as well as the quotation's rhetorical function and impact on the reader (i.e., what it *does*).**

SAY (Quotation and page number)	MEAN (Paraphrase of quotation and/or close reading of its literary and/or rhetorical devices)	MATTER (Connection to the theme and/ or importance of the quotation to the author's purpose)	DO (Rhetorical effect and function of the quotation; impact on reader)
Saki writes, "The children moved listlessly toward the aunt's end of the carriage. Evidently her reputation as a storyteller did not rank high in their estimation" (2).	The word "listlessly"—meaning "slowly" or "without energy"— shows the lack of interest the children have in their aunt's stories, and, in fact, that her stories seem to have a depressing effect on their spirits.	This description is important to the story as a whole for multiple reasons. First, it shows that the children do not respect or admire their aunt and that her moral "instruction" prompts passive resistance, not eager compliance. Second, it shows how poorly she understands the children in her charge; the bachelor has a much better understanding of the children's interests and needs and can meet them appropriately.	The narration slows at this point. The reader doesn't expect anything interesting or exciting to happen while the aunt is telling her story.

Appendix 11

Checklist for Listening to a Think-Aloud: Analyzing Literature Rhetorically

Directions to Students: As you listen to the "Think-Aloud," keep track of what the reader does while analyzing the text rhetorically. Place a check mark by everything you hear the reader do during the demonstration.

___ Identify the subject of the text

___ Postpone judgment

___ Identify figurative language and/or symbolism

___ Notice sentence patterns and choices

___ Identify the context

___ Notice text structure and organization

___ Evaluate the effectiveness of the writer's rhetorical choices

___ Analyze connotations of words

___ Paraphrase key sentences or phrases

___ Summarize the writer's theme or message

___ Identify meaningful repetition

___ Notice inconsistencies or ambiguities

___ Notice what sections of the text say and do

___ Identify the writer's purpose

___ Notice key transitions and shifts

___ Offer a personal response

___ Connect language choices to theme or meaning

___ Look for irony

___ Consider the rhetorical effect of punctuation

Appendix 12

Rhetorical Précis for Caliban's Speech

Textual Analysis Practice

In Act I, scene ii of William Shakespeare's *The Tempest* (1610), Caliban claims that Prospero has stolen the island and his freedom from him, both of which Caliban claims are rightfully his own. Caliban recounts Prospero's kindness towards him at first, despite having taken away his mother; yet now Caliban views his imprisonment on a barren corner of the island as a cruel betrayal by Prospero. Caliban's outburst serves to give another version of the past to the reader, in order to cast a shadow over Prospero and complicate his character. Therefore, the reader is presented with a power imbalance very different from others presented within Act I, and forced to adjust their opinions of Prospero. Shakespeare may be trying to warn those in the audience to beware of those in power, and that all that glitters is not always gold.

Appendix 13

Kairos Analysis

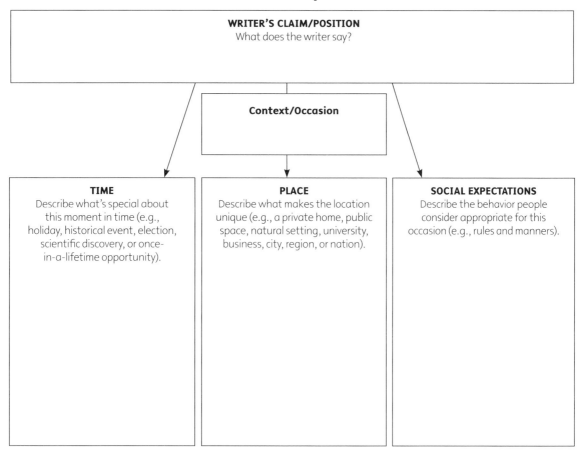

Kairos Analysis

WRITER'S CLAIM/POSITION
What does the writer say?

Context/Occasion

TIME
Describe what's special about this moment in time (e.g., holiday, historical event, election, scientific discovery, or once-in-a-lifetime opportunity).

PLACE
Describe what makes the location unique (e.g., a private home, public space, natural setting, university, business, city, region, or nation).

SOCIAL EXPECTATIONS
Describe the behavior people consider appropriate for this occasion (e.g., rules and manners).

THE LANGUAGE OF *KAIROS*
List any words or phrases in the text that suggest the importance of time.

Quick-Write: How would you describe the *kairos* of this text? How do time, place, and social expectations impact the writer's argument? Do you think the writer has chosen the best opportunity to make his or her argument?

Appendix 14

Comparing and Learning from Communication Autobiographies

"Comparing and Learning from Communication Autobiographies" developed by Dr. Nelson Graff

Author Add the names of those you talk to about that narrative under the author's name.	Problems or Conflicts List problems or conflicts that arose about literacy in the narrative.	Solutions or Resolutions List what the authors did to meet their challenges.	Ideas About Communication List insights the narrative offered you about effective communication.	Reflection List one or two sentences that clearly show reflection in the narrative.	Qualities List characteristics of the narrative that made it effective.
Sherman Alexie					
Amy Tan					
Frederick Douglass					

Appendix 15

Genre Analysis

Genre Analysis

Genre Name: _____

Mentor Texts:
List the titles of several texts that exemplify the key characteristics of this genre.

Purpose:

Organization:	**Language Choices:**	**Writer's Ethos:**
How are texts in this genre generally structured (e.g., chronological order, compare and contrast, etc.)? Are there paragraphs, stanzas, dialogue, chapters, lists, headings, etc.? Do texts usually have a certain kind of beginning or end?	Describe the kinds of words and sentences commonly used in this genre. Is the language typically formal or casual, simple or complex?	How do writers generally present themselves in this genre? What kind of "voice" do they typically use? Do you get to know the writer personally?

Special Features:
List any other conventions or stylistic choices that characterize this genre, including features like documentation style (e.g., MLA), figurative language, pictures, and rhetorical moves.

Context and Audience: In what situations is this type of writing typically used? Who typically reads this genre?

Appendix 16

Genre Feature Analysis Matrix

Genre Feature Analysis Matrix

Name of Genre: _____

Directions to Students: Create a list of 4-6 titles of mentor texts that are examples of the genre you are analyzing. Write the titles of these texts in the far left column. Then, for each mentor text, place a check mark in the box for each genre feature that is a characteristic of that text. Mark all that apply.

Medium	visual rhetoric					
	written communication					
	oral communication					
Context and Community	age-specific					
	time-sensitive					
	broad					
	specialized					
	discipline-specific					
Special Features	stage directions					
	index					
	citations					
	footnotes or endnotes					
	visuals					
	charts or tables					
	dialogue					
Organization	narrative text structure					
	compare and contrast text structure					
	cause and effect text structure					
	stanzas					
	chapters					
	headings					
Language Choices	first-person "I"					
	specialized vocabulary					
	academic English					
	casual diction					
	formal diction					
	complex sentences					
	simple sentences					
Rhetorical and Literary Devices	setting					
	plot					
	symbolism					
	fictional characters					
	personal anecdotes					
	scholarly evidence					
	rhyme scheme					
	imagery					
	figurative language					
Mentor Texts						

Appendix 17

Polar Opposites Guides for Protagonists in YA Literature (Bean and Bishop 1992)

Directions to Students: Place a check mark closest to the adjective that best describes your understanding of each character. Then, in a small-group discussion, defend your choices by using examples from the readings, class discussions, and your outside experiences and observations.

Arnold (*The Absolutely True Diary of a Part-Time Indian*) is...

confident	—	—	—	—	—	insecure
popular	—	—	—	—	—	unpopular
typical	—	—	—	—	—	atypical
supported	—	—	—	—	—	unsupported
included	—	—	—	—	—	excluded
certain	—	—	—	—	—	uncertain
decisive	—	—	—	—	—	indecisive
empowered	—	—	—	—	—	oppressed
transitioning	—	—	—	—	—	settled
mature	—	—	—	—	—	immature
rebellious	—	—	—	—	—	complicit
happy	—	—	—	—	—	unhappy
honest	—	—	—	—	—	dishonest
loyal	—	—	—	—	—	disloyal
traditional	—	—	—	—	—	nontraditional
	5	4	3	2	1	

Appendix 17 — *cont.*

Eddie (*Buried Onions*) is...

confident	—	—	—	—	—	insecure
popular	—	—	—	—	—	unpopular
typical	—	—	—	—	—	atypical
supported	—	—	—	—	—	unsupported
included	—	—	—	—	—	excluded
certain	—	—	—	—	—	uncertain
decisive	—	—	—	—	—	indecisive
empowered	—	—	—	—	—	oppressed
transitioning	—	—	—	—	—	settled
mature	—	—	—	—	—	immature
rebellious	—	—	—	—	—	complicit
happy	—	—	—	—	—	unhappy
honest	—	—	—	—	—	dishonest
loyal	—	—	—	—	—	disloyal
traditional	—	—	—	—	—	nontraditional
	5	4	3	2	1	

Appendix 17 — *cont.*

Delphine (*One Crazy Summer*) **is...**

	5	4	3	2	1	
confident	—	—	—	—	—	insecure
popular	—	—	—	—	—	unpopular
typical	—	—	—	—	—	atypical
supported	—	—	—	—	—	unsupported
included	—	—	—	—	—	excluded
certain	—	—	—	—	—	uncertain
decisive	—	—	—	—	—	indecisive
empowered	—	—	—	—	—	oppressed
transitioning	—	—	—	—	—	settled
mature	—	—	—	—	—	immature
rebellious	—	—	—	—	—	complicit
happy	—	—	—	—	—	unhappy
honest	—	—	—	—	—	dishonest
loyal	—	—	—	—	—	disloyal
traditional	—	—	—	—	—	nontraditional

Appendix 17 — *cont.*

Jin Wang (*American Born Chinese*) is...

	5	4	3	2	1	
confident	—	—	—	—	—	insecure
popular	—	—	—	—	—	unpopular
typical	—	—	—	—	—	atypical
supported	—	—	—	—	—	unsupported
included	—	—	—	—	—	excluded
certain	—	—	—	—	—	uncertain
decisive	—	—	—	—	—	indecisive
empowered	—	—	—	—	—	oppressed
transitioning	—	—	—	—	—	settled
mature	—	—	—	—	—	immature
rebellious	—	—	—	—	—	complicit
happy	—	—	—	—	—	unhappy
honest	—	—	—	—	—	dishonest
loyal	—	—	—	—	—	disloyal
traditional	—	—	—	—	—	nontraditional

Appendix 17 — *cont.*

Jackie (*Brown Girl Dreaming*) is...

	5	4	3	2	1	
confident	—	—	—	—	—	insecure
popular	—	—	—	—	—	unpopular
typical	—	—	—	—	—	atypical
supported	—	—	—	—	—	unsupported
included	—	—	—	—	—	excluded
certain	—	—	—	—	—	uncertain
decisive	—	—	—	—	—	indecisive
empowered	—	—	—	—	—	oppressed
transitioning	—	—	—	—	—	settled
mature	—	—	—	—	—	immature
rebellious	—	—	—	—	—	complicit
happy	—	—	—	—	—	unhappy
honest	—	—	—	—	—	dishonest
loyal	—	—	—	—	—	disloyal
traditional	—	—	—	—	—	nontraditional

Appendix 17 — *cont.*

Esperanza (*The House on Mango Street***) is...**

confident	—	—	—	—	—	insecure
popular	—	—	—	—	—	unpopular
typical	—	—	—	—	—	atypical
supported	—	—	—	—	—	unsupported
included	—	—	—	—	—	excluded
certain	—	—	—	—	—	uncertain
decisive	—	—	—	—	—	indecisive
empowered	—	—	—	—	—	oppressed
transitioning	—	—	—	—	—	settled
mature	—	—	—	—	—	immature
rebellious	—	—	—	—	—	complicit
happy	—	—	—	—	—	unhappy
honest	—	—	—	—	—	dishonest
loyal	—	—	—	—	—	disloyal
traditional	—	—	—	—	—	nontraditional
	5	4	3	2	1	

Appendix 17 — *cont.*

Ender (*Ender's Game*) is...

	5	4	3	2	1	
confident	—	—	—	—	—	insecure
popular	—	—	—	—	—	unpopular
typical	—	—	—	—	—	atypical
supported	—	—	—	—	—	unsupported
included	—	—	—	—	—	excluded
certain	—	—	—	—	—	uncertain
decisive	—	—	—	—	—	indecisive
empowered	—	—	—	—	—	oppressed
transitioning	—	—	—	—	—	settled
mature	—	—	—	—	—	immature
rebellious	—	—	—	—	—	complicit
happy	—	—	—	—	—	unhappy
honest	—	—	—	—	—	dishonest
loyal	—	—	—	—	—	disloyal
traditional	—	—	—	—	—	nontraditional

Appendix 18

Conversation Seating Plan

Appendix 19

Negotiating Voices (Distinguishing Between What a Writer Says and What a Character Says)

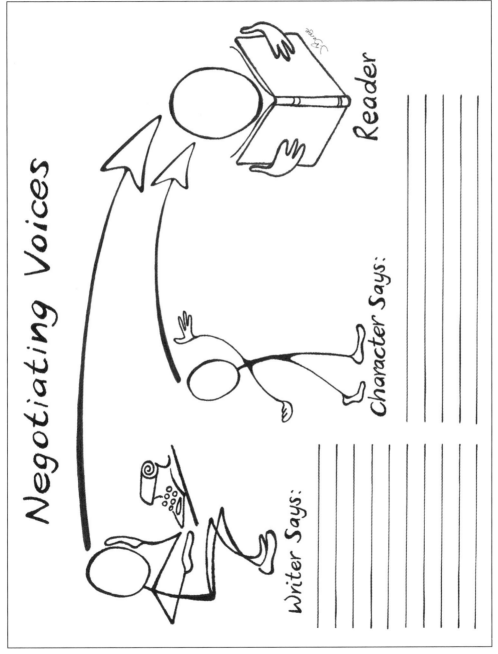

Appendix 20

Polar Opposites Guides for Women in 19th Century Literature (Bean and Bishop 1992)

Directions to Students: Place a check mark closest to the adjective that best describes your understanding of each character. Then, in a small-group discussion, defend your choices by using examples from the readings, class discussions, and your outside experiences and observations.

Elizabeth Bennet is...

confident	—	—	—	—	—	insecure
virtuous	—	—	—	—	—	vicious
conventional	—	—	—	—	—	unconventional
angelic	—	—	—	—	—	"fallen"
chaste	—	—	—	—	—	passionate
warm	—	—	—	—	—	cold
proud	—	—	—	—	—	modest
empowered	—	—	—	—	—	oppressed
rebellious	—	—	—	—	—	compliant
happy	—	—	—	—	—	unhappy
honest	—	—	—	—	—	dishonest
strong	—	—	—	—	—	weak
fulfilled	—	—	—	—	—	unfulfilled
orderly	—	—	—	—	—	disorderly
	5	4	3	2	1	

Jane Eyre is...

confident	—	—	—	—	—	insecure
virtuous	—	—	—	—	—	vicious
conventional	—	—	—	—	—	unconventional

Appendix 20 — cont.

	5	4	3	2	1	
angelic	—	—	—	—	—	"fallen"
chaste	—	—	—	—	—	passionate
warm	—	—	—	—	—	cold
proud	—	—	—	—	—	modest
empowered	—	—	—	—	—	oppressed
rebellious	—	—	—	—	—	compliant
happy	—	—	—	—	—	unhappy
honest	—	—	—	—	—	dishonest
strong	—	—	—	—	—	weak
fulfilled	—	—	—	—	—	unfulfilled
orderly	—	—	—	—	—	disorderly

Catherine Earnshaw Linton is…

confident	—	—	—	—	—	insecure
virtuous	—	—	—	—	—	vicious
conventional	—	—	—	—	—	unconventional
angelic	—	—	—	—	—	"fallen"
chaste	—	—	—	—	—	passionate
warm	—	—	—	—	—	cold
proud	—	—	—	—	—	modest
empowered	—	—	—	—	—	oppressed
rebellious	—	—	—	—	—	compliant
happy	—	—	—	—	—	unhappy
honest	—	—	—	—	—	dishonest

Appendix 20 — cont.

strong	—	—	—	—	—	weak
fulfilled	—	—	—	—	—	unfulfilled
orderly	—	—	—	—	—	disorderly
	5	4	3	2	1	

Hester Prynne is…

confident	—	—	—	—	—	insecure
virtuous	—	—	—	—	—	vicious
conventional	—	—	—	—	—	unconventional
angelic	—	—	—	—	—	"fallen"
chaste	—	—	—	—	—	passionate
warm	—	—	—	—	—	cold
proud	—	—	—	—	—	modest
empowered	—	—	—	—	—	oppressed
rebellious	—	—	—	—	—	compliant
happy	—	—	—	—	—	unhappy
honest	—	—	—	—	—	dishonest
strong	—	—	—	—	—	weak
fulfilled	—	—	—	—	—	unfulfilled
orderly	—	—	—	—	—	disorderly
	5	4	3	2	1	

Appendix 21

Ethos Analysis

Ethos Analysis for Narrators

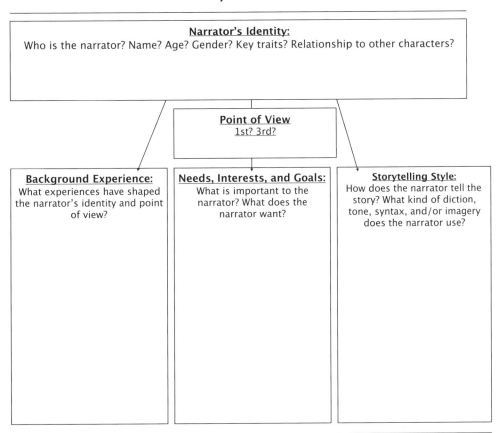

Narrator's Identity:
Who is the narrator? Name? Age? Gender? Key traits? Relationship to other characters?

Point of View
1st? 3rd?

Background Experience:
What experiences have shaped the narrator's identity and point of view?

Needs, Interests, and Goals:
What is important to the narrator? What does the narrator want?

Storytelling Style:
How does the narrator tell the story? What kind of diction, tone, syntax, and/or imagery does the narrator use?

Quick-write: How would you describe the narrator's image or ethos? What adjectives would you use to describe the narrator? Do you trust this person? Do you like or admire this person? To what extent, if any, does the writer seem to share the narrator's views?

Appendix 22

Communication Feature Analysis Matrix

Communication Feature Analysis Matrix

Title and Author of Literary Text: _____

Directions to Students: Create a list of 4-6 characters from a work of literature you are studying. Write the names of these characters in the far left column. Then, for each character, place a check mark in the box for each communication behavior that is typical of that character. Mark all that apply.

Literary Characters	Persuasive Strategies								Collaborative Problem Solving							Listening to Understand					Making Connections						Obstacles to Understanding								Relationship Building				
	supports claims with evidence	shares personal stories	uses humor	uses deductive reasoning (if....then...)	appeals to own authority or power	appeals to fear or anger	appeals to self-interest	negotiates agreements	explores multiple perspectives	contributes own insights	tests different solutions	works to build consensus	compromises	seeks additional information	paraphrases others' words (mirrors)	summarizes others' views	checks for understanding	postpones judgment	asks clarifying questions	reflects on past experiences	draws on prior knowledge	sees similarities and differences	relates to others' experiences	synthesizes information	sees the big picture	interrupts others	deceives self or others	dominates conversations	threatens to harm others	withdraws	insults others or calls others names	uses sarcasm or ridicule	encourages others	validates others	promotes equity of participation	expresses empathy	sets ground rules or norms		

Appendix 23

Reader Annotations for Student Essay on *The Absolutely True Diary of a Part-Time Indian*

In *The Absolutely True Diary of a Part-Time Indian*, Sherman Alexie places the tragedies of the main character, Junior, in direct juxtaposition with his lighthearted tone. This side-by-side comparison allows the reader to learn the truth about how marginalized Junior's life has been, as well as experience the optimism that is the heart of his survival.

Junior begins the novel with an anecdote about how he was born with too much cerebral spinal fluid inside of his skull, forcing him to undergo surgery at six months old that was predicted to have one of two outcomes: his death, or brain damage so severe he would "live the rest of [his] life as a vegetable" (8). Though the content of his anecdote is tragic, his language is full of jokes; he makes fun of himself for being born with a deformity, "But weirdo me, I was born with too much grease inside my skull…" (8), of the deformity itself, "…like my brain was a giant French fry" (8), and of the physical problems resulting from his brain damage, "…I ended up having forty-two teeth… Ten teeth past human" (8-9). In further describing his physical form, he describes his eyes as "so lopsided" (9), being so skinny he'd "turn sideways and disappear (9), and having a head so big "that little Indian skulls orbited around it" (9). He also informs the reader that he had a stutter and a lisp, "Or maybe I should say… a st-st-st-st-stutter and a lishthththp" (9), and that "Everybody on the rez calls [him] a retard about twice a day" (9).

While the anecdote tells the reader that Junior's life has been tragic since he was born, his silly attitude towards his brain damage, and the permanent effects of it, sets the tone for the rest of the book: one that lets the reader know that Junior prefers to laugh at his hardships as opposed to feel pity for himself. His humor is used as a tactic to downplay the severity of his tragedies, making them seem less invasive and impacting on his life.

Handwritten annotations:

precise focus on the purpose and effect of Alexie's choices

right → this is an interesting and important contrast

That's the tension

yes!

This is a compelling reading of the novel

I like how you are describing what Alexie is saying and doing

These examples let your reader appreciate the same edgy humor you describe in your analysis

significant

good word—

anything else?

clear articulation of how these choices impact meaning

I'd want to qualify this statement, too. Alexie doesn't spare his readers the pain of understanding his experiences.

Appendix 24

"Boredom Busters" Anticipation/Reaction Guide

Directions: Read each statement. Then, in column one, write a plus sign if you agree with the statement, a minus sign if you disagree, or a question mark if you are unsure about your opinion. For many statements there are no right answers. At the end of the unit or lesson, you can indicate your reactions in column two.

Agree= +   Disagree= -   Don't know= ?

1. _____ _____ The best way to handle confusion is to just keep reading.

2. _____ _____ It's best to completely ignore personal problems when studying.

3. _____ _____ Having surgery is less stressful than essay tests.

4. _____ _____ Students who are strong in math are usually poor writers.

5. _____ _____ Great writers are born, not made.

6. _____ _____ It's easier to write academic essays if you warm up by reading.

7. _____ _____ I do my best work late at night.

8. _____ _____ I do my best work early in the morning.

9. _____ _____ I often feel sleepy when I try to read academic texts.

10. _____ _____ Reading textbooks is boring.

11. _____ _____ I enjoy writing short stories or autobiographical incidents.

12. _____ _____ Reading literature is boring.

13. _____ _____ It is difficult for me to find time for pleasure reading.

14. _____ _____ Most careers require critical reading and writing skills.

15. _____ _____ Daily writing produces better results than "binge" writing.

16. _____ _____ I consider myself a skilled and competent writer.

17. _____ _____ I find it hard to concentrate when I write essays at home.

18. _____ _____ It's not fun to do something until you're good at it.

19. _____ _____ I enjoy writing poetry or song lyrics.

20. _____ _____ Writing essays takes too much time.

Appendix 25

Transfer of Learning

Transfer of Learning

Preconditions for Transfer	Acts of Tranfer	Transferable Literacy Skills
A mindset toward connection-making	From reading to writing	Assessing the rhetorical situation
An ability to hold onto thinking	From one assignment to the next	Analyzing genres
Rhetorical knowledge and skills	From literary analysis to rhetorical analysis	Reading closely and critically
A habit of creative problem solving	From one class to another	Negotiating voices and perspectives
A habit of leveraging prior knowledge	From high school to college	Communicating with self and others in mind

Appendix 26

Tips for Teaching for Transfer

Tips for Teaching for Transfer

- Help students compare and contrast rhetorical situations.

- Empower students to make effective rhetorical choices.

- Give students opportunities to make transfer choices.

- Make transfer opportunities visible.

References

Abrams, M. H. (1953) 1971. *The Mirror and the Lamp: Romantic Theory and the Critical Tradition*. New York: Oxford University Press.

Acee, Taylor W., et al. 2010. "Academic Boredom in Under- and Over-Challenging Situations." *Contemporary Educational Psychology* 35(1): 17–27.

Ackroyd, Peter. 2005. *Chaucer*. New York: Doubleday.

Adams, Maurianne, Lee Anne Bell, and Pat Griffin. 2007. *Teaching for Diversity and Social Justice*. 2nd edition. New York: Routledge.

Adler-Kassner, Linda. 2017. "Transfer and Educational Reform in the Twenty-First Century." *Understanding Writing Transfer: Implications for Transformative Student Learning in Higher Education*. Sterling, VA: Stylus.

Adler-Kassner, Linda, and Elizabeth Wardle, eds. 2015. *Naming What We Know: Threshold Concepts of Writing Studies*. Boulder: University Press of Colorado.

Alexie, Sherman. 1998. "The Joy of Reading and Writing; Superman and Me." *Los Angeles Times*, April.

———. 2009. *The Absolutely True Diary of a Part-Time Indian*. New York: Little, Brown Books.

Anaya, Rudolfo. 1972. *Bless Me, Ultima*. Berkeley, CA: TQS Publications.

Appleman, Deborah. 2000. *Critical Encounters in High School English: Teaching Literary Theory to Adolescents*. New York: Teachers College Press and the National Council of Teachers of English.

Aristotle. 1984. *The Rhetoric and the Poetics*. Translated by W. Rhys Roberts. New York: McGraw-Hill.

Association of American Colleges and Universities. 2009. "Integrative and Applied Learning VALUE Rubric." www.aacu.org/value/rubrics/integrative-learning.

Atwood, Margaret. 1996. *Power Politics: Poems*. Toronto, ON: House of Anansi Press Inc.

Austen, Jane. (1813) 1985. *Pride and Prejudice*. New York: Penguin Books.

Axelrod, Rise B., Charles Raymond Cooper, and Alison M. Warriner. 2008. *Reading Critically, Writing Well: A Reader and Guide*. 8th ed. Boston: Bedford/St. Martin's.

Bakhtin, Mikhail Mikailovich. 1981. *The Dialogic Imagination: Four Essays by M. M. Bakhtin*. Michael Holquist, ed. Caryl Emerson and Michael Holquist, trans. Austin/University of Texas Press.

Ballenger, Bruce. 2008. *The Curious Writer*. Brief ed., 2nd ed. New York: Pearson.

Barkley, Elizabeth F. 2010. *Student Engagement Techniques: A Handbook for College Faculty*. San Francisco: Jossey-Bass.

Barnet, Sylvan, and Hugo Bedau. 2014. *From Critical Thinking to Argument*. Boston: Bedford/St. Martin's.

Bartholomae, David, and Tony Petrosky. 2002. *Ways of Reading: An Anthology for Writers*. Boston: Bedford/St. Martin's.

Bawarshi, Anis S., and Mary Jo Reif. 2010. *Genre: An Introduction to History, Theory, Research, and Pedagogy*. West Lafayette, IN: Parlor Press.

Bazerman, Charles. 1995. *The Informed Writer: Using Sources in the Disciplines*. 5th ed. Boston: Houghton Mifflin.

———. 2013. *A Rhetoric of Literate Action: Literate Action* Volume 1. Fort Collins, CO: The WAC Clearinghouse and Parlor Press.

Bean, John C., Virginia A. Chappell, and Alice M. Gillam. 2014. *Reading Rhetorically*. 4th ed. Upper Saddle River, NJ: Pearson.

Bean, Thomas and Ashley Bishop. 1992. "Polar Opposites." A Strategy for Guiding Students' Critical Reading and Discussion in Dishner, E., Bean, T., and Readance, J. 1986. *Reading in the Content Areas: Improving Classroom Instruction*. 3rd ed. Kendal/Hunt 247-254.

Beaufort, Anne. 1999. *Writing in the Real World: Making the Transition from School to Work*. New York: Teachers College Press.

Beers, Kylene. 2003. *When Kids Can't Read: What Teachers Can Do*. Portsmouth, NH: Heinemann.

Bennett, William J. 1993. *The Book of Virtues: A Treasury of Great Moral Stories*. New York: Simon and Schuster.

Beowulf. 1977. Translated by Howell D. Chickering. New York: Doubleday.

Beowulf. 2000. Translated and introduction by Seamus Heaney. New York: W. W. Norton.

Bhatia, Vijay. 2014. *Worlds of Written Discourse: A Genre-Based View*. London: Bloomsbury.

Bitzer, Lloyd F. 1999. "The Rhetorical Situation." *Contemporary Rhetorical Theory: A Reader*, eds. John Louis Lucaites, Celeste Michelle Condit, and Sally Caudill. New York: The Guilford Press.

Blau, Sheridan D. 2003. *The Literature Workshop: Teaching Texts and Their Readers*. Portsmouth, NH: Heinemann.

Blauman, Zygmunt. 2007. *Liquid Times: Living in an Age of Uncertainty*. Cambridge, UK: Polity Press.

Booth, Wayne C. [1961] 1983. *The Rhetoric of Fiction*. 2nd ed. Chicago: University of Chicago Press.

———. 1974. *The Rhetoric of Irony*. Chicago: University of Chicago Press.

Brandt, William J. 1970. *The Rhetoric of Argumentation*. Indianapolis, IN: Bobbs-Merrill Co.

Briggs, John C. 2004. "Writing Without Reading: The Decline of Literature in the Composition Classroom." *Forum: A Publication of the Association of Literary Scholars and Critics*.

Bruffee, Kenneth A. 2007. *A Short Course in Writing: Composition, Collaborative Learning, and Constructive Reading*. 4th ed. New York: Pearson Longman.

Burke, Kenneth. 1969. *A Rhetoric of Motives*. Berkeley: University of California Press.

Burns, Robert. 2014. "US Trained Alaskans as Secret 'Stay-Behind Agents.'" Associated Press, August 30.

Bury, Liz. 2013. "Reading Literary Fiction Improves Empathy, Study Finds." *The Guardian*, October. www.theguardian.com/books/booksblog/2013/oct/08/literary-fiction-improves-empathy-study.

California State University, Task Force on Expository Reading and Writing. 2013. *Expository Reading and Writing Course*. 2nd ed. Long Beach: California State University.

Capatides, Christina. 2017. "Badlands National Park Twitter Account Goes Rogue, Starts Tweeting Scientific Facts." *CBS News*, January 24.

Card, Orson Scott. 1985. *Ender's Game*. New York: Tor Books.

Chamberlain, Mike. 2011. "Whales to Windmills: Inventions Inspired by the Sea." *TEDx Talks*. YouTube video, 13:47. November 21. www.youtube.com/watch?v=OpLzI27febM.

Charon, Rita. 2006. *Narrative Medicine: Honoring the Stories of Illness*. New York: Oxford University Press.

Chaucer, Geoffrey. (1387–1400) 1985. *The Canterbury Tales*. Edited by Constance B. Hieatt and A. Kent Hieatt. New York: Bantam Books.

———. (14th century) 1996. *The Wife of Bath*. Edited by Peter G. Beidler. Case Studies in Contemporary Criticism. Boston: Bedford/St. Martin's.

Christenbury, Leila. 2000. *Making the Journey: Being and Becoming a Teacher of English Language Arts*. 2nd edition. Portsmouth, NH: Heinemann.

Coleman, David. 2011. "Bringing the Common Core to Life." Full transcript of webinar. New York State Education Department. http://usny.nysed.gov/rttt/docs/bringingthecommoncoretolife/fulltranscript.pdf

Corbett, Edward P. J., and Rosa A. Eberly. 2000. *The Elements of Reasoning*. 2nd ed. Boston: Allyn and Bacon.

Council of Writing Program Administrators. 2014. *WPA Outcomes Statement for First-Year Composition (3.0)*. http://wpacouncil.org/positions/outcomes.html.

Crosswhite, James. 1996. *The Rhetoric of Reason: Writing and the Attractions of Argument*. Madison: University of Wisconsin Press.

Cunningham, Katie Egan. 2015. *Story: Still the Heart of Literacy Learning*. Portland, ME: Stenhouse.

CWPA, NCTE, and NWP Council of Writing Program Administrators, National Council of Teachers of English, and National Writing Project). 2011. *Framework for Success in Postsecondary Writing*. Berkeley, CA: National Writing Project.

Dewey, John. [1899] 1990. *The School and Society*. Chicago: University of Chicago.

Diaz, John. 2017. "United's 'Hindenburg of Airline Customer Service Episodes.'" *San Francisco Chronicle*, April 11.

Díaz, Junot. 2007. *The Brief Wondrous Life of Oscar Wao*. New York: Riverhead Books.

Dickinson, Emily. 1891. "I'm Nobody! Who Are You?" https://www.poets.org/poetsorg/poem/im-nobody-who-are-you-260.

Dole, Janice, Gerald G. Duffy, Laura R. Roehler, and P. David Pearson. 1991. "Moving from the Old to the New: Research on Reading Comprehension Instruction." *Review of Educational Research* 61,(2): 239–264.

Douglass, Frederick. 1845. *Narrative Of The Life Of Frederick Douglass An American Slave. Written By Himself*. Salt Lake City, UT: Project Gutenberg. www.gutenberg.org.

Duffy, J. and Clauss, P. 2016. "A Brief Essay on the Troubling Distinction Made in the Common Core State Standards for Writing Between Argument and Persuasion," March 23.

Dumas, Firoozeh. 2003. *Funny in Farsi*. New York: Random House.

Dunn, Marcia. 2014. "NASA: There's Your New Spacecraft, America!" Associated Press, December 6.

Dwyer, Colin. 2017. "In Lighthearted Turn/Newspaper Take Crime Report/And Makes Them Haiku." *The Two-Way*. NPR, January 26.

Elbow, Peter. 2000. "The Shifting Relationships Between Speech and Writing." Chap. 7 in *Everyone Can Write: Essays Toward a Hopeful Theory of Writing and Teaching Writing*. New York: Oxford University Press.

Elbow, Peter. *Writing Without Teachers*. 1973/1998. 2nd edition. New York: Oxford University Press.

Elon Statement on Writing Transfer. 2013. www.elon.edu/e-web/academics/teaching/ers/writing_transfer/statement.xhtml.

Ericsson, Stephanie. 1991. "The Ways We Lie." *Utne Reader*. 1992, (54), p. 56.

Farrell, Thomas. 1999. "Practicing the Arts of Rhetoric: Tradition and Invention." *Contemporary Rhetorical Theory: A Reader*, eds. John Louis Lucaites, Celeste Michelle Condit, and Sally Caudill. New York: The Guilford Press.

Fitzgerald, F. Scott. 1925. *The Great Gatsby*. New York: Charles Scribner's Sons.

Fletcher, Jennifer. 2015. *Teaching Arguments: Rhetorical Comprehension, Critique, and Response*. Portland, ME: Stenhouse.

Foster, Thomas C. 2003. *How to Read Literature Like a Professor: A Lively and Entertaining Guide to Reading Between the Lines*. New York: Harper.

Freytag, Gustav. 1896. Translated by Elias J. MacEwan. *Freytag's Technique of the Drama: An Exposition of Dramatic Composition and Art*. 2nd edition. Chicago: S.C. Griggs and Co.

Gage, John T. 2005. *The Shape of Reason*. New York: Pearson.

Gallagher, Kelly. 2004. *Deeper Reading: Comprehending Challenging Texts, 4–12*. Portland, ME: Stenhouse.

———. 2015. *In the Best Interest of Students: Staying True to What Works in the ELA Classroom*. Portland, ME: Stenhouse.

Garcia, Diana. 2014. "On Leaving | On Staying Behind." *Prairie Schooner* 88 (4): 11–13.

Gillespie, Tim. 2010. *Doing Literary Criticism: Helping Students Engage with Challenging Texts*. Portland, ME: Stenhouse.

Golding, William. 1954. *Lord of the Flies*. London, England: Faber and Faber.

Goodman, Andy. 2010. *Storytelling as Best Practice: How Stories Strengthen Your Organization, Engage Your Audience, and Advance Your Mission*. Los Angeles: A. Goodman. www.thegoodmancenter.com/about.

Graff, Gerald. 2003. *Clueless in Academe: How Schooling Obscures the Life of the Mind*. New Haven: Yale University Press.

Graff, Gerald, and Cathy Birkenstein. 2014. *They Say, I Say: The Moves That Matter in Academic Writing*. High school ed. New York: W. W. Norton.

Graff, Nelson. 2010. "Teaching Rhetorical Analysis to Promote Transfer of Learning: This Strategy Has the Potential to Help Students Develop the Rhetorical

Awareness and Meta-knowledge About Writing That Can Help Them Transfer Their Learning About Writing to New Contexts and Tasks." *Journal of Adolescent & Adult Literacy* 53 (5): 376–385.

Grant-Davie, Keith. 1997. "Rhetorical Situations and Their Constituents." *Rhetoric Review* 15 (2): 264–279.

Grassi, Rosanna, and Peter De Blois. 1984. *Composition and Literature: A Rhetoric for Critical Writing*. Englewood Cliffs, NJ: Prentice-Hall.

Gross, Daniel M. 2007. *The Secret History of Emotion: From Aristotle's "Rhetoric" to Modern Brain Science*. Chicago: University of Chicago Press.

Gunn, Tim, with Kate Moloney. 2007. *A Guide to Quality, Taste and Style*. New York: Abrams Image.

Haddon, Mark. 2003. *The Curious Incident of the Dog in the Night-Time*. New York: Vintage.

Hairston, Maxine. 1986. *Contemporary Composition*. Florence, KY: Cengage.

Hand, Elizabeth. 2016. "The Secret Life of Novelizations." By Jesse Brenneman. *On the Media*. WNYC, April 25. www.wnyc.org/story/secret-life-novelizations/.

Harris, Richard. 2014. "Patients Vulnerable When Cash-Strapped Scientists Cut Corners." *Morning Edition*. NPR, September 15. www.npr.org/sections/health-shots/2014/09/15/344084239/patients-vulnerable-when-cash-strapped-scientists-cut-corners.

Haskell, Robert E. 2001. *Transfer of Learning: Cognition, Instruction, and Reasoning*. San Diego, CA: Academic Press.

Heide, Florence Parry, and Sylvia Worth Van Clief. 1978. *Fables You Shouldn't Pay Any Attention To*. Philadelphia: J. B. Lippincott Company.

Hillocks, George, Jr. 2005. "At Last: The Focus on Form vs. Content in Teaching Writing." *Research in the Teaching of English* 40 (2): 238–248.

Houston, Jeanne Wakatsuki, and James D. Houston. 1973. *Farewell to Manzanar*. New York: Bantam Books.

Huff, Darrell. (1954) 1993. *How to Lie with Statistics*. New York: W. W. Norton.

Huxley, Aldous. (1932) 2006. *Brave New World*. New York: HarperCollins.

Intersegmental Committee of the Academic Senates of the California Community Colleges, the California State University, and the University of California. 2002. *Academic Literacy: A Statement of Competencies Expected of Students Entering California's Public Colleges and Universities*. Sacramento, CA: ICAS.

Ishiguro, Kazuo. (1989) 1993. *The Remains of the Day*. New York: Knopf.

Jacobsen, Rowan. 2016. "Obituary: Great Barrier Reef (25 Million BC–2016)." *Outside Online*, October 11. www.outsideonline.com/2112086/obituary-great-barrier-reef-25-million-bc-2016.

James, Missy, and Alan P. Merickel. 2005. *Reading Literature and Writing Argument*. 2nd ed. Upper Saddle River, NJ: Pearson/Prentice Hall.

Jensen, J. Vernon. 1981. *Argumentation: Reasoning in Communication*. Belmont, CA: Wadsworth.

Jetton, Tamara L. and Janice A. Dole, eds. 2004. *Adolescent Literacy Research and Practice*. New York: The Guilford Press.

Johns, A. M. 2008. "Genre Awareness for the Novice Academic Student: An Ongoing Quest." *Language Teaching* 41 (2): 237–252.

Johnson, Alex. 2016. "'California Will Launch Its Own Damn Satellites,' Governor Brown Tells Trump." *NBC News*, December 16. www.nbcnews.com/news/us-news/california-will-launch-its-own-damn-satellites-governor-brown-tells-n696771.

Kennedy, George A. 1994. *A New History of Classical Rhetoric*. Princeton, NJ: Princeton University Press.

Killingsworth, M. Jimmie. 2005. *Appeals in Modern Rhetoric*. Carbondale: Southern Illinois University Press.

Kipling, Rudyard. 1890. "The Road to Mandalay." http://www.kiplingsociety.co.uk/poems_mandalay.htm.

Kittle, Penny. 2013. *Book Love: Developing Depth, Stamina, and Passion in Adolescent Readers*. Portsmouth, NH: Heinemann.

Kogawa, Joy. [1981] 1993. *Obasan*. New York: Anchor.

Lahiri, Jhumpa. 2012. "My Life's Sentences." *Opinionator. New York Times*, March 17. https://opinionator.blogs.nytimes.com/2012/03/17/my-lifes-sentences/.

Lai, Thanhha. 2011. *Inside Out and Back Again*. New York: HarperCollins.

Lane, Barry. 2016. *After the End: Teaching and Learning Creative Revision*. 2nd ed. Portsmouth, NH: Heinemann.

LaSalle, Mick. 2017. "The Best Movies Based on Plays Are Those with Just the Right Changes to the Source Material." *San Francisco Chronicle*, July 9.

Lattimer, Heather. 2003. *Thinking Through Genre: Units of Study in Reading and Writing Workshops, 4–12*. Portland, ME: Stenhouse.

Le Guin, Ursula K. (1969) 1976. *The Left Hand of Darkness*. New York: Ace Books.

Lesesne, Teri S. 2006. *Naked Reading: Uncovering What Tweens Need to Become Lifelong Readers*. Portland, ME: Stenhouse.

Loesberg, Jonathan. 2015. "Wildean Interpretation and Formalist Reading." *Victorian Studies* 58 (1): 9–33.

London, Jack. 1908. "To Build a Fire." First published in *The Century Magazine*, 76, (August): 525-534. http://london.sonoma.edu/writings/LostFace/fire.html.

Makau, Josina M., and Debian L. Marty. 2013. *Dialogue and Deliberation*. Long Grove, IL: Waveland Press.

McClish, Glen. n.d. "Teaching Poetry Rhetorically." Unpublished manuscript.

Meyer, Jan H. F., Ray Land, and Caroline Baillie, eds. 2010. *Threshold Concepts and Transformative Learning*. Rotterdam, The Netherlands: Sense.

Miller, Abby, Katherine Valle, and Jennifer Engle. Institute for Higher Education Policy. 2014. *Access to Attainment: An Access Agenda for 21st Century Students*. www.ihep.org/research/publications/access-attainment-access-agenda-21st-century-college-students.

Moore, Jessie L., and Randall Bass, eds. 2017. *Understanding Writing Transfer: Implications for Transformative Student Learning in Higher Education*. Sterling, VA: Stylus.

National Endowment for the Arts. 2004. *Reading at Risk: A Survey of Literary Reading in America*. Washington, DC: NEA.

———. 2009. *Art-Goers in Their Communities: Patterns of Civic and Social Engagement*. NEA Research Note 18. Washington, DC: NEA.

National Research Council. 2000. *How People Learn: Brain, Mind, Experience, and School*. Washington, DC: National Academies Press.

———. 2012. *Education for Life and Work: Developing Transferable Knowledge and Skills in the 21st Century*. Washington, DC: National Academies Press.

Neebe, Diana, and Jen Roberts. 2015. *Power Up: Making the Shift to 1:1 Teaching and Learning*. Portland, ME: Stenhouse.

Newkirk, Thomas. 2014. *Minds Made for Stories: How We Really Read and Write Informational and Persuasive Texts*. Portsmouth, NH: Heinemann.

Newman, Bruce, and Jeremy C. Owens. 2013. "Amazon Pioneer Joy Covey Dies: Structure She Set Up Still in Place." *San Jose Mercury News*, September 19.

NGA/CCSSO (National Governors Association Center for Best Practices, Council of Chief State School Officers). 2010. *Common Core State Standards for English Language Arts & Literacy in History/Social Studies, Science, and Technological Subjects*. Washington, DC: NGA/CCSSO. www.corestandards.org/read-the-standards.

Norton, Leslie P. 2015. "Yale Goes to Asia." *Barron's* 95 (10) 23–25.

Nowacek, Rebecca S. 2011. *Agents of Integration: Understanding Transfer as a Rhetorical Act*. Carbondale: Southern Illinois University Press.

Panush, Richard. 2008. "Stories in the Service of Making a Better Doctor." *New York Times* (blog), October 24.

Peace Corps. 2016 "Interpreting Behavior: Expanding Our Point of View." www.peacecorps.gov/educators/resources/interpreting-behavior.

Pekrun, Reinhard, et al. 2010. "Boredom in Achievement Settings: Exploring Control-Value Antecedents and Performance Outcomes of a Neglected Emotion." Journal of Educational Psychology 102 (3): 531–549.

Perkins, David N. 2014. *Future Wise: Educating Our Children for a Changing World*. San Francisco: Jossey-Bass.

Perkins, David N., and Gavriel Salomon. 2012. "Knowledge to Go: A Motivational and

Dispositional View of Transfer." *Educational Psychologist* 47 (3): 248–258.

Phelan, James. 1996. *Narrative as Rhetoric: Technique, Audiences, Ethics, and Ideology*. Columbus: The Ohio State University Press.

———. 2007. *Experiencing Fiction: Judgments, Progressions, and the Rhetorical Theory of Narrative*. Columbus: The Ohio State University Press.

———. 2010. "Teaching Narrative as Rhetoric: The Example of Time's Arrow." *Pedagogy* 10 (1): 217–228.

Pride and Prejudice. 1995. DVD. United Kingdom: BBC.

Probst, Robert E. 2004. *Response & Analysis: Teaching Literature in Secondary School*. Portsmouth, NH: Heinemann.

Rabinowitz, Peter J. 1987. *Before Reading: Narrative Conventions and the Politics of Interpretation*. Columbus: The Ohio State University Press.

Ramage, John D., John C. Bean, and June Johnson. 2012. *Writing Arguments: A Rhetoric with Readings*. 9th ed. Boston: Allyn and Bacon.

Richards, I. A. [1936] 1965. *The Philosophy of Rhetoric*. New York: Oxford University Press.

Rieke, Richard D., Malcolm O. Sillars, and Tarla Rai Peterson. 2005. *Argumentation and Critical Decision Making*. 6th edition. Boston: Pearson.

Rosenblatt, Louise M. (1938) 1995. *Literature as Exploration*. New York: Modern Language Association.

Rotelle, John E. 1986. *Augustine Day by Day*. Compiled and edited by John E. Rotelle, O.S.A. Totowa, NJ: Catholic Book Publishing Corporation.

Rowling, J. K. 2005. *Harry Potter and the Half-Blood Prince*. New York: Scholastic.

Roy, Arundhati. 1998. *The God of Small Things*. New York: HarperCollins.

Saki. 1913. "The Storyteller." www.classicshorts.com/stories/Storyteller.html.

Schleppegrell, Mary J. 2004. *The Language of Schooling: A Functional Linguistics Perspective*. Mahway, NJ: Lawrence Erlbaum Associates.

Schreiner, Olive. (1883) 2008. *The Story of an African Farm*. Oxford: Oxford University Press.

Serota, Kim B., Timothy R. Levine, and Franklin J. Boster. 2010. "The Prevalence of Lying in America: Three Studies of Self-Reported Lies." *Human Communication Research* 36: 2–25.

Shakespeare, William. 1998. *As You Like It: With New and Updated Critical Essays and a Revised Bibliography*. Edited by Albert Gilman. With an introduction by Sylvan Barnet. General editor: Sylvan Barnett. New York: Signet Classic.

Shakespeare, William. 2008. *The Norton Shakespeare*. Edited by Stephen Greenblatt, Walter Cohen, Jean E. Howard, and Katherine Eisman Maus. 2nd ed. New York: Oxford University Press.

———. *Hamlet*. 1683–1784.

———. "Sonnet 130." 1990.

———. "Sonnet 15." 1951.

———. *The Tragedy of King Lear*. 2493–2567.

Shelley, Mary. (1818) 1983. *Frankenstein*. New York: Penguin Books.

Shipley Associates. 1985. *Style Guide: Writing in the World of Work*. Bountiful, UT: Shipley Associates.

"Sir Mashalot: Mind-Blowing SIX Country Song Mashup." 2014. YouTube video, November 4. www.youtube.com/watch?v=FY8SwIvxj8o.

Smith, Michael W., Deborah Appleman, and Jeffrey D. Wilhelm. 2014. *Uncommon Core: Where the Authors of the Standards Go Wrong About Instruction—and How You Can Get It Right*. Thousand Oaks, CA: Corwin.

Soto, Gary. 2006. *Buried Onions*. Chicago: HMH Books for Young Readers.

Stedman, Kyle D. 2012. "Why Study Rhetoric? or, What Freestyle Rap Teaches Us About Writing." Writing Commons. https://writingcommons.org/open-text/information-literacy/rhetorical-analysis/582-why-we-study-rhetoric.

Swift, Jonathan. (1726) 2004. *Gulliver's Travels*. New York: Barnes and Noble Books.

Takacs, David. 2003. "How Does Your Positionality Bias Your Epistemology?" *NEA Higher Education Journal.* v19, n1, p 27-38, Summer 2003.

Tan, Amy. 1990. "Mother Tongue." *The Threepenny Review,* 43 (Autumn): 7–8. www.jstor.org/stable/4383908.

Tauber, Daveena. 2016. "Post-Election College Paper Grading Rubric." *McSweeney's,* November 11. www.mcsweeneys.net/articles/post-election-college-paper-grading-rubric.

Thoreau, Henry David. [1854] 1937. *Walden.* New York: The Modern Library.

Todd, Greg. 2015. "You Know Exactly What These 6 Country Songs Have in Common." By Melissa Block. *All Things Considered.* NPR, January 9. www.npr.org/2015/01/09/376145745/you-know-exactly-what-these-six-country-songs-have-in-common.

Toulmin, Stephen E. (1958) 2003. *The Uses of Argument.* Updated ed. New York: Cambridge University Press.

Tovani, Cris. 2000. *I Read It, but I Don't Get It: Comprehension Strategies for Adolescent Readers.* Portland, ME: Stenhouse.

Twain, Mark. (1884) 1995. *Adventures of Huckleberry Finn.* Edited by Gerald Graff and James Phelan. Case Study in Critical Controversy. Boston: Bedford/St. Martin's.

Urioste, Donaldo W., Francisco A. Lomelí, and María Joaquina Villaseñor. 2017. *Historical Dictionary of U.S. Latino Literature.* Lanham, MD: Rowman and Littlefield.

Vatz, Richard E. 1999. "The Myth of the Rhetorical Situation." *Contemporary Rhetorical Theory: A Reader,* eds. John Louis Lucaites, Celeste Michelle Condit, and Sally Caudill. New York: The Guilford Press.

Vedantam, Shankar. 2017. "Researchers Examine the Psychology of Protest Movements." *Hidden Brain.* NPR, April 18. www.npr.org/2017/04/18/524473948/researchers-examine-the-psychology-of-protest-movements.

Wilhelm, Jeffrey D., Michael W. Smith, and James E. Fredricksen. 2012. *Get It Done! Writing and Analyzing Informational Texts to Make Things Happen.* Portsmouth, NH: Heinemann.

Wills, Garry. 2011. *Rome and Rhetoric: Shakespeare's Julius Caesar.* New Haven: Yale University Press.

Wilson, Maja, and Thomas Newark. 2011. "Can Readers Really Stay Within the Standards Lines?" *Education Week,* December 14. http://usny.nysed.gov/rttt/docs/bringingthecommoncoretolife/fulltranscript.pdf.

Wolf, Maryanne. 2008. *Proust and the Squid: The Story and Science of the Reading Brain.* New York: Harper Perennial.

Woodson, Jacqueline. 2014. *Brown Girl Dreaming.* New York: Nancy Paulsen Books.

Yancey, Kathleen Blake, Liane Robertson, and Kara Taczak. 2014. *Writing Across Contexts: Transfer, Composition, and Sites of Writing.* Boulder: University Press of Colorado.

Yang, Gene Luen. 2008. *American Born Chinese.* New York: Square Fish.

Zwiers, Jeff, and Marie Crawford. 2011. *Academic Conversations: Classroom Talk That Fosters Critical Thinking and Content Understanding.* Portland, ME: Stenhouse.

Index